"More Solid Learning"

A Crowd of Authors beseiging the Publishers to prevent the publication of *The Dunciad*. Frontispiece from "Memoir of Pope, with Extracts from His Correspondence," vol. 1 of *The Poetical Works of Alexander Pope,* ed. Robert Carruthers (London: Ingram, Cooke, and Co., 1853).

"More Solid Learning"

New Perspectives on Alexander Pope's *Dunciad*

Edited by
Catherine Ingrassia
Claudia N. Thomas

Lewisburg
Bucknell University Press
London: Associated University Presses

Associated University Presses
440 Forsgate Drive
Cranbury, NJ 08512

Associated University Presses
16 Barter Street
London WC1A 2AH, England

Associated University Presses
P.O. Box 338, Port Credit
Mississauga, Ontario
Canada L5G 4L8

The paper used in this publication meets the requirements of the American National Standard for Permanence of Paper for Printed Library Materials Z39.48-1984.

Library of Congress Cataloging-in-Publication Data

More solid learning : new perspectives on Alexander Pope's Dunciad / edited by Catherine Ingrassia [and] Claudia N. Thomas.
    p.   cm.
    Includes bibliographical references and index.
    ISBN 0-8387-5443-0 (alk. paper)
    1. Pope, Alexander, 1688–1744. Dunciad.   2. Verse satire, English—History and criticism.   I. Ingrassia, Catherine.   II. Thomas, Claudia N., 1951–
PR3625.M67   2000
821'.5—dc21   99-059167

To
Paul and Roberta Ingrassia
and
Peter David Kairoff

Contents

Acknowledgments

THE ENGLISH DEPARTMENT OF VIRGINIA COMMONWEALTH UNIVERSITY and the Dean's Office of Wake Forest University have been gracious in their support of our long-term collaboration.

We would like to thank Ronald Angerer (Wake Forest, Class of 1998) for his invaluable assistance in preparing our manuscript. His technological expertise spared us hours of puzzling over the miscellaneous disks submitted by our farflung colleagues. Michelle Ellwood (Wake Forest, Class of 1999) prepared our final, revised manuscript, for which we are grateful.

Dr. David Levy, chair of the Department of Music at Wake Forest, kindly read and commented on an early draft of Valerie Rumbold's essay on Handel. We thank him for his helpful remarks. Dr. Miles McCrimmon, Catherine's spouse, has been unflagging in his encouragement.

Finally, we dedicate this volume to Catherine's parents and to Claudia's spouse. Without their loving support and encouragement, our careers would be far less joyous and—to borrow a musical metaphor from Peter—harmonious.

"More Solid Learning"

Introduction: "More Solid Learning": Pope, *The Dunciad*, and the Academy

CATHERINE INGRASSIA and CLAUDIA N. THOMAS

ON THE DAY *THE DUNCIAD* WAS FIRST PUBLISHED IN MARCH 1728, according to Richard Savage, a mob of Alexander Pope's literary opponents descended upon his bookseller and attempted to stop sale of the poem.[1] Although we may question whether such a scene ever took place, the image captures the aura of pitched battle that surrounded the poem at its appearance, and that has characterized critical response to Pope's masterpiece ever since. Pope himself set the agenda for aesthetic debate not only over *The Dunciad*, but over many artistic genres. By casting himself as the lone opponent of English cultural decline, Pope synopsized and then perpetuated certain arguments over cultural production. Who has the authority to determine cultural values and standards? Is popular culture inherently less valuable than so-called "high" culture, and what variables determine which is which? What role do aesthetic productions play in a society, and are these productions more influential on or influenced by the historical eras and environments in which they appear? What degree of financial independence ensures an artist's integrity? What level of education is requisite? Is it possible—or desirable—for an artist to produce artifacts that are not implicated in his or her social and political circumstances? Pope's position on most of these questions reflected his opinion that the artist ideally spoke from a privileged position as his culture's representative, and that the progressive marginalization of poets such as himself indicated a decline in public taste and, worse, values. His imaginative reconstruction of this situation as a literal progress of dull writers into the halls of power, with himself as helpless witness of the incursion, not only infuriated competitors but cast aesthetic disagreements as rigidly opposed, and inimical, debates between high and low, immortal and ephemeral, or good and evil.

Pope was undoubtedly influenced by John Dryden's *Mac Fleck-*

13

noe (1682), the droll humor of which diverts the attention of unwary readers from its decidedly apocalyptic undertones. Dryden's Shadwell, for all his alleged ineptitude, is nevertheless at some level the anti-Christ to Flecknoe's anti–St. John the Baptist. Having absorbed so much else in his predecessor's poem, Pope—as Thomas Jemielity demonstrates in this volume—expanded and intensified what was latent in Dryden's satire. In so doing, Pope rendered critical response to *The Dunciad* very difficult. Disagreement with his opinions aligned one with the low, the ephemeral, even the criminal. Under the circumstances, the reply was most often an *ad hominem* attack, intended to oust Pope from his self-appointed post as cultural guardian by proving that he, not his enemies, embodied the infamy he deplored. Throughout Pope's lifetime, the critical attacks of Pope's opponents are nearly always of this *ad hominem* variety. Six volumes of *Popeiana* preserve many of these rebuttals, some still humorous and others downright cruel. One sample, James Ralph's *Sawney: An Heroic Poem,* conveys the tone and argument of many such efforts. In Ralph's recapitulation of Pope's career, the poet, assisted by Swift, Gay, Envy, Fraud, and Dulness herself, has labored to complete his latest project:

> At length, the mighty Task is done, and, from
> Its Authors see the *Dunciad* takes its Name;
> A flight of *Furies* convoy it abroad,
> And *Curiosity* assists the Sale. . . .
>   . . . But, while
> They glory in the monstrous Lay, around
> Th'astonish'd Readers gather in Debate,
> With up-cast Eyes they wonder humane kind
> Can sink so low, that such malicious Thoughts,
> Such nauseous Doggrel, execrable Cant,
> Should blast the Poet's Name: With gen'ral Voice
> Invoke the Injur'd to assert their Cause. . . .[2]

In Ralph's version of *The Dunciad*'s appearance, readers, not anxious literary rivals, gather at the bookseller and deplore the poem's slander. Like many in its initial audience, Ralph apparently believed Swift to be virtual coauthor of the poem. His reply casts the Scriblerians as a malicious club, plotting in Twickenham to strip all competitors of their reputations. Ralph's strategy, by exposing Pope's presumed motive, turned the tables, but in so doing trapped both *The Dunciad*'s author and his opponents in a seemingly endless exchange of recriminations. For close to three hundred years, it has proved nearly impossible to escape from the roles of attacker or defender when writing about *The Dunciad*.

Pope's composition and publication of *The Dunciad*, a project that informs (or for the casual reader defines) the latter part of his career, was in many ways designed to initiate an exchange of recriminations and the positioning of the reader as foe or ally. His 1728 *Dunciad*, like *The Dunciad Variorum* the following year, sprang in part from his personal anger with Lewis Theobald, the original King of the Dunces, and instigated—or in some cases culminated—a sustained published relationship with his literary contemporaries. The original *Dunciad* was very much a part of the Grub Street milieu it depicted, from its plain blue cover to its abundant scatology. Its representation of the literary world was as oppositional as its author's relationships depicted within it. The text was a part of the fray; Pope relished the aura of pitched battle that provided the poem with its vitality. The multiple versions of the poem in the late 1720s function as a mark of the poet's intimate relationship with the world of professional authorship and his still-visceral reaction to the world around him.

Had *The Dunciad* in three books been the only version of the text, the poem would have had a distinctly different influence on the trajectory of Pope's career and the way we understand him as a poet. That text's immediacy, topicality, and personality, coupled with its focus primarily on the literary marketplace, make it, in many ways, a less significant or less weighty (though certainly no less interesting) poem. While a marvelous document of the culture of professional authorship, if not from the most objective observer, *The Dunciad* lacks the cultural resonance provided by Book 4. It also reveals a different side of Pope. In many ways, the Pope of the 1743 *Dunciad* is Pope as Maynard Mack presents him—Christian humanist, *vir bonum*—while the Pope of the 1728 *Dunciad* is the slightly more rough-and-tumble Pope drawn by Sherburn. That is not to say that the 1743 *Dunciad* is removed from the vicissitudes of the marketplace—quite the contrary. James Sutherland suggests that Colley Cibber's pamphlet *A Letter from Mr. Cibber to Mr. Pope* and the Tom Tit episode, which Eric Chandler discusses in this volume, may have been a partial motivation for the revised edition. But despite its continued connection to the culture of professional authorship, the text and its marked change in register with the fourth book complement the careful project of "persona recuperation" Pope undertakes in the 1730s. His *Epistles to Several Persons*, like the

Horatian Imitations, complete the Virgilian career he had cultivated from the beginning. The publication of his strategically revised letters in 1735, like the third edition of his collected works in 1735 (which officially revealed his long-recognized identity as the author of *The Dunciad*), shape the vision of a poet in retirement, removed from the temporal influences of popular culture. *Epistle to Arbuthnot* (1735) fashions Pope as a poet removed from the social aspects of writing, "I ne'er with Wits or Witlings past my days, / To spread about the Itch of Verse and Praise" (223–24), and untouched by the impulses of the literary marketplace:

> Maintain a Poet's Dignity and Ease,
> And see what friends, and read what books I please.
> Above a Patron, tho' I condescend
> Sometimes to call a Minister my Friend:
> I was not born for Courts or great Affairs,
> I pay my Debts, believe, and say my Pray'rs,
> Can sleep without a Poem in my head,
> Nor know, if *Dennis* be alive or dead. (263–70)

That revised poetic stance, coupled with the graver, less personal, or even purely professional tone of the satire, make *The Dunciad in Four Books* a wholly different document than *The Dunciad Variorum*, one distinctly more cultural in its scope. Written on the heels of *Essay on Man*, fragments of which find their way into *The Dunciad*, the satiric poem shares the elevated tone as well as the intertextuality (some might say self-plagiarism) that marked Pope's later career. While Pope certainly has greater cause for cultural anxiety by the early 1740s, we can't read Book 4 as being separate from the poet's own attempt to locate himself and his career, then ending, within the cultural and literary history of his time.

Despite the process of reassessment and recuperation, Pope was trapped himself, as effectually as he entrapped his opponents and readers, by his poem's binary system of cultural values. Of course, the poem's dominant voice in the construction of eighteenth-century literary and cultural hierarchies stems as much from its overwhelming persistence (33 separate editions and almost 60 impressions by 1751) as from its poetic power. Perhaps the irony of this entrapment provided some of the impetus for composing Book 4. From the *Peri Bathous* through successive editions of *The Dunciad*, Pope was excoriated by his enemies for a lack of magnanimity, as well as for turning against his peers.

Book 4 of *The Dunciad* attempts a final response to these charges, while removing to "higher ground" the poem's metaphoric battlefield. Pope still imagines a cultural struggle between forces of opposed value, but he tries to extricate himself from professional confrontations by focusing on the privileged instigators, rather than on the struggling artificers, of decline. Gone in Book 4 are the writers and booksellers; Pope opens with an invocation designed to show "his high respect for *Antiquity* and a *Great Family*, how dull, or dark soever."[3] Pope's first note teases his readers by observing that the author is dealing in *"Mysteries* . . . which he durst not fully reveal," calling attention to the book's libelous potential. Queen Dulness (Caroline?) mounts the throne, her laureate son (George II?) snoring in her lap, providing occasion for an "innocent" Scriblerian jibe at the indolence of king-consorts, as well as for a facetious concession to Colley Cibber's accusation that he had been elevated to the kingship "to catch little readers" (n.20). By merely repeating Cibber's words, Pope implies the unlikeliness of such a motive, again inviting a more political reading.

Pope next presents a tableau of captive arts. Could Grub Street and its Smithfield Muses be responsible for this tragedy? A clue materializes in the "Harlot form" of Opera that minces into the royal presence. As Valerie Rumbold demonstrates in this volume, Pope consciously sacrificed consistency by representing Handel as the opponent of an art form he had helped establish in Britain. In *The Dunciad*, however, Pope fulfilled his own statement in an early "Ode for Musick, on St. Cecilia's Day" that "Musick can soften Pain to ease, / And make Despair and Madness please" (120–21). By lambasting opera, Pope insinuated that the jigs and trills of a foreign medium had lulled the great into ignoring such political realities as Spain's interference with British shipping. The "exile" of Handel, like that of Swift, could then be read as the nation's failure to rise from its opera-induced torpor.

Pope, then, attempted in Book 4 to remove himself from the sphere of his fellow professional writers and to confront in their stead the great, unveiled as the true, culprits in the saga of Britain's cultural decay. In Book 4, the great world is imagined as an enormous Bartholomew Fair populated by "a vast involuntary throng" in which academics, men-about-town, and patrons mix promiscuously with the hack writers they sustain. "There marched the bard and blockhead, side by side, / Who rhym'd for hire, and patroniz'd for pride" (4.101–2). The late headmaster of Westminster School materializes as a bloodthirsty criminal; the

Continental philosophers Crousaz and Burgersdyck have been metamorphosed into huge dray-horses. Cambridge University itself has become a second Grub Street, "Where Bentley late tempestuous wont to sport / In troubled waters, but now sleeps in Port" (4.201–2). Bentley's demise resembles that of the less respectable Orator Henley in Book 2, who "lay inspir'd beside a sink, / And to mere mortals seem'd a priest in drink" (2.425–26). His ensuing speech before Dulness's throne bears a suspicious resemblance to Cibber's boast in Book 1 that his "Prose and Verse were much the same" (1.189); Bentley asserts that "Turn what they will to Verse, their toil is vain, / Critics like me shall make it Prose again" (4.213–14). The scholar who tames Horace and Milton (4.211–12) is accomplishing in the learned sphere what the popular dramatist does with his compound of "Plautus, Fletcher, Shakespear, and Corneille" (1.285) in the vulgar.

By equating Bentley with Cibber, Pope effectively charges Britain's public schools and universities with breeding the decadence of which Grub Street is a mere symptom. As Pat Rogers observes, most of the so-called dunces were in fact university-educated men.[4] Pope creates a "Bentley" whose scholarly labors ("For me, what Virgil, Pliny may deny, / Manilius or Solinus shall supply" [4.225–26]) closely resemble those of "Cibber," glimpsed earlier cobbling plays together in his garret. Likewise, when Bentley rejoices that Isaac Barrow could not "work on ev'ry block" (4.245), and challenges enemies such as Barrow and Atterbury to undo his labors "if you can, / And hew the Block off, and get out the Man" (4.269–70), his metaphor reduces teaching to a perverse kind of sculpture in which minds are encased in cement, resulting in the human equivalents of the "brazen, brainless brothers" sculpted by Cibber's father, Caius (1.32). According to Pope's implied comparison, the scholar is a less successful craftsman than the sculptor he emulates. The nation's undergraduates are similarly equated with Smithfield acrobats; their intellectual skills resemble the antics of a "tumbler thro' the hoops" (4.257). In essence, Pope recapitulates the scenes and imagery of his previous three books, suggesting that the origins of Dulness have all along been on a higher plane and are now trickling downward through society.

Pope's attack on public schools and universities as the wellspring of "dulness" was motivated by personal disappointment as well as political dislike. As with opposition Whigs and disgraced Tories in his Horatian poems, those barred from the establishment were found superior to most of the system's adherents.

Only by discrediting the relevance of—indeed, the possibility of any benefit from—the academies could Pope assert his version of cultural authority. If a university degree made Leonard Welsted a gentleman and Pope an upstart, then the degree had to be discredited. In addition, Pope clearly had a stake in repudiating university education as the basis of his emergent profession. Although he would have despised the analogy, Pope's situation was similar to that of the surgeon whose Continental training proved superior to the medical education at Oxford or Cambridge. While his disgust with privileged education was not novel—many education-writers deplored the incompetence, often exacerbated by cruelty and decadence, of boarding schools and universities— Pope's philosophical disagreements with the system were compounded by accumulated attacks on him as "no gentleman" due to his lack of a degree.

Another, immediate provocation to Book 4 was Oxford's failure to award William Warburton the degree of Doctor of Divinity between 1741–1743, because of which Pope refused to accept an honorary Doctor of Law degree there.[5] Book 4 shows a marked propensity on Pope's part to fight Warburton's battles with fellow academics. In February 1742/3, Pope wrote to the Earl of Orrery, who had tried to procure the Warburton degree:

I dare say your Humanity & Generous Spirit is offended, as well as mine, at such a Demonstration of the Malignity of Dulness, which is never so rancorous as under the Robe of Learning, One would think the Clergy were sworn to hate each other, instead of to love each other. But we have done our best, & must acquiesce under such *Heads* as God is pleased to put over us, that the Weak ones of this world may confound the strong. (4:441)

Despite his proclaimed distaste for what his editor calls "learned Dunces," Pope had engaged Lord Orrery to intercede with the Oxford chancellors on behalf of Warburton (4:436–37). His bitterness at Oxford's failure to award Warburton a degree almost certainly included disappointment at having, as a point of honor, to refuse his own. The rebuff by Oxford provoked Pope to conclude a train of thought, mistrust of the scholar's influence, that had exercised the poet since his *Essay on Criticism*. As he had remarked in the *Epistle to Lord Cobham*, " 'Tis Education forms the common mind, / Just as the Twig is bent, the Tree's inclin'd" (101–2).

In fact, at Warburton's suggestion, Pope had inserted into the

Essay on Man in 1742/3 a passage that might have served as the rationale for Book 4 (see *Corr.*, 4:439). In Epistle 4 of the *Essay on Man*, Pope says of the search for human happiness, "Ask of the Learn'd the way, the Learn'd are blind" (4.19). Later, in a note at line 50, Pope explained that young men are subjected "to the authority of *Systems* in the Universities," which render them incapable of achieving the happiness that results from breadth of vision. Instead, as Silenus remarks in Book 4 of *The Dunciad*, undergraduates are "Bounded by Nature, narrow'd still by Art" (4.503), fit only for duncehood. In fact, according to Pope, Dulness transforms the typical graduate into a variant of Cibber's "brazen, brainless brothers," characterized by either "Firm Impudence, or Stupefaction mild," by "Cibberian forehead, or Cimmerian gloom" (4.530, 32). Pope had not so much extracted himself from the Pamphlet Wars as expanded his offensive to include large portions of the genteel and upper classes, as well as the marginal and middle-class opponents he had earlier compared to Smithfield rabble. The book's imagery pushes all of Pope's enemies into two complementary ranks, leaving the poet to scorn both the poverty that suggests ineptitude and the privilege that implies decadence. Pope leaves himself and sympathetic readers in the position of an ideal middle status, the mean between what he describes as ugly alternatives.

Close attention to the Bartholomew Fair imagery at *The Dunciad*'s conclusion suggests a less tragic interpretation than is sometimes drawn from Pope's final book. Pope's description of the gentry's transformation resembles the bewildering panoply of competing exhibits at a fair. Interest's magic cloak-of-many-colors, the nostrum or "balm" of Dulness, the spectacular but "specious" mysteries of the French chef: each draws the attention for a few moments before the onlooker turns toward fresh attractions. As in Book 2, Dulness proves an indulgent judge of her children's accomplishments; all are blessed with titles and degrees. Here, Pope merges his Smithfield and academic themes, reserving the universities' honorary degrees for the most sought-after duncical rewards. The awards ceremony itself resembles a graduation, complete with an address: "To Practise now from Theory repair" (4.580). But the aristocratic students have "graduated" a mirror image of the plebeian station whose amusements they patronize and emulate. As the Twickenham editors observe at line 592, Pope here echoes a trend that discouraged genteel participation in plebeian amusements, but Dulness's commands reiterate the imagery of his entire poem:

The Cap and Switch be sacred to his Grace;
With Staff and Pumps the Marquis leads the race;
From Stage to Stage the licens'd Earl may run,
Pair'd with his Fellow-Charioteer the Sun;
The learned Baron Butterflies design,
Or draw to silk Arachne's subtile line;
The Judge to dance his brother Sergeant call;
The Senator at Cricket urge the Ball. . . . (4.585–92)

The bishop becomes a cook; the king, a fiddler. Dulness "makes one Mighty Dunciad of the Land" (4.604) by reducing the gentry to so many weavers and stagecoach drivers, rolling up their sleeves to indulge in a horse or a foot race, a jig, or a cricket match.

The close of Book 2 had featured a "waking contest," in which Dulness promised that anyone who could stay awake throughout the recited works of Henley and Blackmore would acquire "Full and eternal privilege of tongue" (2.378). Nobody, of course, had withstood "the drowsy God" (2.396), and all had collapsed, sleeping, in the street. The close of Book 4 is ostensibly more sinister, as the Arts and Sciences themselves fade into oblivion, while there is no comforting intimation, as in the three-book *Dunciad*, that the vision is false. On the other hand, the conclusion of the great yawn is described much as Pope had earlier satirized the farces of Cibber and Rich. The enormous sable thrones of Night and Chaos, the meteoric flare of Wit, the subjugation of Argus by Hermes: all these scenes and effects, as well as the representation of Truth flying to her Cavern, shrinking philosophy, and flying Mathematics, are worthy of the Drury Lane opera. When the dreadful empire of Chaos has usurped the final scene, the lights have gone out, and Dulness "lets the curtain fall" (4.655), we have either witnessed a prophetic vision of imminent uncreation, or been spectators at an operatic production designed to shock us into sharing Pope's opinions about his culture. The "Universal Darkness" may be no more than the theater's darkness at the end of a frightening spectacle. Something like computer instruction designed to appeal to the Nintendo generation, *The Dunciad* swept readers into a giant spectacle intended to make them critical of spectacles.

Before Pope added Book 4 to *The Dunciad*, he had announced publicly his "resolution to publish no more" as "a sort of *Protest* against the insuperable corruption and depravity of manners, which he had been so unhappy as to live to see" (final note, *Epi-*

logue to the Satires: Dialogue II). The Twickenham editors suggest that one reason for Pope's resolution was the Whigs' renewed fervor in prosecuting libels. But in January 1741/2, shortly before Book 4's publication, Pope wrote his friend Bethel in a feisty tone:

> I little thought 3 months ago to have drawn the whole polite world upon me, (as I formerly did the Dunces of a lower Species) as I certainly shall whenever I publish this poem. An Army of Virtuosi, Medalists, Ciceroni, Royal Society-men, Schools, Universities, even Florists, Free thinkers, & Free masons, will incompass me with fury: It will be once more, *Concurre Bellum atque Virum*. But a Good Conscience a bold Spirit, & Zeal for Truth, at whatsoever Expence, of whatever Pretenders to Science, or of all Imposition either Literary, Moral, or Political; these animated me, & these will Support me. (4:377)

Neither his proclaimed despair nor presumed fear of prosecution apparently dissuaded Pope from the final campaign of his "warfare upon earth." When in January 1743/4 Colley Cibber prepared to publish his second *Occasional Letter* challenging his promotion to King Dunce, Pope remarked to Warburton that the attack would "be more to me than a dose of Hartshorn" (*Corr.*, 4:492). Unfortunately, Cibber's pamphlet proved an ineffectual remedy for Pope's dire physical infirmities. He soon lapsed into his final illness, and died three months after confiding to Bethel that "I have lived long enough, when I have lived to despise & lament the Worthlessness, Perfidiousness, & Meanness of half my Acquaintance . . ." (*Corr.*, 4:499).

Pope did not end his career of warfare upon earth, however, without a final battle. Instead of retreating as promised into silence, he deliberately provoked "the whole polite world" in a last gesture of defiance. The four-book *Dunciad* draws a line between Pope and his adherents and those who patronized or supplied much of the polite as well as popular culture in his day. While the three-book *Dunciad* deplored what he perceived as the growing confusion of popular and genteel tastes, Book 4 declares the fusion nearly complete and dismisses the avocations of all but a saving remnant. The resulting satire appeared to contemporaries extreme but also sublime; it was and remains difficult to dispute the poet's vision without including oneself among the dunces he defies. Throughout the eighteenth century, nevertheless, readers continued either to take issue with Pope's dismissal of popular and polite culture, and his prediction of Britain's speedy decline, or to imagine Pope assessing the current cultural scene from some Valhalla reserved for visionary poets.

The Dunciad remains a critical and interpretative minefield. It still provokes strong reactions, in part, because it questions the nature of literary value, authorial responsibility, and cultural transformation in a way that transcends eighteenth-century studies. Though Pope would have resisted the impulse for the on-going re-examination of the canon, his text addresses issues at the heart of that debate. Whether approached from the perspective of student or scholar, the act of reading the poem potentially reinscribes its literary hierarchy. The text often proves daunting and threatens to exclude those who lack the biblical, classical, and historical knowledge central to its meaning. Yet if we feel overwhelmed by the poem's enormity (in every sense of the word), perhaps we risk being positioned as one of the dunces Pope scorns. Just as the eighteenth-century reader unfamiliar with the personalities of Grub Street required (and requested) Edmund Curll's multiple "keys" to the poems, so too the modern reader looks to the "keys" within the Twickenham edition with the same desire for clarity of allusion. Our very dependence on (or, perhaps, contributions to) the (ever-expanding) supplements to the text dangerously allies us with the pedants Pope portrays. The act of reading can make the poem seem an impenetrable literary history rather than an accessible object of popular culture. This problem is particularly true of Book 4, with its series of allusions that, to some scholars' minds, displays the influence of Pope's friendship with Warburton. "Pope may sometimes have failed to realize" writes Sutherland, "that what, after due explanation, was crystal clear to his friend, might not be readily intelligible to the general public who had not Warburton's advantage."[6] At the same time, however, the seductive momentum of Pope's couplets traps the reader within the poem and often softens the obscurity of a line or allusion. That is the genius of the text. A piece of writing inextricably tied to the impulses and passions of popular and consumer culture appears elevated, transhistorical, and canonized.

Although modern readers encounter the multiple texts that comprise *The Dunciad*—Pope's poem, Pope's footnotes, and the scholarly apparatus appended to both—they were, until recently, read largely within the frame established by the poet. As Samuel

Richardson, another writer preoccupied with shepherding his readers to the "correct" interpretation, observed, the poem's successive editions ensured a certain amount of interpretive control (or at least the illusion of the same): "Mr. Pope in the Height of his Fame, tho' he had made himself, by Arts only He (as a Man of Genius) could stoop to, the Fashion, could not trust his Works with the Vulgar without Notes longer than the Work, and Self-praises, to tell them what he meant, and that he had a Meaning, in this or that Place. And thus every-one was taught to read with his Eyes."[7] Pope's "Fame" necessarily makes him the "Fashion," though he proves unwilling to liberate his poem interpretively to the "vulgar"; he insists on his meaning as the "man of Genius."

Literary scholarship on *The Dunciad* perpetuates Pope's model and potentially replicates the binaries he constructs within the poem. Scholars are perceived as advocates of the poet perpetuating the evaluative cultural construct he offered, or antagonists attempting to locate the poet and his poem more fully within its social, economic, and commercial environment. For a long period, there was a tacit acceptance of Pope's classification of "dunces," which now seems unexamined and perhaps "old-fashioned." Yet a re-evaluation of the professional authors he characterized as "hacks" is, itself, an act of literary history that challenges or revises Pope's interpretation of events. Work of the dominant Pope scholars of this century, which enabled subsequent generations of scholarship, largely maintained the attitudes or standards Pope established in his poem.

John Butt's Twickenham edition of the complete works (and within that James Sutherland's edition of *The Dunciad*), George Sherburn's biography of Pope's early career and his edition of the letters, and Maynard Mack's extensive work including the biography, provided the bibliographic, biographic, and philological rigor on which subsequent studies still depend. William K. Wimsatt's *The Portraits of Alexander Pope* (1965), Mack's *The Garden and the City* (1969) and the essays collected in his *Essential Articles for the Study of Alexander Pope* (1968), Reuben Brower's *Alexander Pope: The Poetry of Allusion* (1959), and Marjorie Nicolson and G. S. Rousseau's *"This Long Disease, My Life"* (1968) are still indispensable. Similarly, Emrys Jones's "Pope and Dulness" (1969), Elias Mengel's "The *Dunciad* Illustrations" (1973), or John Sitter's *The Poetry of Pope's Dunciad* (1971) retain their power and relevance.[8] This work, founded on literary-historical or generic models, stood in sharp contrast to the efforts of the new critics who ignored Pope's life and read or taught his poems primarily from an aesthetic perspective. Similarly, some later attempts to "deconstruct" *The Dunciad*, such as G. Douglas Atkins's treatment in *Quests of Difference* (1986), illustrate why such referential poetry eludes that kind of discussion.[9]

While the value of traditional scholarship on Pope remains unquestioned (and for some, unsurpassed), these scholars primarily read the poet as he wished to be read—as a man more sinned against than sinning, the moral exemplar from Twickenham. "Their" *Dunciad*, then, is Pope's *Dunciad*—a poem emerging from a justifiable frustration with the expanding cultural debasement and a personal desire to even the literary score. Pope's act of narrative self-creation through his poetry, his (heavily revised) letters, and his persona become accepted as the "real" man, not as a discursively constructed subject. Such work offers a humanist vision of Pope, a portrait that ultimately harmonizes any tensions between the poet and his poem. While many recognized the contradictions that marked Pope's existence—and by extension, *The Dunciad*, the poem that arguably characterizes him best—they were largely recuperated into the familiar portrait of the poet. The dazzling maneuvers of Pope's verse also eased any ideological or personal inconsistencies that might appear. Consequently, such scholars perpetuate and substantiate Pope's literary history, one largely consonant with the traditional notions of "Augustan" culture.

The nature of Pope's allusive and topical work demanded scholarship that, in some ways, anticipated the impulse of the new historicism and cultural studies. Howard Erskine-Hill's *The Social Milieu of Alexander Pope* (1975) provides socioeconomic information crucial to an informed and engaged reading of the *Epistles to Several Persons*.[10] His detailed cultural history carefully reconstructs the ideological, political, and material contexts for Pope's poems. However, the serious consideration Erskine-Hill granted to, say, the "false steward" Peter Walter wasn't really granted to a "false wit" like Theobald or Cibber. Pope's classification of his literary competitors as "dunces" remained too powerful. Pat Rogers's *Grub Street: Studies in a Subculture* (1972) wonderfully explores the social, literary, and topographical milieu of professional authorship but restricts its vision to Pope's purview. The study remains a crucial resource for reading *The Dunciad*, but it never departs from the hierarchy of the poem. J. V. Guerinot's *Pamphlet Attacks on Alexander Pope, 1711–1744* (1969) compiles an exhaustive descriptive bibliography of the Grub Street pamphlet attacks, but limits its discussion to the bibliographic.[11] Ironically, his study, as he acknowledges, continues the project Pope himself initiated when he included as Appendix II in *The Dunciad Variorum* "A List of Books, Papers, and Verses, in which our Author was abused." Pope's gesture ultimately preserved and publicized the work of his enemies. As one of Pope's first bibliographers, Reginald H. Griffith, observed, "If Pope is not the greatest among English poets, he is the greatest advertiser and publisher among them."[12] The dunces, or abusers, were listed by name; no one really attempted a thorough reconsideration of their "literary" or scholarly work. While history might suggest that Pope was inaccurate in his assessment of Defoe, Bentley, or the editorial skills of Theobald, until recently little had been done to recuperate the work of Eliza Haywood, Colley Cibber, or Elizabeth Thomas. The poem's monolithic characterization of eighteenth-century literary culture remained essentially unchallenged; a hegemonic voice worked in service of the largely monologic reading of the poem.

The years surrounding the 1988 tercentenary introduced new cadences to this voice. Indeed, the decade proved a transitional period, with the publication of a work that culminated a long (and fading) tradition of Pope scholarship, and one that initiated a completely different critical discourse: Maynard Mack's *Alexander Pope: A Life* (1985) and Peter Stallybrass and Allon White's *The Politics and Poetics of Transgression* (1986).[13] The first Pope biography in more than fifty years, *Alexander Pope: A Life* was a monumental tribute to the poet's life, and, in a sense, to Mack's since it was the culmination of a life's work. In his review for *South Atlantic Quarterly*, George Rousseau, dwelling on the biography's "threnodic" tone, describes it as "possessing a finality in that it necessarily performs closure on a whole era of Pope scholarship."[14] The affectionate description and exhaustive detail synthesized a substantial body of knowledge on Pope into a readable, accessible, and invaluable narrative. Nevertheless, the definitive nature of the book more firmly erected the traditional (in other words, Augustan, Popeian) version of the poet.[15] That is not to say that Mack is not savvy about Pope's strategic manipulation of his work, his colleagues, and his enemies in service of his own poetic image; rather, Mack's sympathetic attitude dominates even the most revealing material. Though, like all Mack's work, it is essential to the study of Pope, the biography, intentionally or not, potentially overwhelmed dissenting voices that complicated his persona. James Winn's *A Window in the Bosom* (1977), Dus-

tin Griffin's *Alexander Pope: The Poet in the Poems* (1978), or
James Grantham Turner's essay on "Pope's Libertine Self-fash-
ioning" (1988) are at odds with and in some ways subsumed by
Mack's portrait.[16]

Appearing within a year of Mack's biography, Peter Stallybrass
and Allon White's *The Politics and Poetics of Transgression*
starkly contrasted with the tenor of his scholarship. If Mack's
work was a latter-day *apologia* for the master of Twickenham,
Stallybrass and White's theorized and authorized the dunces as
it explored *The Dunciad*'s dialogic nature. The study radically
shifted the perspective of the poet and the poem. Though the
book devoted only one chapter to Pope in its more wide-ranging
approach, it redefined the boundaries of Pope scholarship and
opened *The Dunciad* to inventive and revealing examinations.
The discussion of authorship in the eighteenth century, "The
Grotesque Body and the Smithfield Muse," marked scholars' increasing interest in the marginalized voices of the poem (as the
recent critical work on a "dunce" like Eliza Haywood vividly illustrates). Using Bakhtin's concept of classical and carnivalesque, as well as grotesque realism, the study examines the
relational nature of high and low culture, and the necessary seep-
ages and links between the two. It introduced the concept of
transgression into a poetic world previously read as ordered and
stable. That volume, which informed a number of essays in this
collection, offered the opportunity to regard the pamphlet wars,
the dunces, and even Pope's body as something central to understanding the poem. Subsequent work such as Helen Deutsch's illuminating *Resemblance & Disgrace* (1996) is enabled by this
type of approach.

Stallybrass and White's re-examination of the received truths
about Pope and *The Dunciad* emerged at a time when eighteenth-
century literary studies re-examined itself and experienced fundamental theoretical and philosophical shifts. A mark of the
changing nature of scholarship was Laura Brown's controversial
Alexander Pope (1985). Part of Terry Eagleton's Rereading Literature series for Blackwell, her Marxist critique offered a Pope
whose embrace of the ideology of mercantile capitalism informed
all his poems. In her reading, the "main explicit enterprise" of
The Dunciad is an "attack on the capitalization of the printing
industry and hence of literature itself."[17] Her attempt to "demys-
tify" the poet and the ideological structures in which he existed,
though resisted by more traditional scholars, further opened the
poet to new kinds of approaches. This text shares a theoretical

preoccupation with the collection Brown edited with Felicity Nussbaum, *The New Eighteenth Century* (1987) (although that collection includes multiple theoretical approaches, not just Marxist).[18] The volume's stated aim, "the revision or problematization of period, canon, tradition, and genre" (14), helped redefine the culture of eighteenth-century literary studies. The resulting furor threatened to (and in many ways did) reinscribe, albeit in different terms, some of the tensions and antagonisms that Pope created in *The Dunciad*; the profession revisited a kind of "ancients" versus "moderns" (or "old" versus "new" eighteenth century) battle. The "new" scholars sought a more egalitarian, less hierarchical, and appropriately theorized "eighteenth century"; like the dunces, as constructed by Pope, they questioned the dominant literary history and construction of eighteenth-century studies. Lance Bertelsen suggestively observes how the notion of a "smart" or " new" academic can be seen to refigure the concept of a "dunce":

> As anyone who stalks the halls knows, nothing more admiring can be said of a colleague or a colleague's work than that he, she, or it is "smart." By "smart" we mean . . . "up-to-date," full of "invention" . . . "[S]mart" also implies a certain associative sprezzetura and delight in mental acrobatics. . . . In other words, "smart" means today (with rhetorical adjustments) what "dunce" meant to Pope: the aspiration to fulfill, through flexible and everchanging discursive practice, the will to literary power.[19]

Proponents of the "old" eighteenth century, by contrast, insisted on the stability of their period and their field. While the volume did not include an essay on Pope, the introduction of new critical practices and the re-examination of the canon implicated him, as the prototypical voice of Augustan culture. The nature of this work, like Stallybrass and White's, has profoundly influenced a generation of eighteenth-century scholars who really cannot read Pope without incorporating the knowledge of the gaps, inconsistencies, and machinery of the constructed persona that exists within the poems. Obviously, pitfalls exist for the scholar who relies solely on work following the "new" eighteenth century since it, of course, provides a vision of the period as constructed and calculated as Pope's. And consistently, the most nuanced work on Pope balances the persona and the man, poetic voice and professional practice. The "revisions" of Pope make little sense without a firm understanding of the original "text."

The New Eighteenth Century became a lightning rod (or catch phrase) for theoretically informed approaches to canonical and noncanonical eighteenth-century texts, and its impulses were consistent with contemporaneous scholarship. The period from the late 1980s to the present saw increased work on Pope from previously untapped critical directions. Feminist reconsiderations of Pope's work have had arguably as profound an effect on the reshaping of Pope studies as approaches following the "new" eighteenth century. Studies by Felicity Nussbaum, Ellen Pollak, Carole Fabricant, and Valerie Rumbold began an intense examination of the representation of gender and the construction of women within Pope's work.[20] Yet *The Dunciad*, despite the female figure at the center of poem, largely escaped feminist treatment.[21] Similarly, Carolyn Williams's *Pope, Homer, and Manliness* (1993) and Kristina Straub's chapters on Pope in *Sexual Suspects* (1992) explore Pope's use of gender and issues of sexuality (including his own).[22] Dennis Todd's *Imagining Monsters* (1995) locates Pope and his body within the cultural anxieties about the transgressive power of imagination; his discussion of *The Dunciad* suggests that Dulness embodies the force of the imagination that threatens personal identity. Recent work on authorship and copyright such as Mark Rose's *Authors and Owners* (1993) or Marlon Ross's essay on "Authority and Authenticity" suggest how the legal construction of authorship affected Pope, a particularly relevant subject for *The Dunciad*.[23] Though from an earlier decade, David Morris's emphasis on Pope's preoccupation with refinement and revision ensures *Alexander Pope, The Genius of Sense* (1984) a place alongside current studies.[24] While this impressive body of work addresses issues related to or touching on *The Dunciad*, the poem itself often escapes extended discussion.

Despite its intimate relationship with issues central to our profession and to understanding Pope's career, *The Dunciad* seems slowest to receive the theoretical treatment that has marked other eighteenth-century scholarship. Ironically, a fairly traditional bibliographic study cast into sharp relief some of the contradictions within *The Dunciad* and redirected attention to that poem and Pope's activities in the print trade. David Foxon's *Pope and the Early Eighteenth-Century Book Trade* (1991) reveals Pope's intimate involvement in the production of his own books.[25] Describing a Pope as financially motivated as many of the dunces he reviled, Foxon complicates our understanding of the poet who pretended to eschew such material concerns. As Foxon's volume makes clear, the more we learn about the material conditions of production, the more fully we can understand a poem like *The Dunciad*, so inextricably linked to that world.

No collection has yet focused exclusively on *The Dunciad*. The seeming resistance to engage the poem belies its centrality within eighteenth-century culture. Like *Gulliver's Travels* or *The Beggar's Opera*, the poem's hybridity actually changes and improves upon the forms it parodically controls. But unlike those texts, it proves difficult to teach, despite its multiple points of entry. Its allusive text and extensive reading apparatus can seem labyrinthine; it seems, at times, an eighteenth-century hypertext offering embedded explication, commentary, and directions to additional or secondary texts. The essays in this volume approach the poem from a variety of perspectives and, in doing so, illuminate its role as literary history, cultural artifact, and material object. They suggest ways the poem interacts with and influences the dynamic milieu from which it springs. Because of the poem's centrality in eighteenth-century culture (literary and otherwise), the essays in some cases look beyond the poem at the cultural forces with which it interacts.

For example, George Rousseau's essay explores the relationship between Pope's psychosexual development and his antipathy to opera. Approaching this understudied Popeian aversion from a second perspective, Valerie Rumbold explores the theme of opera within *The Dunciad in Four Books* to reveal internal tensions and complicated examples of shared authorship within the poem. Her essay illustrates the challenge historical analysis poses to the tradition of reading the poem as an expression of absolutes. Laura Rosenthal's and Eric Chandler's essays each examine, in different terms, the construction of masculinity and its role in the textual relationship between Cibber and Pope in the 1740s. Similarly, Linda Zionkowski discusses Pope's centrality in the debates over the often gendered nature of literary labor, and his repudiation in Book 4 of *The Dunciad* of the concepts of masculine conduct from which he was excluded. Catherine Ingrassia looks at the reconstruction of Pope's body and persona (both suffering from a compromised masculinity) in Edmund Curll's pamphlets responding to the 1728 *Dunciad*.

To some degree, these essays explore Pope's paradoxical query whether "the Poem was not made for these Authors, but these Authors for the Poem."[26] They share a concern with unveiling Pope's inextricable connection to the duncean "other" that resembles another version of the poet himself, a resemblance the poem simultaneously embraces and effaces. Though their treatment of the published *ad hominem* attacks on Pope seemingly privileges the voices of Pope's enemies, the essays expand the context for understanding the poem and, perhaps, underscore the reasons for the poem's dominance over these dissenting voices. As Helen Deutsch asks, "What better way to show their insignificance and mark his own enduring value than to confine the dunces to the hell of historical particularity?"[27] This "particularity" necessitates a rehearsal of original responses to the poems, a critical approach that the poem, in a sense, forces on the reader who desires a full understanding of the text. While we may not always agree with Pope's assessment of the dunces, without knowledge of their published interaction with him we must simply take him at his word. A re-examination of these texts also makes it apparent why Pope's poem works, literarily and historically, in a way these ephemeral attacks do not. In addition to possessing greater cultural authority, publishing acumen, and textual control, Pope, as cannot be denied by even the most produncean among us, also had superior poetic powers that ultimately ensured the predominance of his poem. The material and the imaginative conspired to ensure his success. The hybridity of the poem, the linking of high and low, that marks *The Dunciad* is completely lacking in these adversarial texts: while they attack the elevated and transhistorical on which Pope drew, they cannot escape the metaphor and resonance that might be characterized as the "low" and topical. They become victims of their *own* particularity, not just Pope's. Consequently, this volume's preoccupation with the oppositional voices not only serves to contextualize the poem within the discourse of professional authorship (at all levels), but, in the process, explore some reasons for Pope's ultimate success.

Other essays approach issues of literary form and print culture in specific historical moments. Thomas Jemielity reads *The Dunciad* as "mock-apocalypse" and suggests how such a reading complicates the poem's satiric structure. Claudia Thomas's discussion of the poem's Rabelaisian qualities goes beyond Stallybrass and White's or Bakhtin's use of that term; rather, she is concerned with the "Rabelaisian" in terms of the imagery and purpose of the Renaissance satirist.

The variety of essays in this collection indicates that the poem remains a vital and exciting text that invites—indeed requires—new perspectives and critical approaches. At the same time, the essays share a common concern for locating the poem in its social, cultural, and economic milieu, for understanding the text as a cultural object, and for teasing out the implications of these revisionings for Pope's persona. The appearance of a collection on *The Dunciad* more than a decade after the tercentenary suggests the poem's continued vitality and, more important, its centrality to understanding the culture of eighteenth-century England: it remains a touchstone because it captured the tenor of the period it helped create. The poem's canonical status—albeit often as excerpted in an anthology—might prompt us to ask why the poem has survived. Its calculated obscurity, its superior tone, and its binary cultural vision might mark it for extinction. Our repeated return to the poem, however, suggests that the cultural work it performs remains current for a society increasingly defined by commerce, popular culture, and rampant consumerism (which now can be satisfied through multiple media). The tensions the poem revisits are ever-modern in a world confronted by efforts to quantify and categorize "culture" in response to the perceived disintegration of "cultural values" stemming from the interrogation of their underlying ideological assumptions. Perhaps Pope's poem prompts us not only to re-evaluate the poet, but to visit our own culture anew.

"et in Arcadia homo": Opera, Gender, and Sexual Politics in *The Dunciad*

G. S. Rousseau

I

Pope's perpetually perplexing sexuality—biographical and representational—has endured among the most-vexed topics before and after Maynard Mack's landmark biography published in 1985. Yet even in this *ne plus ultra* of apparently definitive pronouncements composed of almost one thousand pages and almost three hundred thousand words, the poet's sexuality remains nebulous: at times burstingly heterosexual, yet paradoxically homosocial at others; patently recalcitrant, tentative, and even nebulous on the biographer's part; in any case, utterly unrelated to Pope's final poetic will and testament, *The New Dunciad*. The inherently amusing nature of this contradiction should not be overlooked even by Pope's modern devotees. After all, in the end, a group of cloistered (possibly even closeted) scholars speculate on others' sexual experience and its symbolic representations. Still, Mack accepted Pope's "homosociality," if his index provides a clue; in his text, Mack merely describes Pope's warm feelings for literary advisors like Trumbull and Congreve and deep attachments to older "brother types" like Bathurst, while continuing to uphold the fiction of a heterosexual Pope incapable of finding the right woman. Even when commenting on the sexual energies of Pope's *Dunciad*, Mack is silent.

These may have been characteristically cautious and wise observations in 1985, but, even then, they were less than brave in their tendency to tame Pope's life and his work more than a cultural context different from Mack's would warrant. Since 1985, scholarship and criticism have amended this record, particularly in the appearance of studies of *The Dunciad*'s great goddess and her followers, and among the new breed of feminists, masculinists, gender critics, and gay cultural historians attempting to

pinpoint more explicitly than Mack the poet's experienced sexual
state of mind. Bravery and cowardice may not seem the most appropriate dichotomy to capture "then and now." Some may deem
it more fitting to present self-engrossed contemporary theorists
more concerned with their own agendas than Pope's historico-
biographical one. Nevertheless, early in the 1970s, I myself attempted to affix a sexual label to Pope's sensibility after collecting
everything pertinent to his sexuality, and by assessing everything
written about it before and after his death in 1744. But I could
not "prove" a homosexual Pope by any reasonable definition of
the word, and ceased the pursuit.[1] A few years later, after the appearance of Mack's biography, I concurred with his conclusion
that Pope was *not* homosexual, but rather homosocial, and I
abandoned the matter there.[2] That moment merely represented
the first stage of a project of retrieval, the first part of which appears here.

The record of commentary from 1744 onward had been pal-
try—anything but reliable or abundant. The view of the 1740s
was that of an almost genderless Pope—the asexual creature caricatured by his enemies as stinking and stung himself—taking his
final pot shots: an alienated and sexless misfit. Since the appearance of the *Essay on Man* in 1733, he slowly had grown increasingly disaffected: the "wicked wasp of Twickenham" venting his
spleen on amanuenses, servants, friends, family, everyone, only
to terminate his poetic career in an apocalyptic vision—the most
gloomy imaginable—of universal chaos in which the world virtually comes to an end. In the *Essay*, Pope, although no Enlightenment chaologist, had shown himself to be deeply interested in
theories of order and chaos in relation to their Lucretian, Bacon-
ian, Newtonian, and Leibnizian heritages.

But chaos—the history of the idea, the Renaissance allegory,
and the Western myth constituting the mighty subject of Pope's
last published major poem (*The New Dunciad*)—is a more complex matter than has been recognized, even among the current
milieu of chaos theorists, for whom it has a totally different resonance in almost every sense from Pope's chaos. Even more differ-
entially, chaos in the last decade has become a metaphor, of
course, for virtually everything known or knowable: chaos theory, complexity theory, the new realism, and so forth. I claim in
this essay that Pope's chaos, as he idiosyncratically configured it,
rather than our modern chaos theory, has profound implications
for his *sexuality* and especially for what I call *et in Arcadia homo*,
by which I designate the poet's deep homosocial *yearning*—not

merely the fact of his homosociality and the myth he erected that, in the next, eternal world, he would become a better man, with the better body he sought all along, but also including its resonances. And this is why his "arcadia" here is suggestive and associative of a mental landscape rather than a concrete place with a specific name. Pope's varied Grubbean settings in *The Dunciad* constantly imply rustic realms through opposition, but it is not an antithesis any sensible reader would wish to exploit or push to the limits of the explicit. His places and settings, whether Grubbean or antithetically arcadian, are subservient in *The Dunciad* to a myth of self-creation that intensified rather than diminished with age. This is perhaps the force—again by association—of his "ego" not merely in the state of arcadia but also as "homo," as self-regenerating male poet living through his art.

Still, my larger aim in this essay entails the demonstration that Pope's Chaos (despite its vast distance from our chaos theory) is complex *precisely* because it was gendered. It was gendered in ways Pope thought some of his readers (then and perhaps in posterity, but surely not all) would have understood, especially in his view that Italian opera (as *distinct* from English and in the totality of its spectacle as drama, story, music, costume, setting) was a precondition for this copula of chaos and sexuality. It was so, as Pope claims in his *Dunciad*, simply because opera was a *female* "Harlot form." Italian opera, on the other hand, is not so pronounced in *The Dunciad* as to become a major theme—such a claim would entail exaggeration—but its stunningly dramatic appearance is calculated in ways making clear that it has practically become synonymous for Pope with the primary force of female chaos. This convergence of Italian art form transplanted on to foreign soil, and its symbolisms and representations there (in Britain), forms as crucial a strain in this essay as any attention devoted to the biographical poet and his famous poem. Finally, Pope's belief that the sociocultural disturbances elicited by this vicious import to England, especially through opera's castrati and eunuchs, were among the most vexing events of his adult experience.

Considering his physical oddities and the massive sexual toll they took on his self-identity, it is difficult to imagine that the appearance of castrati and eunuchs in England would *not* prove troubling to his sexual psyche and symbolic imaginative life; as Mack so shrewdly pronounces, not only is a poet's life symbolic, but it was particularly in Pope's symbolic view of reality that he had calibrated so much of his poetic resonance.[3] *Au fin*, Italian opera as a sociocultural phenomenon profoundly troubled him, despite the great likelihood from the mass of available evidence that he himself *never* saw one staged, and disturbed him more than has been acknowledged by some of his finest critics. Every aspect of the castrati, even their high fees and relation to female courtiers, disturbed the Pope who was so curious about them. He saw performances of Gay's *Beggar's Opera* and Handel's *Esther* or *Semele*, but did not witness the live production of any *Italian* opera (French operas were not then performed in London and differed, in any case, *vis-à-vis* castrati from Italian): a bare-bones fact that underlied the nature and context of his negative attitude to the new entertainment and that seems to have eluded even those who have written explicitly about his relation to Italian opera. My aim here is to adumbrate the artistic and biographical consequences of these anxieties, as well as their cultural resonances.[4]

Today, at the end of the twentieth century, we tend to construe opera's "disturbances" (whether Italian or German or in any other national form) as virtually nonexistent. For example, our general sense of the legacy of Italian opera—from Mozart and Rossini to Verdi and Puccini—embraces bel canto arias, exquisite melodies, high drama, visual spectacle, and (in the all-important category of story) a libretto recounting some tragically flawed romantic love in which desire, disease, and death combine to abort almost every pair of lovers.[5] One could claim, epigrammatically, that the form consists of these three Ds: so indigenous are they to its existence. And there are few exceptions to the norm. Italian opera by now is so well-established in all Western countries and their opera houses that its stars and productions, divas and producers, receive all the attention rather than the original composers or librettists. Wayne Koestenbaum makes the point in *The Queen's Throat: Opera, Homosexuality, and the Mystery of Desire* (1993), where he elevates opera's threshold by constructing his own self-indulgent contemporary mindset—especially in his own biographical development—and demonstrates opera's affinities with romantic temperament and thwarted love: an essence of the homosocial matrix.[6] But the introduction of Italian opera into England in the eighteenth century represented much more of a sociocultural disturbance, and embedded all personal responses, such as Pope's, within a cultural–political context. A century later, English social commentators were still denouncing its deleterious effects on its first audiences, and William Hazlitt, no friend of perceived debauchery, considered it to be the ultimate form of "intellectual prostitution." Within these often fierce attacks lurked unidentified ambiguities: Which aspects of its formal existence? Its national site? Its lewd characters? The excesses of its spectacle? The libretti it imported? The lives of its composers? And so forth. Among these, the castrati especially were sites of terrific tension within a culture already stretched to the limit by gender stress.[7] Within a generation—from roughly the 1660s to the late 1690s—sexuality's ethos had proceeded from extreme toleration toward unbridled libertinism to restraint and caution; and in the next—when Pope was born and maturing—into gender ambiguity and serious doubt.

The maturing Pope, as even Mack so brilliantly chronicles, could not help but see himself refracted through these anatomic ambiguities and gender stresses. It was not merely his physical deformity, as so many commentators by now have noted, which confused and even deranged Pope, as his pathetic outpourings to Lady Mary make evident, but the implications of the *specific* source and site of his own biographical deformity: the anatomical groin, the penis.[8] Eventually Pope's numerous enemies feminized him in ways extending far beyond the human groin. Even so, students of Pope's deformity (including myself) often overlook the fact that, whatever his psychosexual mindset may have been, he *must* have been conscious of his symbolic phallic incongruity: this is the culmination of the accident at eight and his endless urethral constrictions. Whatever the accident with the cow in the field actually was; whatever Pope's own construction of, and coping with, his difficulty in passing water and possibly even masturbating; he *must* have realized, despite his silences and (his physician) Cheselden's later testimony, that it was the result of gonorrhea, the limitations of his genital capability. He may not have connected the accident or his adolescent dwarfdom with his genital incapacity as cause and effect; but later in life, certainly by the late 1730s, he must have known that his phallic apparatus was defective both anatomically and in its ability to perform. What he thought earlier, in his "rake days," is another matter; before his thirties, he posed as a heterosexual rake, boasting of visits to prostitutes and dreaming of the legendary sexual prowess of dwarves like himself. All these tensions were precisely the ones refracted in the figures of the castrati who were somewhat like him. The uncertain matter regards Pope's self-positioning in this capacity. Some castrati claimed to be sexually functional, others not, and the truth of the matter and its precise anatomy can be hard to gauge. The surgical operation varied in its results, leaving some with a very small mutilated penis of sorts but no visible testicles, others with virtually nothing except a tiny lump of flesh to micturate. Pope, unlike them, apparently *had* a penis to insert, but if it was as defective and painful as he gave out biographically, the similarities were all too palpable. Hence, like him, they were of a different kind of anatomical man: physically differentiated, anatomically deviant, symbolically monstrous, sexually ambiguous, perhaps—in the apt words of Carol Flynn, who borrows from Pope himself—a "softer kind of man."[9]

The Italian opera had also introduced eunuchs into the popular English imagination (earlier, they had been restricted to a few plays on the stage), and here too Pope saw himself reflected in an anatomical mirror. Biographically, he had done what he could to assert his physical manliness, but his inner self—the part outraged at caricatures of him as a type of eunuch-castrato—knew. And this inner Pope, so to speak, was the imaginative one harnessing the sexual politics of Italian opera to the grotesque lampoon that constitutes his most original poem(s): *The Dunciad* and *The New Dunciad*. Here opera, as introduced by Johann Heidegger and others into England in the second decade of the eighteenth century, is included as a major topos, particularly the sociocultural circumstances on which its content is based.

But if these biocultural circumstances are valid, why should chaos feature so centrally in Pope's poetic vision, other than for its apparent Homeric and Miltonic energies? Do *opera* and *chaos* share common ground? Is there a sense in which they both create something (*poiesis*) out of nothing? Most fundamentally, they would seem to be incommensurate: the former an entertainment (even if imported); the latter a vast concept, if not a perpetual region of the literate Western mind. I argue that they were intermixed, with opera as the necessary condition—for Pope—for the establishment of modern chaos (Dulness's kingdom), and for the "Universal Darkness" that buries all. Universal dullness, social and poetic, constitutes the proof. The fact that Italian opera could succeed in England was proof for Pope, not merely of a pervasive dullness, but (concomitantly) of the "gender trouble" that personally vexed him. Pope's general disgust with his society is too well known to require commentary here—the Pope whose self-confessional tropes abound with dismay as he composes his last poem: "my Heart is sick of This bad World, (as Cato said) and I see it daily growing worse."[10] His imagination of chaos must add in the next sentence: "If there were to be Another Deluge, I protest I don't know more than One Noah; and his Wife, (for he happens to have no children) whom I could expect God would save: I hope He will live forty years however, to preach in, before it comes." Seven days later, again to Allen: "Once more I tell you, I am sick of *this* World and the Great ones of it, tho they have been my intimate Acquaintance."[11]

The poet doth perhaps protest too much: it was *he himself*, especially his sickly phallic carcass, he was "sick of." His disgust as he trounced Italian opera in a poem he had conceptualized as an "abuse" on "Travelling"[12] was shaped by, even determined by, anxiety over his own anatomy. Nothing reminded him more of the defect than the eunuchs and castrati strutting about in Italian operas. That Pope was in touch with his emotional psyche cannot be doubted: he transformed it poetically and mythologically into Cybele, the Galli, and other castrated hacks of *The Dunciad*. Clark Lawlor, drawing on the brilliant detective work of Faulkner and Blair, has clinched the copula of chaos and the opera:

> The poem [*The Dunciad*], although driven by Dulness as the great female monster, also constructs the male grotesque body, and it does this in terms of gender. Dulness's offspring, the dunces, parallel the servants of Cybele, the Great Mother, in their intellectual sterility. Faulkner and Blair explain that the Galli, mendicant priests of Cybele, were eunuchs, castration being part of the initiation into the cult (233–36). Named after the River Gallus, whose waters were said to induce lunacy, they would travel in processions through the towns dancing ecstatically and making a great commotion. Amongst other practices, their secret sacrifices were considered obscene and orgiastic in nature. Faulkner and Blair note that "classical writers looked upon the cult as generally offensive and lewd, and described the sexless priests as tricksters, vagabonds, and swindlers (235)."[13]

II

Other contexts may also have impinged on Pope's imagination of chaos and the sexual energies he amalgamated to it. Ovid's famous description in the *Metamorphoses* was the staple but John Ray's *Three Physico-Theological Discourses* (1713) provided eighteenth-century readers with didactic knowledge about physical chaos, citing Hesiod's *Theogony* and Ovid's *Metamorphoses*. Ray quoted Hesiod's *Theogonia*: "*First of all there was a Chaos*," and claimed of the ancient cosmologies: "*From* Chaos *proceeded* Hell, *and* Night, [or Darkness] which seems to have its Foundation or

Occasion from the second Verse of the first Chapter of *Genesis;
And the Earth was without Form, and void; and Darkness was
upon the Face of the Deep.*"[14]

However, Ray lamented the absence of (almost Foucauldian?)
origins in these ancient accounts. "That which I chiefly dislike in
this Opinion of theirs, is, that they make no mention of the Creation of this *Chaos*, but seem to look upon it as self-existent and
improduced."[15] The notion that God created chaos without motive, or for unknown reasons, dissatisfied Ray's inquisitive mind
about the natural universe. To resolve the dilemma, he combed
ancient authors other than Hesiod in search of valid parentage.
Ray discovered much, yet appears unaware of the tradition in
which Chaos (here with upper case in view of its coexistence with
Eros) had been coeval with Eros before the formal creation of the
world. As N. Katherine Hayles observes in tracing the historical
origins of modern chaos theory:

> The tradition that identified Chaos as that which existed when the
> world did not continued at least through the Renaissance. In *Para-
> dise Lost*, God creates his world not out of nothing but out of Chaos,
> the primeval *materia* of the universe before it was invested with
> spirit. Also continuing into the Renaissance was the apposition be-
> tween Eros and Chaos as the two primeval forces of the world. It oc-
> curs in Shakespeare, for example, although the tonalities are
> significantly darker than in Hesiod. In Shakespeare a return to Chaos
> signals a failure of love, as though the universe were disintegrating
> back to where it was before Eros appeared.[16]

Yet still another allegorical tradition existed in which Chaos
was the offspring of Eros and Strife. In this version the four elements floated into two enveloping media—Eros and Strife—
which acted as material forces on them. Love initially prevailed
and kept Strife on the periphery of the egg of the world, but eventually Strife absorbed or swallowed the four elements and drove
out Eros, thereby creating Chaos. This view had its spokesmen
in late Renaissance alchemists, especially in the tradition from
Paracelsus and the Hermeticists to Athenasius Kircher.[17] What
Ray absorbed from these thinkers, or Pope, must not deflect us
from the larger matter: the genealogies of chaos Pope adjudged
he could reunite with their ancient erotic counterparts, hence his
dunciadic cults of Cybele and her castrated eunuchs in Book 2.[18]

By ca. 1700, the consortium of Chaos and Eros seems to have
grown obscure, eventually disappearing, and Chaos parentage
shrunk to an all-time low: so low that Pope may be the last poet

to have made Chaos a god. As the offspring of Eros and Strife, or (in yet another tradition) Eros and Anteros, the chaos of Pope's world represented the forces of sexual love and its antithesis, barrenness.[19] This latter lineage produced a hermaphroditic child, Chaos, whose saturnian countenance continued after Pope's lifetime, as when Vala reinforces Blake's conception of Satan as thoroughly hermaphroditic.[20] Both Pope and Blake knew (as did Jung much later) that throughout history the cosmogonic gods had been hermaphroditic and androgynous. In a countertradition, hermaphroditism symbolized ultimate perfection: almost as an alchemical alloy, endowing the form with eternal unity precisely because it lay beyond the human one. But for Blake, as perhaps for Pope, the hermaphrodite was emblematic of a vile chaos and radical *deviance* precisely because it collided with expectations of human and divine form. So too the vile form of Chaos's gender: an unnatural amalgam of warring principles, especially manly and epicene. These mythographic riddles troubled Pope, I believe, throughout his life, albeit transformed from cosmogonic into anatomic contexts. It was one thing to be dwarfed as a male; another, like Dulness, to be monstrous as a grotesque female; much worse, a *hermaphroditic* freak, as Pope's body symbolized to his contemporaries, a view that redounded on himself.[21] No wonder he complained that he never enjoyed three days' health from this "crazy carcass."

These hermaphroditic contexts bore on Chaos's lineage, even in its post-Miltonic decline. The lowering of Chaos's stature from a god to a mere force was particularly noteworthy. Milton had created the world, as Hayles comments, out of chaos, the primary material of creation before mind was infused into it. The competing Ovidian view, that chaos was confused genderless matter, as Sandys notes in his translation of the *Metamorphoses*, appears to have gained ground during the Restoration and eighteenth century. By the 1720s Pope could dramatize Chaos as the inseminator of "eternal Night" by whom was produced a monstrous female creature called Dulness: a deformed and unnatural birth (like the change-of-life baby born in 1688, Alexander Pope); a creature almost without precedent in the ancient pantheon and certainly unparalleled for its grotesquerie in the poet's work.

Moreover, Chaos's progeny, Dulness, was as monstrous in the ancient theology as Chaos itself: specifically configured as a female monster whose paradoxical power was both effeminizing and emasculating. But if Dulness was grotesque, she was equally aberrant in her radical potency: the *femme fatale* who could spawn the sickliest of poetic creatures as proof of her moral inversion. As Aubrey Williams notes, Pope's Dulness is the "Mighty Mother and ponderous matriarch," and the "maternal source from which everything arose."[22] Black night from Homer to Milton had always produced freaks and monsters, and it is hardly surprising that Dulness should have sprung from her specific parents: "Chaos" and "Eternal Night." Pope's dunces, like the Galli, produce hideous dins as they learn "the wond'rous pow'r of Noise" (B.2.222). The Galli also cross-dressed as women and wore long mantles, one of several reasons Lucian considered them "mountebanks and effeminate fellows."[23] In parallel, Pope's dunces are characterized as effeminate, castrated, and locked in homosexual acts: "Behold yon Pair, in strict embraces join'd" (B. 3. 179). If Faulkner and Blair are correct about these classical resonances of Pope's Dulness, then Chaos becomes all the more surcharged in its post-Miltonic lineage because of its gender transformation.

Furthermore, in classical and Renaissance theogonies the precondition for the instauration of Chaos was familial: as we have seen, the progeny of two such antithetical forces as Eros and its opposite (Anteros). Pope's extraordinary superimposition was cultural: the extension of chaos to culture—almost as a cultural norm or barometer—and the refinement of its precondition as more specifically gendered than any previous notion. Dulness reigns throughout *The Dunciad* of 1728–29 and in *The New Dunciad* of 1742, but it is the cultural dislocations of gender, as witnessed in the vulgar importation of Italian opera, that compel "Universal Darkness" to "bury all." Nowhere was the horror of gender trouble more evident, Pope thought, than in the luxuriousness and effeminacy of Italian opera with its prancing castrati and Galli-like eunuchs. To many English viewers, like Pope,[24] this corrupting spectacle imported from the Mediterranean land of Catholic lewdness and buggery was proof that gender relations had degenerated beyond the pale at home. It provided them with armor to buttress charges of the declining moral fibre of the nation, and permitted many of them to rankle in the spirit of Bolingbrokean patriotism that it was reducing the nation to degeneracy.[25]

This corrupting luxury and its inevitable effeminacy sprung forward from larger realms political and cultural, with which cosmic chaos had its direct parallels. *The Dunciad*'s Twickenham editor calls attention to this constellation of cultural forces of which Italian opera constitutes such an integral part. "Pope is looking

critically at contemporary England after twenty years of Walpole's administration," James Sutherland comments, "and
exposing the nation's follies and stupidities one after another: the
decay of the theatres, of the schools and universities, of the aristocracy, of the arts and sciences, of the Church, of public and private morality, of liberty; the growth of luxury, of free thinking,
of political corruption; the follies of virtuosi, of young peers who
patronize the Opera or who make the Grand Tour, of pedantic
scholars, of gourmets, of freemasons. . . ."[26]

Sutherland's map is of a dispersive cultural milieu perhaps
grasped best by travel outside the realm. These operatic "young
peers" reflected at home the corruptions of the Grand Tour
(hence Pope's sense of *The Dunciad* as a satire on the "abuses
of travel"): both opera and travel played their parts—the line of
argument went—in perverting the genders through Italian
means. Nevertheless, so much has been written about Italian
opera during Pope's adult life that it need not be rehearsed here:
its arrival on English soil during the decade of the 1720s, its collapse in the 1730s as a result of the famous quarrel between two
rival companies, and its relation to English opera. Much less has
been culled, however, first about its corrupting influence (here
Pope's *Dunciad* remains the major statement despite others), and
secondly, and more germane here, opera's sexual symbols and
what I am calling its sexual politics. The latter camp—symbols
and politics—particularly spoke to the dwarfish Pope of impaired
genitals who saw, or was forced to see, himself reflected in its eunuchs and castrati. Our generation has identified opera's participants, economies, performers, performances, and even its early
audiences. But its associations with gender politics—a long-term
developing Italian xenophobia ever since foreign travel heated up
after the Treaty of Utrecht, exotic Italian sexuality, Italy as the
preternatural home of sodomy, and, of course her native castrati—continue to remain ignored topics.[27]

III

The predominant (Protestant) English view was that the
(Catholic) Italians had yielded themselves entirely to the gratification and vice of the senses. Even in Pope's formative years, wit
upon wit, scribbler after scribbler, perceived Italy and the Italians as the landfolk of decadence *par excellence* where decadent
values flourished, and opera was the national Italian codified art

form sanctioning these values. Gray and Walpole almost certainly never saw an opera while in Italy but they sent home accounts of their 1742 "Grand Tour" just as Pope was composing *The New Dunciad*;[28] so lurid are their vignettes of Italian lust that they may as well have been a couple of debauched young Venetians themselves. This in contrast to the noble young Romans of Virgil's epic, as Howard Erskine-Hill has shrewdly compared these Aeneases *de ses jours* with reference to the famous passage in *The Dunciad*'s Book 2 about Italy's "Tyber, now no longer Roman" (4. 299).[29] Erskine-Hill also cites the Pope–Warburton explanatory note to the passage: "This [Venetian] Republic heretofore the most considerable in Europe, for her Naval Force and the extent of her Commerce; now illustrious for her *Carnivals*." The two Popeian collaborators may as well have included opera as salient among the "carnivals." Still worse, Europe has followed suit, constructing "a moral landscape so beautiful because they [the inhabitants] have yielded themselves up to the gratification of the senses, yet the true result is the 'smooth Eunuch and enamour'd swain' rather than the vitality of a true love."[30]

Medico-anatomical contexts for this degeneracy theory also existed. By the early eighteenth century a view of the anatomical degeneracy of *homo sapiens* had developed,[31] although it fell short of the post-Darwinian discourse that pushed it to its logical conclusion (the eventual decline of mankind itself) and accounted for it as the malady of travel, western and eastern.[32] The figure of the eunuch was central to this discourse, especially in such extensive anatomical treatises as Charles d'Ancillon's *Traité des Eunuques* (1707),[33] which described the physical operation, chronicled its hot bathtubs leading to nervous insensibility, explained how the ducts to the testicles were severed, the testicles themselves made to shrivel and disappear. Ancillon and others explained that the operation had, for all its cruelty, surprisingly little effect on the subject's health and robustness. Indeed, the eunuchs often possessed voracious sexual appetites afterward that enjoyed remarkable and inexplicable longevity. In some cases the operation intensified the eunuch's sexual impulses and heightened his intellectual capacity. What damage there was seems to have been psychological in an era when virility—especially virility in Italy—was accounted such a sovereign virtue. Years later, Charles Burney attempted to discover where these surgical procedures were conducted so that he could observe one, but was unable.[34] Pope may not have known about this lore. If he did, he may have been jealous of all these attributes, not least their sexual competitiveness (he himself ever-ready to assert his virility) and longevity (he would not have known, of course, that he would die at fifty-six).

Moreover, if some eunuchs were demonstrably sodomitical in their practices, the great majority continued to lust after women. The main criticisms hurled were economic, sodomitical, and especially flung on grounds of a surfeit of conceit: an air of arrogance, which women especially found insufferable, perhaps out of spite and jealousy. The economic complaint was coupled to their degeneracy, as in Abel Evans's *The Apparition* (1710) where he lamented that:

> For Faults, like these, from France the Dancers came,
> And Eunuch Singing Choristers, from Rome:
> At vast Expence those Epicures are fed;
> The Poets, Players, justly want their bread.

Evans continued by implicating homosexual lewdness:

> With Prudence then, divert th'impending Blow,
> Some Moderation in your Madness show:
> For Lewdness, for discreeter Lewdness call;
> For Modest Vice:—or else the stage will fall.[35]

The rivalry between the eunuchs-castrati and female singers was legion, all the more so in that even the very best female singers—as the well-known Pietro Tosi attested[36]—were never more competent than inferior castrati.[37] This must have galled the women and aroused their envy. Besides, before approximately 1700, few female opera singers of any renown could be found in Italy: most were men, most of the sopranos castrati. The Catholic church forbade them to marry and overlooked the attacks and assaults made upon them, but they could make fortunes in no time, and when no longer able to sing they routinely attached themselves to courts as *virtuosi di camera*, celebrated figures often feared and revered. One would wish to have had accounts of their plight preserved, but only one autobiography of a castratus has survived.[38] Courts, Catholics, bachelors, envy, spite, money, virility, fame, fierce female rivalry, genital operations, bodily deformity: can Pope have been blind to *all* these parallels? Did he see none of these analogues?[39] No one should argue for one explanation to the exclusion of the rest, but the weight of evidence is on the broad spectrum rather than the particulars of one or another.

The advent of Italian opera in London renewed the topicality of the medical accounts (those like Ancillon's), especially when they explained how the castrati-eunuchs sang so well. But the moralists only recounted their seduction of London's *men*. "They were often castigated as evil creatures," historian Angus Heriot claims, "who lured men into homosexuality—and there were admittedly homosexual castrati, as Casanova's accounts bear witness."[40] The anonymous author of *Hell upon Earth*, published within months of Pope's first three books of *The Dunciad* in 1729, devoted an entire third chapter to Italian opera as the single cause of the sudden rise of sodomy in England, claiming that "since the Introduction of Italian Opera's [sic] here, our Men are grown insensibly more and more *Effeminate* ..." and names the "womanish eunuchs" and debauched castrati who lure unsuspecting young men into their nets.[41] Column after column in the newspapers and magazines asserted that Italian opera was a "sick" and "unnatural" entertainment.[42]

Historically, the eunuchs arose in the Orient and Levant to perform menial services for the emperors and harems. But the pan-European Catholic church elevated them and displayed a hypocritical attitude: outlawing the surgical castration on one hand and rendering it punishable by excommunication, while installing a eunuch in every Roman chapel, on the other, including the pope's own private chapel in the Vatican, which (during the other Pope's adult years in the 1720 and 1730s) boasted well over two hundred.[43] During Pope's lifetime, castrati males sang Italian opera in England in exclusively *male* parts (they also performed in France but under different conditions). The spectacular sight of this stunned (think of the film *Farinelli* in our time) abundant British travelers abroad into recording their impressions of the native soil of these creatures: Charles Burney, Horace Mann, Horace Walpole.[44] These reports were generally positive, as Heriot notes; the famous Goethe being among the most enthusiastic at the end of the eighteenth century via a rather concocted theory of mimesis within double-entendre: specifically, that they afforded spectators "*double pleasure* by not being women themselves but by mastering the female's part."[45] Long before inveterate travelers to Italy such as Goethe and d'Archenholz (1791) expressed their delight in watching the castrati, the Count Pollnitz (Frederick the Great's favorite plaything for a time) objected on grounds that the castrati were anatomically inferior men to be eradicated. Shades here, perhaps, of Lady Mary's "third sex" quip that there were three genders, not two: men, women, and Herveys.

A number of traditions converged here: first the visual, where audiences were deranged by the castrati's new ocular sensations in flamboyant costume, coiffure, jewelry, feathers, and furs. One charge was that these audiences were all too willing to pander to an erotics of submission. In England, where a national stage tradition was already well developed by the 1730s, a further accusation was that the castrati were subverting good home-grown English theater. Even in Roman times there were caricatures of the castrati, as Heriot notes,[46] resembling those in the era of Pope as the deformed poet-statesman (i.e., the effeminate statesman as deformed as if he had been castrated)—and at least some of the Roman-Augustan analogues could not have escaped Pope. For example, Salvator Rosa, the fanatical Italian patriot, isolated the castrati as the symbol par excellence of Italy's degradation, and in his satire on music—*Satire di S. Rosa, dedicate a Settano*—vented his bitterest venom on them.[47] Pope may not have known Rosa's satires (Sutherland and Mack are uncertain), but Rosa's notions of Italian debasement were at the expense of English guineas (Farinelli was the highest-paid castrato in Europe, paid in English currency).[48]

Even more pressing were the issues of nationalism, economy, religion, xenophobia, and the spread of the miasma of Italian degeneracy, as they impinged on this negative construction of the castratus/eunuch as an emblem of the new degeneracy.[49] John Abell's death (1660–1736?), the English male soprano singer who had trained in Italy and thought to be a castrato, caused a stir in Pope's London precisely because he typified the pollution of Italian contagion.[50] Abell was sent as a boy to Italy by Charles II to cultivate his voice; it remained so high throughout his life that English audiences deemed him a castrato and attributed to him all sorts of secret powers for such preservation until old age.[51] These English audiences again and again—and this is the means to comprehend the context of Pope's own absorption—hold the key to understanding the castrati's success. Heriot's conclusion, based on the popular press of the 1730s, was that the castrato's gender ambiguity played a dual function in both alienating *and* serving the audiences for whom he performed:

> It is difficult to believe that these practices arose altogether from necessity, and one can only conclude that such ambiguities were valued for lending a spice of double-entendre, even to the most tragic situations. . . . Tastes change, and today this may seem tediously silly and out of keep with the dignity of serious art; but it must be remem-

bered that an opera of Scarlatti or Hasse fulfilled the functions, not
only of "Tristan" or "Aida" today, but also those of "Oklahoma" and
"The Merry Widow," and there was no distinction between brows of
varying heights.[52]

The position is apt so far as it goes but may not proceed far
enough. Italian opera, after all, was—in England—a thoroughly
new and highly exotic entertainment, and as such succeeded or
failed by its ability to tap into an audience *already* prepared to
covet and pay for it. Beyond this, however, is the documented fact
that the court and aristocracy were paying the exorbitant prices
commanded by the castrati in what must be counted as the first
appearance of international stars. Heriot is right to emphasize
that they were, moreover, "the only international stars of the
epoch."[53] But his salient point, underpinning my argument about
Pope's sexual politics of opera and the castrati, is this: "the most
important part, however, is that Italian opera was, till the *late*
eighteenth century, almost synonymous with the castrati, and
that Italian opera was the opera that really mattered."[54]

If Heriot is right, particularly about the gender derangements
of Italian opera, then we can see how its reception in England fed
into the new androgyny perceived during Pope's lifetime. Androgyny, and its attendant bisexual energies, had been strong in
England from the Restoration onward, formally having been almost unknown during the Revolution and Interregnum, but the
generation between the 1690s—in Pope's childhood—and the
South Sea Bubble campaigned against it as part of the new morality contra lewdness on and off the stage. Historians of gender arrangements such as Trumbach and Garber have confirmed this
sense, but omitted Italian opera from their discussion. Nevertheless, one reason for its almost instantaneous success was the inherent androgynous dimension, as evidenced by the fact that
these castrated males sang male parts *exclusively*, as we have
noted, yet possessed the high soprano range of females and in
some cases could reach higher notes. Thus visual males possessing female voices combined into androgynous theatrical spectacles. Even Swift, no shrewd observer of operas, complained in the
Intelligencer 3 of London's being "over-run with *Italian Effeminacy*, and *Italian Nonsense*"—an outcry against vice not at all of
the sort made about that other indigenous "opera" by Gay. The
gender arrangements in Gay were hard and fast in comparison.[55]

IV

Such gender fluidity acknowledges the varieties of Georgian eunuchism, as Germaine Greer long ago suggested in other contexts (*The Female Eunuch*, 1970) and as we do today when we widely recognize a broad spectrum of homosexual types rather than a monolithic gay stereotype: biological, psychological, even homosexuals of the mind. It also suggests that Pope, who, as we have said, may never have actually seen an Italian opera yet who was fiercely opposed to the form, somehow absorbed many of its energies into his own larger-than-life spectacle. My point has not merely been the absorption but also its formalistic representations. For example, in Italian opera, as we have just seen, the castrati play the central roles within the performances. So too in *The Dunciad* where Dulness commands her castrated votives, as well as other female grotesques. Both the historical Italian opera and Pope's poem incorporating it made much of the sibyls' relation to the castrati. As Clark Lawlor comments, the main ones are "Cloacina, the 'slip-shod Sibyl,' and the related form of Opera."[56] Indeed, it is "Opera" who "prepares the way" (B.3.301) for Dulness: not merely as conduit but as grotesque female form "filled," as Lawlor claims, "with notions of her own self-importance and prepared to supply the audience with anything it desires." And as Pope's Dulness boasts her castrated Galli/dunces, so Opera had her high priests—the castrati—who appeared in scenes as grotesque as Hercules singing in high soprano voice. What better strategy to force "normal" male singers out of their proper roles?[57] Parallels such as these typify Dulness and her Popeian maker. Opera, on the other hand, similar to her analogous goddess Dulness, lords over emasculated male servants: the castrati of Italy and eunuchs who had been servants in the harems of the Middle East. These analogies—Opera and Dulness—are imperfect, but they are Pope's not ours, and are sufficiently abundant to confirm that Pope knew what he was about in this dimension of his great satiric lampoon.

In the category of monstrosity, in whose representational history *The Dunciad* must also be construed as an artifact, these deformed operatic creatures doubtlessly also deeply impressed Pope. Here too both lampoon and musical form shared in the "Phantom Opera's" representations. First and foremost, the castrati of opera were demonized as unnatural monsters, for some of the reasons already provided, but also in view of their protean

sexual ambiguity—what today might be termed gender liminal-
ity. Ness and others observe that they occasionally acted *en
travesti*, in what part they pleased, as men or as women.[58] The
basic distinction—sexual difference—was blurred in monstrous
ways among the castrati precisely because of their protean ability
to disguise themselves. In their epicene appeal, they usurped the
position of "legitimate" humans, becoming obscene symbols, for
Pope and others, of the kind of "amphibiousness" that heralds
chaos.[59] Here, in the blending of chaos and monstrosity, resides a
further copula connecting them. Catherine Ingrassia connects
them thus: "Pope's description of the Phantom of Opera indicates the ambiguous, corrupt sexuality Opera also engenders in
the real world; the castrati willingly mutilate themselves, sacri-
ficing their virility in pursuit of profit."[60] Sexual amphibiousness
(with which Pope had already charged Hervey in the famous
Sporus passage in *Epistle to Dr Arbuthnot*) and an environment
of chaos would also seem to be found among unnatural monsters.[61] Then, continuing, no leap of faith is needed to understand
how they combined to produce an obscene symbol of ultimate degeneracy for Pope—hence the Phantom of Opera within Pope's
order of Chaos.

The basic distinction about gender difference was blurred in
the castrati. In their epicene reach-out, they usurped the position
of legitimate humans. Like the Galli, who worshipped Magna
Mater, the castrati emasculated themselves to demonstrate their
devotion to a feminized aesthetic. Dennis followed this line of attack in his *Essay on Operas*: "And as soft and delicious Musick,
by soothing the Senses, and making a Man too much in love with
himself, makes him too little fond of the Publick; and so by *emasculating* and dissolving the Mind, it shakes the very Foundation
of Fortitude, and so is destructive of both branches of the Publick
spirit" (emphasis in original).[62] Here, amphibian sexuality and
Dulness share common borders: by transgressing gender boundaries they contribute to a larger cultural confusion. As Ingrassia
notes, "Like the dunces, they happily live within a world of ambiguous sexuality, subverted power relations, and threatening social incoherence."[63]

V

It is well known that opera audiences in our age consist of large
numbers of homosexual patrons, although ballet and Broadway

musicals also draw out huge crowds. The fact need not be statistically validated because it is obvious to those opera patrons capable of decoding (in many cases) the homosexual's body/sign language. Terrence McNally exploits the comic side of this fact of contemporary cultural life in a series of plays—*Lisbon Traviata*, and *Master Class*, the latter about the contemporary homosexual following of Maria Callas—reconstructing how this cult came into existence almost with an historian's shrewd eye. The question poses formidable hurdles: does the genre (opera) draw particular audiences (gays), or does the audience gravitate to the genre? I have already commented on the personal input to the equation by Wayne Koestenbaum in *The Queen's Throat*.[64]

Playwright and commentators all suggest in their own ways that opera speaks so directly to modern homosexuals because it places their plight and tragedy—as outsiders normally and tragically incapable of sustained love through the combined forms of music, drama, poetry, spectacle, costume, setting; virtually appealing to all five senses all the time—directly before them. This is not to deny the modern homosexual's genuine delight in Italian opera's monumental aesthetic achievement. Nor is this the appropriate place to divagate on this fascinating and complex subject at large, except to comment that Pope and Handel and the castrati played an important role at the beginning of the process. Pope ranted against the new entertainment at the moment of its introduction to his own country precisely because it touched so many of his own nerves. Without ever seeing one, he chastised the mode at large: the literal story or libretto, the score, the setting and costume, the singers, the chorus, everything. After all, his sexuality, like that of the eunuchs in Italian opera, was troubled; his masculinity forever called into question.[65]

David Morris aptly epitomizes *The Dunciad* as "an anatomy of the irrational."[66] If it is that, it also captures—more specifically within the precincts of the poet's own imagination—a dark zone of psychosexual politics in which the night of a particular mind (Pope's) encounters a more frightening realm of mental darkness. Eternal night pervades the poem, like death and annihilation, and is ultimately more frightening than any sexual politics instaurated by the Phantom Opera. Yet the Pope responding to the operatic tensions of the 1730s and imagining his *New Dunciad* (where Italy and all things Italian loom large), smarted from the assaults on his manliness. Whatever offenses Cibber and others had given, none were greater than the implications made of Pope's genital incapacity: a matter polite scholarship could not address until our generation because it cut so close to the heart of phallic privacy.

Yet phallic privacy, however cumbersome a phrase and concept, lies at the heart of the anatomical eunuch: genitally castrated, sexually amphibious (as Pope had charged Hervey with being while actually indicting himself), feminine in voice (Pope's voice was high, according to Spence), compensatorily cast of a masculine mind forever asserting its maleness, desirous yet apparently incapable of heterosexual intercourse, symbolically a deviant hermaphrodite through and through. By these symbolic processes, Pope has ironically become one of Dulness's own emasculated men: effeminate, eunuch-like, robbed by 1742 of the poetic virility he had generated for himself in his earlier poetry. His sublimation of manhood into satire—even great poetic satire—was one thing, but not even the javelin thrust of vigorous satire could compensate for the tug of his heart and mind. Every great poet, such as Pope was, knows that his art *is* his life but also recognizes, perhaps less symbolically, the something beyond his art— his life. Earlier he could cathect his rage on to "spores" like Hervey; now *"The Dunciad* returns him to the Orphic body of his real life"—a grotesque, anatomic fragment body to be laughed at by women, or, worse yet, ridiculed by men. That is, street women, rather than fashionable ladies. The earlier vicious laughter of *femmes fatales* like Lady Mary is, at least in Pope's psyche and in the brave new world of his *Dunciad*, transformed into the claw-like violence of Thracian women. "Pope's symbolic classical body" is rent apart by "a deterritorialized feminine power" capable of castrating him. Hence the depiction of the grotesque Goddess Dulness: a vast Lucretian-like feminine power that may constitute "Pope's greatest poetic achievement."[67]

Pope's inevitable anatomical tragedy, like the archetypal eunuch's, always originated in bodily dysfunction. William Heming's play *The Eunuch*, performed during the 1670s but probably written earlier, defectively dramatized some of these tensions.[68] But no matter how psychological the consequences of such anatomic difference, the greatest offense remained to the male body itself: its unseen cavity and the mutations known only to the self. Real eunuchs, so to speak, in staged operas often compensated for their loss—perhaps like Farinelli—by lavishing their wealth on fineries other than those of the flesh, although they tried to assert their manliness (again like Farinelli) there as well. Pope, no less than these real eunuchs and castrati, attempted from his early years to prove his manliness, and where it failed him, to compensate his loss in other domains: realms of charm and chivalry, romance with the Blount girls, Lady Mary, and even dowagers—if not also sublimated in the pursuit of such avocations as drawing, gardening, and landscape architecture. His greatest outlet, however, remained the quill: thus forming a link between body and literary vocation that requires no higher feminist bouillon à la Kaja Silverman to be fed.[69] No one wants to make the biographical Pope *entirely* dependent on the literal identification of his own "crazy carcass"—his phrase—and opera's castrati, yet it is irresponsible to suppress the many connections that would have been obvious even to him. This is why Kaja Silverman, who writes about the "phallus of malice"—denoting the phallus as signifier of ultimate male authority rather than anatomic penis—unknowingly touches on something vital to Georgian England's greatest poetic satirist. Reputed to be the literary lion of his era, Pope did everything he could to reinforce the reality behind the legend. Readers of Pope need only consult the "Phantom of the Opera" in Pope's poem to see how sharply he himself had drawn some of these analogies. His (defective) phallus as (powerful) quill was necessary as a precondition and for a number of psychological reasons, as we have seen. The tensions created by Italian opera in Georgian England permitted him to see the connections in sharper focus.[70]

One development in the new cultural musicology of our time pertaining to Handel's sexuality impinges on these matters. Gary Thomas and others recently made a valiant case for Handel's homosexuality, valiant because they braved a hypothesis that cannot be proved but for which a surfeit of evidence exists, if it will just be marshalled.[71] The evidence is controversial, but enough exists to raise the possibility that Pope knew very well what he was about when he banished Handel from *The Dunciad*. And it is as a gloss on that famous passage that this essay serves, in large part, to document: the poet's accusation that opera is an explicitly *female* "Harlot form." The high drama of Pope's moment, as the harlot-opera surmounts the stage, indicates with what ambivalence of sexual expectation and sexual boundaries the biographical Pope construed these matters. One need not wax anachronistic by citing Freud and the Freudians, who have claimed that throughout history humans have chided in others what they most loathe in themselves. This is the celebrated doctrine of internalized self-hatred. The sexually starved Pope, whose romantic heart had been twisted and turned from early maturity onward, as his best biographer (Mack) argues, would consciously have deplored being associated with anything we today could conjure as homosexual, let alone sodomitical. His adult life amounted to a Temple of Industry dedicated to the *annihilation* of such a possibility. Besides, he was merely one in a long series of talented bachelors in his generation and down through the whole eighteenth century; one can conjecture that the symbolism of his sexual monstrosity was merely a *symptom* of the larger cultural contortions of gender and sex distributed throughout his society. There is no contradiction here, merely paradox and the incommensurability of unconscious desire and conscious will: the fact that Pope wanted so much to be loved by women, yet found himself perpetually attracted to (usually older) men.

Yet in his dwarfism and compromised sexuality, and in the degree to which his anatomy and ill health *consciously* vexed him, Pope could not have failed to notice his similarity with the castrati. All he had was his pen, not his penis, as surrogate quill. If women loved him, like them (the castrati), it could not be for his genital might. In this sense, Handel may have unconsciously served as a type of alter-ego: Handel, the other immensely talented bachelor of his generation, also cultivated by the Burlingtons and Bathursts, for whatever reason also steeped in bachelordom but whose body formed no "crazy carcass," as did Pope's. Could Pope be jealous of Handel?

But it is *Pope*, not Handel, who imagined *The Dunciad*, containing the most sustained female monster in English poetry until then. Here, too, in this concoction, opera played its part, even if unconsciously in Pope's imagination. On stage, deformity and deviance rippled out of the castrati's body: the symmetrical male build emitting high soprano shrieks. The castrato's visible body was often large and fat (as in Hogarth's *Marriage A-la-Mode*), surgery having activated the secretion of glands. But the castrato could also be a model of exterior male perfection. The interior body invisible to the gazing eye was imperfect, or at least nonexistent. Audiences in England often were awed by the castrato's grotesque body size and, paradoxically, his bel canto voice, but also devalued the castrato's presentation as the result of incongruity. That is, true manliness would display a perfection of interior *and* exterior zones.

Catherine Ingrassia astutely observes that the term "feminization," certainly not unique to eighteenth-century studies, stems from the exclusionary practice social scientist Andreas Huyssen identifies as "the persistent gendering as feminine of that which is devalued."[72] But the term "feminized" also includes a perception of the erosion of traditional masculine values, as Ingrassia suggests, and cultural practices that are replaced with characteristics culturally defined as feminine, such as passion, sentiment, fancy, and emotion. For these reasons, in addition to the autobiographical and anatomic ones, Italian opera was one of the most feminizing (and effeminate) art forms available in Pope's adult lifetime; not the only cultural force against which a heterosexist masculinity would define itself against both women and sodomites (there were others), but doubtless one of the most vital. Like all things Italian, it was opprobrious because it was *both* cause and effect. It was, as Ingrassia again shrewdly notices, both "a cause and symptom of feminization."[73] Italian opera is the ultimate "Harlot form soft sliding by" (B.4.45) because it represents the worst aspects of all *domains female*: especially the soft interior body, with its cavities and empty spaces and lack of a steel-like shaft. This difference is what eventually gets transformed in Pope's psyche into his Silvermanian phallus of malice: those quills, so to speak, perceived by his contemporaries as coming from the Wicked Wasp of Twickenham. Hence—in Pope's mind— opera thankfully had been banished from England before the appearance of *The New Dunciad*.

Pope may have complained that the depiction of characters of the opposite sex in Italian opera blurred the boundaries of gender, or that its allure of spectacle was superficial, although one wonders how he justified that charge in view of his own resort to spectacle in *The Dunciad*. Nevertheless, it was Italian opera's gender trouble, as I have been somewhat infelicitously calling his anxiety, that was most monstrous. The implication is of a new sexual breed no better than a monster itself. Monstrosity was then (and long since had been) a region of the mind. The burst Bubble, the inquisitions against the Atterburyan Catholics, the Walpolian nightmare, the new sodomy of *Hell upon Earth*: all were monstrous in some genuine way for Pope. Indeed, the 1720s held up monstrosities of every type: public and personal. Even abnormal births qualified, as in the celebrated case of Mary Tofts, the "rabbit breeder" about whom Pope himself had become so engrossed and wrote so wittily in his poetry. These became rampant: a matter for the most rancorous disputes among the learned "doctors." It is no surprise that Sporus-Hervey, the fattened courtier featured as grotesquely epicene "Amphibious Thing," could be imaged, like the eunuchs of opera, as an anatomical deviant: all "painted" and decked out in flaming costume, "now master up, now miss, and he himself one vile Antithesis."

Painted Hervey was not the only "operatic" figure at court. The King (George I) and his corpulent Attis-like consort (Caroline) also possessed deviant bodies like the castrated Attis of the Cybele/Magna Mater cult, who, as Ness says, "gathers a band of followers, who raise their barbaric music in the temple of the Goddess."[74] The king's body was a taboo subject, but it, too, was privately said to be deviant. And the dwarfish poet who held the last pen for freedom, as "Alexander the Little" so often proclaimed he did, also recorded with equal vigilance the new perversions of the town among the genders. More egregiously, they broke his Arbuthnot-like peace and arcadian calm. This disturbance to personal tranquility, however, can flex either way: to his advantage, in which case Pope's calm would reap harvest in the form of poetic fruit, or disadvantage, wherein he would break down and dissipate. The turning point is reached when the poet confronts his own solitude, mirrored as silence in his poem. How will the poet's imagination respond to sudden disturbance and the breaking of silence? How will his shift of mood invade his artistic decisions at the moment of disturbance? These questions would appear to be less pressing if they did not impinge on a poet writing about the birth of the world and the origins of cosmology. In view of *The Dunciad*'s preoccupation with the rebirth of chaos and the rise of culture it is hardly arbitrary that Pope's own autobiographical solitude and silence in the creative act should mirror the universe's. The poet's interruption resembles the crisis moment in postmodern chaos theory—Chaos or chaos again—as when Alvin Toffler describes Ilya Prigogine's chaos model.[75] To paraphrase Toffler, at the revolutionary moment or bifurcation point, it is inherently impossible to determine in advance which direction the change will take. That is, whether the system will disintegrate into chaos or leap higher to a new, more differentiated, level of "order" or organization, which Prigogine calls the "dissipative structure." No one wants to graft contemporary chaos theories wholesale onto Pope's classical ones: Pope, not Prigogine, remains our subject. But the analogies are intriguing, not least because Pope's 1742 poem provides the coda to his silences in the *Epistle to Dr Arbuthnot*. Sporus may "tremble" (insect) and "stink" (perfume), but the one charge that could not be levelled against the biographical Sporus—Hervey—was the one about castration.

Hence the "dissipative moment" for Pope entailed the recognition of his own symbolic castration. If chaos incorporates the realms of psychic calm and physical void *before* creation, its disruptions must have been as vexing to Pope as his private parts. His self-image as eunuch is essentially one of defect: as anatomical deviant, further suggesting a Pope profoundly interrupted by the tensions threatening his tranquility. Pervasive in what has been called his late poetry of retirement—from the opening lines of *Dr Arbuthnot* to the castrated priests of Cybele in *The Dunciad*—gender ambiguity invades his psychological space. He himself often accounts for the *fons et origo* in other terms and through other realms: poetasters aiming to gain his patronage, dullards screaming and scribbling in Grub Street. But the tension arises, first and foremost, from a protean anxiety coloring his sense of manliness that does not abate so long as castrati and eunuchs remind him of it. Universal darkness *must* bury all, so long as Italy and her foul operas remain in England. They were the true scourge, the concrete reminder of the anatomical limits forming the basis for much of his feminization: a lapse he could never accept, and for which he would see the whole of civilization expire rather than concede his ambiguous anatomy. Perhaps this is also why no portraits exist, among many hundred, painted from the waist down, an extraordinary fact of the history of Georgian portraiture of celebrities.[76] Yet here in the mental mindset of castrati, chaos, and all things grotesquely phallic, lay the core of the true politics of sexuality in the brave new world of *The Dunciad* because it was the one hitting closest to home.

VI

My main point then about "Pope's arcadia"—or, more precisely, his *sexual Arcadia* and his "ego" within it—is fundamentally homosocial and phallocentric in just the way the feminist gynocritics configure the concept. Its literal and symbolic centerpiece is a male body without whose central organ—the penis—there can be neither sex nor associated sexuality.[77] Nor can the point have eluded the sagacious little poet himself, whose life was played out on the daily reminder of "this long disease, my life," as he dubbed it in his familiar homoerotic letters. The biographical evidence is pervasive: in the correspondence, in Spence, in the fine print of the vast collaborative notes written with Warburton. Those with certain (anti-feminist and boldly heterosexual) ideologies may choose not to confront it, but it is there.

Furthermore, the disturbances to his tranquility while writing *The New Dunciad* prompted Pope to see a large chunk of himself anew: as if looking in a mirror and seeing afresh the grotesque body he had been all along, let alone what he had now become. A mature poet suffused with images of the Noachian deluge, conflagration, and (C)haos, now in my typographical alteration, to reflect the combined historical chaos Pope inherited with our own mindsets on which chaos theory is indelible. They equal a unique Popeian imagination of Night suffused with sexual resonance. Historically, nighttime never has been free of erotic charge, nor was it for Pope as he had brilliantly demonstrated in *Eloisa to Abelard*. So, while in the thick of his poetically surcharged (C)haos in *The New Dunciad*, Pope wrote to Allen his much cited *cri de coeur* about being "sick of *this* World and the Great ones of it."[78] The tropes were mannered and premeditated, uttered in the manicured epistolary cadences Pope had practiced throughout his life. But they also contain deep-layer content: an almost existential imagination glimpsing no exit, which therefore must bury all in "Universal Night." The neoclassical symmetries of Tom Stoppard's *Arcadia* are witty and tempered compared to this stark vision of self created out of Spenserian fantasy commingled with apocalyptic Blakeian passion.

Whether Popeian or Stoppardian, Arcadia had always been an ancient Grecian place, no matter how modern its trappings: for long that edenic region of the mind where passionate shepherds piped out homosocial desire, as did Alexis and Corydon in the bucolic fields of Theocritus and Virgil. Arcadia concurrently served many ends: real, imagined, political, metaphorical. Yet it endured as a nostalgic zone where desire could be indulged under many protean guises—literary, musical, erotic, social, even military—as well as pursued by the Ganymedes of Anacreon and the Professor Bernard Nightingales of Tom Stoppard. Those cultivating pastoral literary forms, in music as well as literature, had succumbed to Arcadia's lure, not least among them Pope and Handel. In its verdant pastures, the "loves" of innocent swains were laid bare on a border of potentiality: the sense that desire could be transformed into the homosexual. This gender ambiguity also constituted their deepest tension.[79]

Hence the homosexual potential of Arcadia also lay near the surface of the participant's imagination, and it is this imagination I have been attempting to describe as the context for Pope's massive attack on the new art form—Italian opera—he most likely had never seen. Gary Thomas expresses the notion as eloquently as anyone: "Although not the sole property of gay people, the idea of Arcadia, that mythic-pastoral *locus amoenus* (pleasant place) populated by shepherds and shepherdesses, has a long and richly established history of homosexual appropriation."[80] I think Thomas's point is that arcadian pleasures were unique *precisely because* their eroticism required so little covert coding. The vast, almost Lucretian, spaces of *The Dunciad* are hardly arcadian: they are far too gloomy for Arcadia's sunny optimism about its future. Yet through inversion they (the spaces) appropriate these tensions and potential for gender transformation. Pope excelled in adroitly maneuvering through such territories: in poetry as well as letters. Hence when writing to Teresa Blount about "lying together" at Lord Burlington's: "I am to pass three or four days in high luxury, with some company at my Lord Burlington's. We are to walk, ride, ramble, dine, drink, and lie together. His gardens are delightful, his music ravishing."[81] Here too, in the arcadian country, was potential and possibility.

It is tempting to drop Silverman's gynocritical "phallus of malice" and masculinist Raymond Stephanson's "phallus as quill," a subject that will figure in his book-in-progress on Pope's masculinity. These tropes, both symbolic but utterly different, have been invoked in so many different guises over the last decade—at large and specifically in relation to Pope—that they represent something in our common psyche at the end of the twentieth century. The former—Silverman—designates a particular feminist position articulated as artillery of defense against specific masculine prejudices. Its fertile suggestions of "malice" toward the gendered Other may open up avenues of exploration for Pope: his rage and spite were downplayed by Mack, whose wisdom as biographer-critic lay, in part, in letting these qualities sleep for fear that exposure could fatally damage the protagonist's integrity.[82]

The "phallus as quill"—this "last pen for freedom"—is surely the more potential and enticing for Pope. Jonathan Goldberg already has traced the propinquity of hand and sexual organ in the Renaissance; more recently, in *Sodometries* he continues this line of historical argument to show that writers—especially gay writers—were sensible of the analogies.[83] I do not claim that Pope belongs in the milieu of *Sodometries*: he was neither sodomitical nor homosexual in my view. But his nongenital, erotic bonds with other males were so powerful that he may as well have been homosexual had it not been for "this crazy constitution which. . . ." This corporeal infirmity, as profoundly as any homoeroticism, taught Pope that his penis had disciplined his hand, and even

ruled it. His groin and his verbal disclosures were never very far
apart, and he was forever completing the sentence in daydreams:
with one organ or another. And therefore it makes perfect sense
to explore "the quill as phallus" and vice versa in the fullest detail possible. D. H. Lawrence, another homoerotic sensibility at
the other end of the rainbow, has told us why. "Our old show will
come flop," the narrator-mouthpiece of *Lady Chatterley's Lover*
reveals for Lawrence; "Our civilization is going to fall. It's going
down the bottomless pit, down the chasm. And believe me, the
only bridge across the chasm will be the phallus . . . the phallus is
the bridge to what comes next."[84] For Pope, no "next" existed.
His dunciadic "Universal Night" *was* the end, "when darkness
buries all."

Finally, the issue arises of the much-neglected *Dunciad* in our
time in relation to these matters and Pope's Arcadia. It has been
ruefully claimed that this vast couplet lampoon extant in so many
recensions now gathers dust: an unreadable poem for a multitude
of reasons ranging from its hundreds of allusions and references
to its elliptical grammar and mordant syntax. Swift had prognos-
ticated this neglect in posterity, but Pope was unrelenting. In our
generation, a number of attempts have been made to reclaim the
work—mostly among students—most of which have failed. One
way to reaffirm its vitality lies in relating it to another art form—
opera—whose status has gone in the opposite direction and is
much elevated in our time; try to understand, perhaps in the psychological sense, why a poet of two centuries ago can have railed
so vigorously against a form we now take for granted as "great."
The disparity is extraordinary: we embrace opera, even enthusiastically cultivate it by paying small fortunes to attend it as the
entertainment of sophisticates *par excellence*; simultaneously we
dispraise satire for all sorts of reasons, even more so specific satire such as *The Dunciad*.

Broadly speaking, the crux may entail a psychological approach
to the sister arts and the role of performance. But I think it also
amounts to something rather more specific. The warfare within
The Dunciad has been viewed as derisive of the cackling dunces:
braying asses all, according to Pope. Yet it is also a psychomachia
within which Pope "outs" himself, not merely the poet claiming
to stand alone against the mass of print culture but exposing and
outing *himself*. Pope's deformity and sexuality must have been
vulnerable indeed if he could lay such claims for (C)chaos on the
Italian opera. Nothing in familiar realms political, social, or eco-

nomic border on this degree of opera's pathology: the only force capable of obliterating civilization.

In Pope's version, sexual politics exceeds the worst nightmares of his recent commentators. Things sodomitical and eunuch-like lead to opera. Opera leads to (C)chaos; indeed it is the precondition. (C)chaos leads to the disintegration of society through anarchy and dissolution of quality in the arts. Disintegration leads to the end of the world and the consequential demise of the poet creating and mediating that world. Authority and transgression have collided through the menace of the new Italian entertainment.

Lawrence was right: the symbolic phallus based on the anatomic penis *was* the bridge. But for Pope no bridge existed, nor could there be one. Arcadia for him was an imaginary place where one could be built if only his "ego" could cross it. But the "ego" would not: instead it coyly hovered on one side or the other, forever tormented by the perils of the other. Pope's great psychosexual angst lay in the space between his deformed physical body and perceived poetic might: the one a contorted dwarf, the other a proclaimed titan. These were the antipodes of his tortured and unintegrated psyche. Unable to enter Arcadia by himself, either as lover of women or lover of men, he instead quashed the symbolic world he had created: symbolically murdered and cast it into "Universal Night." The other side of his paradise embraced the Arcadia he dreamed he might enter someday as the man he longed to be. There he would be both poet and lover combined in a perfect male human form. There, no symbolic phalluses would be necessary. He would be no eunuch or castrato in Arcadia. Such were the terrific sexual anxieties and gender ambivalences aroused in him by the *female* "Harlot form." Opera had become his symbolic nemesis.

Ideology and Opportunism:
The Role of Handel in Pope's
The Dunciad in Four Books

VALERIE RUMBOLD

CONTEXTUALIZATION HAS OFTEN BEEN USED MORE TO ILLUSTRATE the constructions of cultural issues in Pope's *Dunciad*s than to question them. Yet Pope is plainly tendentious in his assertions: hardly any scholar today would seriously subscribe, for example, to his negative evaluation of natural history, or to his rejection of historicist textual scholarship. Knowing to what he refers is important not so much because it proves (or even disproves) his claims as because it provides a framework for assessing what is at stake for him, and why he constructs the issues as he does.

However, to contextualize Pope's claims involves reading them against independent testimony, and we necessarily read this testimony through the scholarship of our own historical moment. The effect is obvious when we look at the annotations of past generations, shaped, often in ways we no longer find acceptable, by the then-standard accounts of the fields in which the text finds its contexts. Within fifty years or so, most standard accounts are superseded, their claims of increased rigor and relevance in turn overtaken. Thus there is a problem for readers not only in what they choose to do with contextual knowledge, but also in the knowledge itself, which cannot ultimately represent an objective standard against which judgments about the text's construction of issues can be made.

The treatment of opera in *The Dunciad in Four Books* is an interesting case in point. Though in some ways a hackneyed subject for interpretation, it has usually been approached from the assumption that Pope's negative judgment is essentially correct. The operatic theme, prepared by passing allusions in Books 1–3, culminates in Book 4, in the speech of Opera personified:

> When lo! a Harlot form soft sliding by,
> With mincing step, small voice, and languid eye;

Foreign her air, her robe's discordant pride
In patch-work flutt'ring, and her head aside:
By singing Peers up-held on either hand,
She tripp'd and laugh'd, too pretty much to stand;
Cast on the prostrate Nine a scornful look,
Then thus in quaint Recitativo spoke.
O *Cara! Cara!* silence all that train:
Joy to great Chaos! let Division reign:
Chromatic tortures soon shall drive them hence,
Break all their nerves, and fritter all their sense:
One Trill shall harmonize joy, grief, and rage,
Wake the dull Church, and lull the ranting Stage;
To the same notes thy sons shall hum, or snore,
And all thy yawning daughters cry, *encore.*
Another Phoebus, thy own Phoebus, reigns,
Joys in my jiggs, and dances in my chains.
But soon, ah soon Rebellion will commence,
If Music meanly borrows aid from Sense:
Strong in new Arms, lo! Giant Handel stands,
Like bold Briareus, with a hundred hands;
To stir, to rouze, to shake the Soul he comes,
And Jove's own Thunders follow Mars's Drums.
Arrest him Empress; or you sleep no more—
She heard, and drove him to th' Hibernian shore.[1]

What makes the attack on opera so interesting is not only its intrinsic importance in Pope's wider construction of cultural, aesthetic, and religious issues, but also the fact that it impinges on an area in which scholarly attitudes have changed radically in the very recent past. For two hundred years after the publication of *The Dunciad in Four Books, opera seria* was virtually unknown except from hostile commentary, while Handelian oratorio, which Opera cites by implication as the principal threat to Dulness's empire, was generally regarded as, for good or ill, a bulwark of English culture.[2] These assumptions have remained surprisingly current in readings of *The Dunciad in Four Books*, despite the revival of *opera seria* through scholarship and performance and the parallel transformation of performance style in oratorio, developments which have, since the 1970s, transformed the general perception of Handel and his age.[3] The sharpness and suddenness of these changes can, however, make it possible to see from a fresh perspective how Pope's treatment is constructed and what functions it serves. Without deceiving ourselves that we have reached the final truth about eighteenth-century opera and oratorio, we can now see aspects of both that were not available to previous generations of readers. Such a marked discontinuity in what counts as contextual knowledge, the recognition that we can no longer dismiss *opera seria* as intrinsically preposterous, compels a more explicit attention to the "how" and "why" of *The Dunciad in Four Books'* construction of its cultural context.

It might seem natural to suppose that strong feelings about opera would have their origin in aesthetic response to the experience of seeing and hearing it. Pope did have at least one first-hand experience of an operatic performance: in 1727 he attended Handel's *Admeto*, although the Earl of Oxford suggested to Swift that the experience of "staying out a whole opera" was partly to blame for Pope's being "very much out of order" afterwards.[4] The context, Oxford's discussion of Pope's apparently deliberate absence from the coronation of George II, juxtaposes the favorite royal entertainment with a ceremony crucial to the politics of the *Dunciad*s, and politics seems from the beginning to have been central to the role designed for opera in the work. In an early manuscript draft of a version of Book 2—which may even date from before the publication of the first *Dunciad* in 1728—the "Directors of Musick," the aristocrats whose financial support made opera seasons possible, are made to join university dons, tutors of noblemen on the Grand Tour and virtuosi in the fine arts in a procession to the throne of the new king—the motif that was, in time, to provide the framework for Book 4.[5] The sketch envisages the directors "with all their Set of fine Gentlemen of Taste. All telling Dullness & their King Tibbalds what they will perform with [their] Lives and Fortunes for her, & what they have done in bringing up yᵉ Youth to such Ends for yᵉ Next Age." Opera thus makes its first appearance in Pope's plans for the *Dunciad*s alongside the perversion of education, and takes its place as one of the absorbing hobbies that divert Dulness's elite disciples, thus educated, from their proper responsibilities. Meanwhile, although Pope withheld this material until 1743, the notion of opera as an effeminating influence on a national spirit conceived as manly and martial was becoming an established commonplace of cultural criticism, sharpened by the emergence in the 1730s of the Patriot movement as focus for opposition to the alleged corruption of Walpole's regime.[6] When, therefore, Pope finally presented his personification of Opera in 1743 as feeble in herself and enfeebling of the nation's guardians, he was inviting his readers to place the depiction within a politicized interpretive framework which was already thoroughly familiar.

Pope's feelings for music as such were evidently not intense.

Although Morris Brownell demonstrates the implausibility of the long-standing assumption that Pope was absolutely incapable of appreciating music, it remains striking that in comparison with his active involvement in painting and in gardening, he never sought instruction in either the theory or practice of music. When Spence asked him in 1744 about his musical knowledge, his reply was categorical:

> "Did you ever learn anything of music?"
> "Never, but I had naturally a very good ear, and have often judged right of the best compositions in music by the force of that."[7]

There is no hint of enjoyment, nor even of regret at not having learned more. It is a response that seems both lukewarm and complacent.

His commitment to words, on the other hand, was passionate, and connected at a deep level with his beliefs about God, creation, and the role of the poet. *The Dunciad in Four Books*, and particularly its new fourth book, works out more fully than previous *Dunciad*s the humanist assumption that verbal art, conceived as echoing the creation of the world by the divine Word, stands at the apex of human endeavor. It is the possibility of such art, and the mythic act from which it draws its authority, that Dulness's yawn, her "uncreating word," aims to undo (4.654). In this foundation myth, world springs from word, confirming the centrality of words as a human concern, and privileging the poetic vocation for its potential to make good the deficiencies of fallen human language. Seventeenth-century grammarians had explored a range of possibilities for the construction of new languages or the understanding of elements in existing ones that might provide a motivated rather than an arbitrary connection between signifier and signified. Simon Alderson argues that it was in response to this debate that Pope throughout his career gave a high priority to the practice of iconic versification, the choice of vocabulary and of metrical and verbal patterns calculated to serve precisely expressive ends, thus vindicating the capacity of the English language to provide a referentiality that was not simply arbitrary.[8] Pope drew attention to this practice by the index to "VERSIFICATION/ Expressing in the Sound the Thing describ'd," that he provided for his translation of the *Iliad*; he felt, however, that his efforts in this direction were not well appreciated by most of his readers:

I have followed that (the significance of the numbers and the adapting them to the sense) much more even than Dryden, and much oftener than anyone minds it: particularly in the translations of Homer, where 'twas most necessary to do so and in the *Dunciad* often, and indeed in all my poems.[9]

He had lamented in the *Essay on Criticism* that many readers were more interested in beauty of sound ("But most by *Numbers* judge a Poet's Song / And *smooth* or *rough*, with them, is *right* or *wrong*") than in the exactness with which words executed their (for him) definitive function of expressing things ("The *Sound* must seem an *Echo* to the *Sense*").[10] This alleged taste is in some ways akin to that which would draw audiences to a form of opera—and beyond that, in the later part of the century, to the new extended forms of purely instrumental music—which was conditioned more by the inner logic and development of its musical structures than by any attempt to imitate extramusical phenomena.[11] In effect, Pope's attitude to opera is typically English in its conservative appeal to Renaissance notions of the supremacy of the word.[12]

Music and poetry, inseparable in the earliest cultures, had long ceased to be so. In the words of James Winn, "Musical composition and performance, once wedded to poetic texts, had gained independence but lost prestige," and the ancient tradition by which the poet is a singer and his poem a song worked increasingly as a figure in which the associative benefits were all in one direction.[13] For Pope, whose epigraph to *The Dunciad in Four Books* parallels him with Orpheus, to speak of "song" and "singer" in this sense is simply to appropriate the creative ordering power of an art that poetry has in effect abandoned.[14] Although it was still possible in the late seventeenth and early eighteenth centuries to invoke harmony as cosmic principle (as in Dryden's *A Song for St. Cecilia's Day, 1687*), or as symbol of the ordering of chaos by art and civilization (as in the miraculous song of Amphion in Pope's *Temple of Fame*, lines 85–92), practical music-making had long since moved away from such speculative theory, and poetry was increasingly uninterested in invoking these doctrines for any serious purpose. Practical music was for conservatives like Pope most acceptable when it followed quasi-rhetorical formulae traditionally believed to evoke particular passions, or when it set words of approved merit in accordance with recognized expressive conventions.[15]

The problem with opera, however, was not simply that it subordinated poetry to music, but also that it activated Pope's wider reservations about stage drama. His sense of poetry as the supreme vocation rendered even spoken drama problematic, since dramatic verse could only be realized on stage, and consequently in a theatrical marketplace. He felt threatened by the obvious need for the dramatic poet to please managers, actors and audiences, telling Spence he had decided not to write for the stage "from seeing how much everybody that did . . . was obliged to subject themselves to the players and the town."[16] In his own career, he had found through his Homer subscriptions a way of buying exemption from pressures inimical to creative independence; but when he looked at Shakespeare, however, he lamented, in contrast, a poet led into betraying his own standards of taste by the need to please audiences and actors. In the theatre seasons mounted by contemporary managers, he saw art corrupted by the need to woo audiences obsessed with novelty and spectacle.[17]

Even more than ordinary stage plays, *opera seria* offended at every point against Pope's belief in the supremacy of the poet's verbal art: opera was an ephemeral experience rather than an achieved text, a continuously shifting interplay between music, words, scenery, and action, changing from production to production according to the singers and other resources available. Although the name of the librettist conventionally took precedence over the composer's on the title of the published text (where the work was described not as the composer's "opera" but as the poet's "dramma per musica," set to music by the composer), the poet generally worked from a preexisting libretto, and was expected to adapt it according to what singers were available, what political constructions were likely to be placed upon the subject, and what the market demanded.[18] Since English audiences knew little or no Italian (although bilingual libretti could be studied in advance and followed during the performance), librettists were under pressure to cut down on plot development transacted through the medium of recitative (which presented relatively little melodic interest), a constraint that ruled out much of the subtlety and intricacy usually taken for granted in the London theater.[19] The *da capo* aria demonstrated the essentially musical motivation of its ABÁ form by its unsuitability for detailing substantial movement along plot lines, given that the text of the first section had to be repeated to an ornamented version of its original melody at the close: such musical exploration of contrasted emotional responses, however enthralling to committed opera subscribers, could satisfy only one aspect of conventional dramatic expectations. Later in the century, indeed, Charles Burney was to make clear by his extensive treatment of London's Italian opera in the *A General History of Music* his view of the form's central importance in the development of modern music. He prefaced his account of his own century with an "Essay on the Euphony or Sweetness of Languages and their Fitness for Music," which gives the preference to Italian over English and envisages the librettist as working within a prescribed range of phonetic procedures determined by the demands of voice production.[20] Although Pope and his contemporaries were not exposed to such explicit and authoritative theorizing of the subordination of poetry to music, the tendency of operatic practice in that direction was already clear. The Italian opera cast an implicit slur on the authority of the dramatic poet, and lent itself to incorporation in the allegation that elite taste was now no more rational or refined than the popular entertainments of Bartholomew Fair.

Thus it is no surprise that Pope should attack opera. The surprise is rather that, throughout the process of his *Dunciad*s, his attacks never allude to Handel, and that in *The Dunciad in Four Books* he eulogizes him as opera's opponent. On the face of it, the charges that could have been brought against Handel seem overwhelming. He was the most important opera composer in early eighteenth-century London, having been appointed principal composer to the Royal Academy, set up in 1719 to mount regular Italian opera seasons.[21] He had been a frequent collaborator with the librettist Paolo Rolli (attacked at 2.203 and note), and he regularly worked with the Swiss entrepreneur John James Heidegger (whose notorious ugliness is implicated in the descent of the Unholy Spirit of Dulness's trinity at 1.290 and note). The fact that he was German, like the Hanoverian royal family who gave the lead to his English aristocratic patrons, might also have been expected to discredit him. In 1733, moreover, the Prince of Wales, figurehead of the Patriot group to which Pope was broadly sympathetic if not absolutely committed, gave his support to the Opera of the Nobility, which mounted seasons in rivalry with Handel's; and Pope's friends Bathurst and Burlington became directors of the new company. Handel could therefore have been identified from this point on with an especially objectionable grouping within the operatic world. Such factors, however, can be overemphasized: party-political reasons for attacking Handel in the 1730s were by no means as compelling as is sometimes implied, and he himself seems not to have been particularly concerned with the politics of the texts he set.[22] Moreover, although the Pa-

triots were perceived as opposing Handel because of the patronage his operas received from George II and Queen Caroline, both
Prince Frederick and the Burlingtons continued to support him
even after they had expressed their support for the Patriots by
becoming patrons of the rival Opera of the Nobility.[23] Pope had
apparently decided, right from the first *Dunciad* of 1728, not to
implicate Handel in his attacks on opera, and these additional
factors were evidently not sufficient to change his mind. Despite
the *Dunciads'* investment from their earliest stages in anti-operatic satire, those who did not already know of Handel's operatic
career would not find it mentioned, either for praise or for blame,
in any of the *Dunciad*s. Only in a footnote to 4.54 in *The Dunciad
in Four Books* is there the merest hint from which a careful
reader might infer that Handel had once been an opera composer—and even that, it is tempting to speculate, may be a slip
on the part of Warburton, a relative newcomer to the project.

The Dunciad in Four Books recruits Handel for the forces of
good on the grounds of his new career in English oratorio. The
references in Opera's speech to Handel's "hundred hands" and
his "Thunders" and "Drums" (lines 66, 68), supported by the
"fuller Chorus" with "Drums and Cannon" of the note to line 54,
fix the allusion to oratorio (since opera had no chorus, and was
correspondingly lightly orchestrated), and specifically to the ket-
tle-drums (not actual cannons) borrowed from the Tower of London in 1739 for use in *Saul*: these could be called "Mars's
Drums" in a particular sense, since they had reputedly been captured by Marlborough at Malplaquet. As Smith points out, Handel is "one of the very few recipients of praise in the fourth book
of the *Dunciad*."[24] Indeed, presented as he is so near the beginning of the book, in the keynote speech of the leader of the procession of Dulness's faithful, he could almost be seen as the hero of
The Dunciad, Dulness's chosen victim, the only one who at this
late stage seems—until despatched to Ireland—to pose a significant threat. Given his massive involvement in opera, which had
finally ceased only with the production of *Deidamia* in 1741, the
harangue against him that Pope puts into Opera's mouth demonstrates just how significant his recent experiments with oratorio
must have seemed, since they were sufficient to outweigh all his
years of serving "singing Peers" and the London audiences who
followed in their wake (4.49).[25]

In the light of recent scholarship, the long-held belief that Handel's turn from opera to oratorio reflected a penitent's desire to
stoop to truth and moralize his song is no longer plausible: the

dwindling market for opera and the humiliating experience of manipulation by aristocratic patrons, rather than any aesthetic or moral conversion experience, now seem to have been the salient factors.[26] From this perspective, it becomes easier to see how *The Dunciad in Four Books* assisted in constructing the long-lived interpretation of Handel that implied by its focus on English sacred oratorio a polarization of his manly, English, and reverent music against the effeminate, foreign, and frivolous music of the opera—making it almost incredible that Handel could have had anything to do with the latter. Paradoxically, *The Dunciad in Four Books'* very refusal to use the actual word "oratorio"— which might have compromised a tone of lofty generality by using terminology reminiscent of the consumer world in which rival opera and oratorio seasons had been marketed—further smoothes the acceptance of this vision of Handel by implying that he is essentially, and not only in one division of his output, the composer of English sacred oratorio.

The most likely cause of Pope's decision to leave Handel out of the satire of the early *Dunciad*s and to celebrate his turn to oratorio in 1743 is an experience, dating back to 1718, of what collaboration between an English poet and a composer might ideally be. In that year, Pope's close friends Gay and Arbuthnot had been with Handel at Cannons, the home of Handel's patron James Brydges (later Duke of Chandos), and it was rumored at the time that Pope too was involved with Handel's English masque *Acis and Galatea*, composed to a text by Gay and first performed, privately, in that year.[27] This collaboration between Gay and Handel would surely have appealed to a poet of Pope's outlook as the kind of music-drama in which a poet could involve himself without compromising the dignity of his calling: English words are set with care for expressiveness and the discrimination of character; and the casting of the piece, based largely on the resources of Brydges's all-male chapel choir, is weighted toward natural male voices, in contrast with opera's domination by fashionable soprano and castrato soloists. While *Acis and Galatea* is never explicitly invoked in the *Dunciad*s, two near-references suggest that Gay and Handel remained fundamental to his thinking on music-drama. In 1729 he introduced a long note to 3.330 eulogizing Gay, in which he proclaimed the triumph of *The Beggar's Opera*—another English work, this time set to unpretentiously familiar tunes—over Italian opera: "That idol of the Nobility and the people . . . was demolished by a single stroke of this gentleman's pen." In 1743 he added to 3.305 a gibe relating to Porpora's *Polifemo*, an opera on the same subject as *Acis* with which Cibber (but not, significantly, Handel) had been associated. Cibber, accused of mistranslating the libretto into English, is exhorted, "Teach thou the warbling Polypheme to roar": his translation instructs the blinded giant what to cry in his agony, but because Cibber does not grasp the Homeric joke (whereby Odysseus calls himself Nobody, and Poliphemus tells his friends that nobody has injured him), his words make no sense. Behind the line echoes irresistibly Handel's treatment of the giant, particularly the number "O ruddier than the cherry," in which, at an earlier stage of the story, the giant really does warble, attempting the delicacy of a lover with calculatedly expressive incongruity. Pope's line centers, in effect, on notions of expressiveness and decorum crucial to his conception of the artist's role, and hence crucial to the acclaim with which he later greeted Handel's oratorios. Indeed, it seems likely that, at about the same time as *Acis,* Pope too had composed a libretto for Handel, for a project that began like *Acis* as a privately performed masque, but that was later reworked for public performance in 1732 as the oratorio *Esther*.[28]

Oratorio probably appealed to Handel in the late 1730s partly because it was a kind of music-drama he could mount independently, without becoming once more entrammelled in the increasingly impracticable schemes of the aristocratic opera directors so prominent in Pope's conception of Dulness's "instruments, the Great." Pope, who had himself crafted a career largely independent of aristocratic patronage by shrewd manipulation of the developing commercial market in leisure and the arts, may well have noticed and approved of this aspect of Handel's change of direction. More importantly, however, Handel's English oratorios, unlike his operas, could be seen as addressing a range of concerns of compelling importance to the traditional Christian humanist agenda, and, in particular, to that agenda as assimilated to the concerns of the Patriot opposition. As Smith demonstrates, a well-articulated demand existed for a kind of music-drama that would vindicate English identity, assert manly authority, insist—notably through a formal choric element—on the moral and political purposes of art, and, essential to all these, make explicit a conception of music as the handmaid, not the mistress, of meaning. Handel well knew how to capitalize on such attitudes, as he was to show by appealing to his audience's patriotic pride in their language when in 1744/5 he reproached them for their failure to support his oratorio season:

As I perceived, that joining good Sense and significant Words to Musick, was the best Method of recommending *this* to an English Audience; I have directed my Studies that way, and endeavour'd to shew, that the English Language, which is so expressive of the sublimest Sentiments, is the best adapted of any to the full and solemn kind of Musick.[29]

The text Pope may have provided for *Esther* suggests another factor that probably affected his response to Handel's oratorios of the late 1730s. Biblical narratives were open to political reading, and Smith suggests a possible interpretation of the story of Esther that could connect plausibly with Pope's Roman Catholicism: in the reign of James II, Mary of Modena had been identified with Esther, and the English Roman Catholics with the Jewish minority whose protection she sought from her royal husband. In comparison, Smith suggests that the 1732 revision of the work, which was patronized by George and Caroline and included anthems composed for their coronation, represents "a hasty attempt at allegorical takeover" incapable of concealing "joins in the scissors-and-paste treatment." The spectacle of Hanoverian enthusiasm for a work on this potentially subversive subject, especially given that Pope had probably written the original version, recalls his triumph in stage-managing the presentation of *The Dunciad Variorum* to the king by Walpole, which allegedly gave its author the ironic satisfaction of being regarded by his uncomprehending royal victim as "a very honest Man."[30] Whether Pope actually heard *Esther* and other oratorios is unclear, but, particularly in view of his less-than-enthusiastic response to music generally, it seems unlikely that he was an assiduous attender. Conversely, it would probably not have been necessary for him actually to hear the works to feel strongly in their favor: the new oratorios were common topics of journalism and conversation, and their wordbooks could be purchased independently of attending a performance. Indeed, the importance of the text in this new kind of music-drama, arguably the main reason for Pope's approval, was emphasized by commentators who advised audiences to study the wordbook in advance of the performance to appreciate the full effect of its setting.[31]

The oratorios most likely to have helped form the view of Handel presented in *The New Dunciad* in 1742 and incorporated into *The Dunciad in Four Books* in 1743 are *Saul* and *Israel in Egypt*, both performed for the first time in 1739; of their two wordbooks, one was definitely and one very probably by the Jacobite and Anglican traditionalist Charles Jennens, and both contain much to appeal to audiences of a conservative outlook. *Saul*, the oratorio most clearly alluded to in Opera's speech, takes a story that had been subject to political appropriation by diverse interests and reshapes it toward a meditation on the evil of killing a king. The libretto concludes with David's execution of the Amalekite who has killed Saul, a text sanctified by Tory piety, since it figured in the Anglican commemoration of Charles King and Martyr.[32] Conversely, Saul's attack on the musician David could also be read in a Patriot sense as an attack on Walpole's attempts to suppress opposition writers. Furthermore, while such anti-regicide and anti-Walpole readings would presumably have recommended themselves to Pope, particularly in view of Jennens's very obvious use of Cowley's royalist epic *Davideis*, the wordbook would perhaps have seemed more significant still for the underlying values it expressed. The action of the individual characters is embedded in a communal context, emphasizing the role of the chorus—a major desideratum of the classically orientated critique of drama—as the nation of Israel, and using the figure of the High Priest as an additional chorus figure through whom the action can be interpreted. Although David is principally characterized as the champion appointed by God, he is also presented (in a sequence printed in the wordbook but apparently omitted from early performances) as emblem of human creativity, master of a song whose power echoes the composing Word in the creation of the world from chaos. After David's triumph in soothing the deranged Saul by his music, the High Priest restates the traditional metaphor:

> *Recitative*
> This but the smallest Part of Harmony,
> Great Attribute of Attributes Divine,
> And Center of the Rest, where all agree:
> Whose wond'rous Force what great Effects proclaim.
> *Accompagnato*
> By thee this Universal Frame
> From its Almighty Maker's Hand,
> In primitive Perfection came,
> By thee produc'd, in thee contain'd:
> No sooner did th' Eternal Word dispense
> Thy vast mysterious Influence,
> Than Chaos his old Discord ceas'd.
> Nature began of labour eas'd,
> Her latent Beauties to disclose,

A fair harmonious World arose;
And tho' by diabolick guile,
Disorder Lord it for awhile,
The Time will come,
When Nature shall her pristine Form regain,
And Harmony for ever reign.[33]

By the middle of the eighteenth century, this solemn deploy-
ment of musical symbolism was distinctly outmoded: it appealed
to conservative values by appropriating music mythically to "th'
Eternal Word," rather than conceding the practical independence
from text that actually marks the development of musical form in
the period.[34] Opera, in effect, speaks for that independence, for
the supremacy of music uninhibited by referentiality; and thus
she aligns herself with Dulness's subversion of the mythic claim
of language to recapitulate the divine ordering of the world. Jennens's old-fashioned, Tory and Jacobite text unites religious and
aesthetic values in an implicit rejection of the modernizing regime under which kings, poets, and the values they traditionally
represented have lost their centrality.

Israel in Egypt was first performed later in 1739, when Patriot
claims that the Spanish were enslaving British sailors led to pressure for war, and it was revived after war had been declared.[35]
Although the work never achieved popular success in Handel's
lifetime, it too presented features potentially congenial to traditionally minded opponents of opera. Pope could hardly have been
unaware, as familiar as he was with Patriot politics, that the biblical episode was being used in the press as an allegory of Britain's salvation from Spanish oppression; nor could he have failed
to notice that the figure of Moses could be read as the new leader
demanded by the Patriots as essential to Britain's revival
(whether that leader was identified as Prince Frederick or the
Pretender, as Jennens, the probable compiler of the libretto,
would have preferred; for both, like Moses, could be said to have
been brought up in foreign courts, unnaturally separated from
their destined subjects).

Yet here too the underlying mythic resonances of the work and
its conformity with idealized notions of dramatic representation
may have been more significant for Pope. Whereas *opera seria*
emphasizes solo voices as trained in a continental tradition and
has no chorus, *Israel in Egypt* is set almost entirely for chorus
and can be seen as a development from the English anthem tradition (especially in the light of Handel's re-use of his funeral an-

them for Queen Caroline, an appropriation of Hanoverian panegyric that Patriots presumably found gratifyingly subversive).[36] Its disposition of forces speaks of a communal faith, and draws on the hallowed associations of the English choral foundations from which Handel drew many of his singers to produce an effective union of the pious and the patriotic. Solo voices in this work speak from and for the chorus; solos and duets display the distinctive timbres of alto, tenor, and bass voices equally with the soprano. It is particularly striking that when a named female character briefly takes center stage in the final ensemble, it is as Miriam the prophetess, whose role is to lead the antiphonal song of praise with a melodic line of triumphant and emphatic simplicity already stated by male voices and answered by the full chorus.[37] There could hardly be a more striking contrast with the operatic world of high-pitched solo virtuosity than this reintegration of the female into community and hierarchy. Also redefined is the convention, familiar to audiences as a means of transacting the business of operatic plots, which Pope ridicules as "quaint Recitativo," but which Handel transforms into a medium for emphatic choral statement (4.52). In the choral setting of a text such as "And Israel saw that great work that the Lord did upon th' Egyptians; and the people feared the Lord," the shape of the line and the coloring of words by chromatic movement combine with the density of the choral texture to express the awe of a complex but unified community.[38] Even the artifice of fugal layering can be seen in this work as less a display of virtuosity than a means of evoking an emotional response from the listener, as voice after voice and the final coming together of voices reinforce a subject crafted to emphasize key words and feelings—as in the repeated rhythmic blows of the entries on "They oppressed them with burdens," or the layering of chromatic misgivings in "They loathed to drink of the river: He turned their waters into blood."[39]

Although *Israel in Egypt* has often been enjoyed for its more obvious mimetic effects (such as hopping frogs, buzzing flies, and bouncing hailstones), its commitment to expressive setting of English biblical words also makes a deeper appeal to traditional notions relating the expressiveness of language and the authority of the poet to the performative language of God in creation.[40] Not only is the whole text selected to praise the saving acts of God, but specific tributes are made to such images of potency as God's breath ("with the blast of thy nostrils the waters were gathered together"; "Thou didst blow with the wind"), his right hand ("Thy right hand, O Lord, is become glorious in power"), the fire of his anger ("Thou sentest forth thy wrath, which consumed them as stubble"), and his prowess in warfare ("The Lord is a man of war"), expressed for the most part by male voices or full chorus.[41] In the account of the plagues, number after number begins with a formula emphasizing God as subject of the verb, fully underwritten by the musical emphasis ("He gave them hail-stones," "He sent a thick darkness," "He smote all the first-born," etc.).[42] The text comes very close to the central myth of divine performative language in the account of the plague of flies: "He spake the word" is given out in a measured monotone by male voices, echoed by the brass that plays so unusually prominent a part in the work; and the result of the edict, "And there came all manner of flies," is taken up in contrast by staccato female voices accompanied by whirring violins.[43] Such conventional ways of figuring divine and human, masculine and feminine, with all their associated hierarchies, are part of the traditional system of values that Dulness comes to undo. Opera is thus entirely accurate in exhorting her to fear a composer who sets important words in a manner calculated to "stir," "rouze" and "shake the Soul" into the reassertion of the implicitly natural and essential values traditionally discerned in such texts (lines 67–68). The speech reaches a fitting climax with the claim that in Handel's music "Jove's own Thunders follow Mars's Drums," for in *Israel in Egypt* the Lord is not only the "man of war" celebrated in the blare of trumpets, but also the God whose hailstorms are accompanied by the thunderous roll of drums, assimilated by neoclassical convention to the mythic language of the classical sky-god who speaks in the thunder. Such symbolism is also recalled earlier in the speech when Handel is called "bold Briareus," in allusion to the hundred-armed monster who defended Zeus against Titans and Olympians.[44]

Dulness's response suggests that the threat posed by Handel has been decisively dealt with: "She heard, and drove him to th'-Hibernian shore" (line 70). The implications of this statement are taken up by Sherburn, who contextualizes it with the statement that, when the lines were written, Handel was "bankrupt and in Ireland."[45] Yet this is misleading. Handel was certainly in Ireland between November 1741 and August 1742, and had apparently experienced some financial difficulty in the late 1730s as opera seasons became less and less viable, but he was never bankrupt, and his decision to go to Dublin for the winter season—which may have been prompted by an official invitation by the lord lieutenant—and subsequently to extend his stay into the following summer seems to represent a pragmatic judgment of relative advantage rather than a gesture of despair at his prospects in London.[46] Taylor suggests that the reference in the note to line 45 to Handel's oratorios' being "too manly for the fine Gentlemen of his age" is a reference to the aristocratic would-be directors and their potential subscribers whom Handel had recently crossed by declining to involve himself with new opera projects: certainly in his Index, Pope gives the reference "HANDEL, an excellent musician, banished to Ireland by the English Nobility, iv. 65." From this point of view, some exaggeration of Handel's distress might have seemed in order, but it could also be that Pope was simply responding to alarmist rumor in the press. A letter in the *London Daily Post* of April 1741 not only mentions "the Gentlemen who have taken Offence at any Part of this great Man's Conduct" (also called "so many Gentlemen of Figure and Weight"), but also cites the activities of "those little Vermin, who, taking Advantage of their Displeasure, pull down even his Bills as fast as he has them pasted up," and suggests that the public should support Handel's next oratorio performance, "if Report be true, probably his last for ever in this Country."[47]

By the time Handel returned to London in August 1742, a few months after the publication of *The New Dunciad* in which Opera's speech was first used, *The Dunciad in Four Books* was substantially complete, and the printer had begun work.[48] By its publication in 1743, therefore, events had moved beyond the framework set by Pope's gloomy prophecy: although Handel's 1745–1746 oratorio season was to be financially difficult, in the longer term his oratorio seasons were to open the possibility of profits vastly larger in proportion to the number of performances than he had ever achieved with opera.[49] The operatic theme in the *Dunciad*s had in fact from the beginning encapsulated the problem of a text that, revision by revision, pursued contemporary trends in quest of eternal verities: even the most resonant prophecies rested on people who might die and circumstances that might change while the text was in press. Sometimes events seemed made for the text, as when Cibber was elected laureate, or Handel went to Ireland; but sometimes events were less easy to accommodate, as when Walpole fell from power and Handel came back from Dublin to work toward his period of greatest commercial success. In such cases, the mythic underpinning of the claim that "the *poem was not made for these authors, but these authors for the poem*" is revealed in a more problematic light; and from this perspective we can recognize the potential

datedness, by 1743, of the entire argument against opera, whic
had its origin in the experience of the late 1720s, when the firs
triumph of the Royal Academy seasons was eclipsed by the scan
dal of quarreling between its leading ladies and the triumph o
The Beggar's Opera.[50] Without the opportunity that oratorio fur
nished to refocus and refurbish the anti-operatic theme, Pope's
decision in the early 1740s to personify Opera at the head of the
procession to the throne could have risked a somewhat untopica
revival of his early plan.

Pope's evocation of the resonant affirmations of Handel's oratorio is impressive, and must have seemed especially so for English readers caught up in the gargantuan religiosity of the
massed oratorio performances that came to represent Handel's
achievement in the two centuries after his death. Yet now that we
again take seriously the notion that *opera seria* was in its time a
viable artistic medium, and have adjusted to a less solemn and
weighty style of oratorio performance, we may also be more open
to the possibility that in this passage Pope maneuvered himself
into a not entirely consistent position. In Book 2, after all, the
noise-making competition had been inherently ludicrous; but
now, with reference to oratorio, Pope seems dangerously close to
equating sheer volume of sound with manly virtue. Indeed, the
assonance as well as the vocabulary of the claim that "Jove's own
Thunders follow Mars's Drums" chimes uncomfortably with
Pope's earlier satire of Blackmore's adulation of George II's heroic prowess:

Rend with tremendous Sound your ears asunder,
    With Gun, Drum, Trumpet, Blunderbuss & Thunder? (*Imitations
    of Horace*: *Satires* II.i.25–26)

Blackmore is writing on the wrong side, but, as winner of the
braying section of the noise-making competition (2.245–68), his
example prompts the reflection that in the contest between opera
and oratorio, it is not the thing in itself that matters, but the
function it is made to perform in a complex of polarized values.
Oratorio could have been presented less as opera's opposite than
as simply another phase in Handel's career.[51] An alternative construction of the supposed opposition could have promoted the purity of opera, the singleness of its concentration on the quality of
the individual voice, its thorough absorption in the elegant styli-
zation of emotion in and between characters, the space its conventions clear for the display of formal inventiveness and

refinement by composer and singer. Lady Lucy Wentworth speaks for a perception opposite to Pope's when she criticizes a church service that she found too noisy for including "drums and Trumpets as loud as an Oritoria," and when she responds to the news of Handel's borrowing drums from the Tower for *Saul* with the anticipation that "it will be most excessive noisy with a bad set off singers."[52] For Lady Irwin, the forces assembled for oratorio were less evocative of English manliness than of the oppressive racket of a common French eating house: " 'tis excessive noisy, a vast number of instruments and voices, who all perform at a time, and is in music what I fancy a French ordinary in conversation."[53] As Pope himself had admitted in other contexts, loudness is no guarantee of truth or virtue.

A final irony is provided by a reference toward the end of the poem that reactivates once more the theme with which Pope's attack on opera had originated in his manuscript draft, the notion that opera was seducing the ruling class away from its duty. The reference is teasingly half-concealed in a note jointly composed by Pope and Warburton on lines that might otherwise pass unremarked in this connection:

> Unfinish'd Treaties in each Office slept;
> And Chiefless Armies doz'd out the Campaign;
> And Navies yawn'd for Orders on the Main.

These Verses were written many years ago, and may be found in the State Poems of that time. So that Scriblerus is mistaken, or whoever else have imagined this Poem of a fresher date.[54]

The denial of contemporary reference invites the reader both to apply the lines to current affairs and to remember where he has read them before. The allusion is to a poem called "Orpheus and Margarita," published forty years earlier, which compares the power of Orpheus over inanimate objects with the power of the singer Margherita de l'Epine over her highly placed lovers:

> And since the tawny *Tuscan* rais'd her Strain,
> R—k furls his Sails, and dozes on the Main;
> Treaties unfinish'd in the Office sleep,
> And *Sh—el* yawns for Orders on the Deep.[55]

The corrupting effect of the "Harlot form" is thus presented as dating right back to the first decade of the century, when continental opera stars first appeared on the English stage, and readers who had once found the poem in their copies of the 1704 *Poems on Affairs of State* would also have been reminded that another poem in the same volume described l'Epine's rivalry with the English prima donna Catherine Tofts in terms of national and party-political polarities that clearly anticipated more recent polemic.[56]

Yet l'Epine, whose characterization in *Poems on Affairs of State* as the dangerous foreign siren Pope and Warburton chose to embed in their commentary, was probably the singer who created the role of Galatea in the Cannons *Acis and Galatea*, that touchstone of English word-setting.[57] She had from an early stage of her career sung not only Handel's English works, but also songs by Purcell and other authentically English composers; she married Pepusch, who arranged the music for *The Beggar's Opera*, so lauded in Pope's commentary; and she settled permanently in England, being particularly noted for her playing on the harpsichord of pieces from the quintessentially English compilation now known as the Fitzwilliam Virginal Book.[58] To list these facts about her life is to construct a very different image, almost the polar opposite of the first. This is just one instance of how artful, interested, and opportunistic *The Dunciad in Four Books* is in its constructions of the contemporary scene: the more closely we examine the events and personalities on which it draws, the more clearly it appears that things could have been represented quite otherwise.

"Trials of Manhood": Cibber, *The Dunciad*, and the Masculine Self

LAURA J. ROSENTHAL

IN RESPONDING TO THE FAMOUS RIVALRY BETWEEN COLLEY CIBBER and Alexander Pope, few scholars have much trouble in choosing a side. The bulk of Pope criticism accepts the poet's signification of his rivals as "dunces" and explores his scathing brilliance in exposing their flaws. Feminist scholars provide the most notable exception by protesting Pope's banishment of women writers into the filth of Grub Street, by clearing *The Dunciad*'s muck from their reputations, and by salvaging these figures for serious and deserved attention. Catherine Ingrassia, in fact, represents Pope as attacking not from a perception of his own strength, but from a sense of the encroachment of women writers and the feminine in general.[1] But while we begin to consider the possibility that Pope's prejudices shaped his judgment of Eliza Haywood and Susanna Centlivre, few question his ridicule of the male Grub Street authors.[2] Theobald may have cut a relatively minor figure on the literary landscape, but Colley Cibber wrote numerous popular plays, became a widely respected actor and powerful manager, composed a witty autobiography and, as *The Dunciad* reminds us, served as England's poet laureate.

It would be impossible to defend Cibber on aesthetic grounds—not because his writing is obviously "bad," but because Pope in many ways helped define the eighteenth-century aesthetic itself and located Cibber and others outside it. Departing from traditional views of the aesthetic, Lance Bertelsen insists that it is time "to rethink what it means to be a 'dunce.' "[3] Bertelsen suggests that the (anti-)aesthetic of "duncehood" described by Pope and Swift characterizes a transgressive carnivalesque that need not be assumed negative from our perspective: "the breaching of traditional boundaries of social and generic decorum (of which all dunces were accused) could be seen as a testing of new voices, new associational liberties, new economic opportunities, new re-

lations between classes."[4] *The Dunciad* genders these oppositions: as Valerie Rumbold argues, "that Dulness herself is female
is one of the most important facts about her."[5] Marilyn Francus
goes even further in suggesting that in *"The Dunciad,* the female
appropriation of male hierarchy is the centerpiece of the text, as
the now absent father is replaced completely by subservient, incompetent sons."[6] In a sense we even can see the dunces themselves, and especially Cibber, as feminized by the poem, for their
identities become inseparable from that of their Goddess: "In
each she marks her Image full exprest, / But chief in BAYS's monster-breeding breast."[7] Elsewhere, the Dunces bray like "long-
ear'd milky mothers" waiting for absent foals (307). Putting
these observations together suggests a hostility in *The Dunciad*
toward Cibber as somehow associated with women, and one reading of the Cibber–Pope rivalry might be to see Pope as staking out
elite aesthetics and dominant masculinity, while reviving Cibber
as a figure of the carnivalesque, the feminine, and a transgress-
ively heteroglossic popular culture.

Yet reversing the valuation of these binaries—high culture/
popular culture; masculine/feminine; order/carnivalesque; Pope/
Cibber—not only preserves them, but it also preserves a characterization of the difference between Pope and Cibber (and fellow
Dunces) that cannot entirely be supported. Pope, as *The Dunciad*
itself evidences, generated as well as denigrated carnivalesque; in
his plays, Cibber both indulged in campy excess and insisted on
domestic order. Both Pope and Cibber were successful professionals, accumulating various sorts of economic and symbolic capital.
The texts that their rivalry produced evidence both personal difference and participation in the same general discourse with similar terms of attack and vulnerabilities of the authors. To offer
one brief example, James Ralph unflatteringly described Pope as:

> —Fam'd among Fops and Beaus,
> For Poetry and Sense, or, in effect,
> For *stealing* other Mens; he next usurps
> A Sovereign Rule, and, in *Apollo*'s stead,
> Becomes the Tyrant of his fellow Bards
> Hemh! he begins, attend ye Criticks, hear
> Ye Poets what by him the *God* ordains.
> " '*Tis hard to say if greater want of Skill
> Appears in writing, or in stealing ill.*"[8]

Both plagiarism and fame among beaus and fops became important ways in which Pope defined Cibber's dullness. To suggest

that while the two writers faced similar accusations their difference lies in accomplishment—that, in other words, Pope was indisputably the more talented one—does not solve the problem
either, for as Dennis Todd argues, the greatest threat to *The Dunciad* lies in its potential triviality of subject.[9] If Cibber was really
so dull, what made him worth attacking so furiously? Why, if Dulness is a woman and Pope attacked the feminization of culture,
did he make *Cibber*—and not a woman—the final hero?[10] However subsequent canon-makers may have treated these two writers, Cibber's importance in the eighteenth century is beyond
dispute. Further, Pope's selection of a male chief dunce and
mostly male auxiliary dunces in a poem rife with images of monstrous femininity evidences not the absence of significant women
writers in the culture, but rather a more immediate concern (although not necessarily a conscious one) with defining gender itself—and, in particular, masculinity—over attacking women.[11]

In this essay, I argue that Pope and Cibber both responded to
changing forms of masculinity that became respectively associated in eighteenth-century culture with print and theater. The
intensity of their rivalry emanated not from a clear opposition between masculine genius and feminine dullness, but from differences within masculine possibilities. Kristina Straub shows how
both Pope and Cibber faced profound challenges to their masculinity, but for different reasons. Not only did Pope's ailing body
leave him vulnerable to attacks on the basis of his masculinity,
but so did his religion. Catholic men, she points out, were satirized for failing to control their wives and daughters, and anti-
Catholic propaganda regularly linked "papacy" to sodomy.[12] Cibber had similar vulnerabilities from different sources: as an actor,
he faced the specularization generally reserved for women in the
eighteenth century, and his *Apology* constitutes an attempt, according to Straub, to reclaim control of this feminized abjection.[13]
"Power over sexuality and language," she argues, "is . . . the primary issue in the quarrel between Cibber and Pope," both of
whom use homophobic images to suggest the compromised masculinity of the other.[14]

While I agree that Pope and Cibber attacked each other on the
grounds of masculinity, in what follows I would like to pursue another of Straub's suggestions that in the end we *can* see differences in Pope's and Cibber's constructions of gender, despite
their many similarities and their participation in the same discourse. For Straub this becomes apparent in Pope's total abjection of the homoeroticized schoolboy figure compared to Cibber's

abjection *and* identification—a "slamming door" as opposed to one that "swings both ways."[15] I argue that, even more than its attack on women and the feminine, *The Dunciad* attacks what it defines as a defective version of masculinity. This defective masculinity has less to do with resembling women than with failing to establish impenetrable boundaries, often represented in the poem as the failure of separation from an engulfing other. While this is not necessarily an expression of homophobia in particular, it nevertheless articulates related anxieties about masculine vulnerability. Returning to Bertelsen's suggestion that we might find something positive in duncehood, I suggest that Colley Cibber and "dunce subjectivity" in general resemble what feminist psychoanalytic critic Jessica Benjamin advocates as intersubjectivity, an alternative to the emphasis in classic psychoanalysis of achieving separation. While *The Dunciad* points by negation toward an independence and interiority potentially enabled by the proper relationship to print culture, Cibber, by contrast, maintains a theatricalized subjectivity that unabashedly depends on the admiring gaze of the other. In this respect, I believe that Pope offered an accurate impression of Cibber. While in many ways Pope and Cibber attacked each other on the same terms, Cibber became chief of the dunces for his self-assured adherence to this alternative intersubjective model, despite his conformity in so many other ways.[16] His famed relish of display was not just making a virtue of necessity, but a performance of masculine selfhood genuinely different from the aesthetic individualism called for, but entirely absent from, *The Dunciad*. So while Pope represented masculine intersubjectivity as the horror of indistinction and engulfment by the Other, Cibber performed this masculinity as a relish of the pleasure of the Other's gaze. The *Apology* thus proved infuriating for so many contemporaries not for its recuperation of a more acceptable version of male authority, as Straub suggests, but for its refusal to apologize.

Before turning to *The Dunciad,* however, let me briefly explain the unlikely usefulness of contemporary feminist psychoanalysis to an eighteenth-century dispute. Jessica Benjamin's critique of classic psychoanalysis cannot help but recall for students of the eighteenth century Pope's striking images of engulfing maternal power in *The Dunciad*. According to Benjamin, both Freud and ego psychology characterize a child's process of coming into identity as the painful and violent liberation of the self from dependence: "[t]he classic psychoanalytic viewpoint did not see differentiation as a balance, but as a process of disentanglement.

Thus it cast experiences of union, merger, and self-other harmony as regressive opposites to differentiation and self-other distinction."[17] While other feminist critics notice the way Freud's normal individual is defined as masculine, Benjamin further points out that the Oedipal paradigm crucially erases the subjectivity of the mother and inscribes her as the object from which the child must separate himself to achieve identity. This model of individualism inscribes male domination through the primary importance of a subject–object division, with the mother as the first object: "the vulnerability of a masculinity that is forged in the crucible of femininity, the 'great task' of separation that is so seldom completed, lays the groundwork for the later objectification of women. The mother stands as the prototype of the undifferentiated object. She serves men as their other, their counterpart, the side of themselves they repress" (77). While the goal of individual autonomy has been naturalized, Benjamin suggests that, from the perspective of intersubjective theory, "which sees the relationship between self and other, with its tension between sameness and difference, as a continual exchange of influence" (49), other human possibilities become apparent. The current valuation of individual autonomy, however, structures masculinity as dominant by defining full subjectivity as the extent to which one can escape the engulfing and border-destroying mother through her objectification.

While Benjamin criticizes classic psychoanalysis for its failure to recognize the possibilities of intersubjectivity, Carol Barash suggests the usefulness of recovering some of the cultural possibilities that preceded this model. She characterizes "classic psychoanalytic theory" as producing "a universal(izing) account of heterosexual norms from a much more unwieldy, historically specific set of sexual narratives;" for Barash, the eighteenth-century novel articulated "new bourgeois norms" that nevertheless remained "in tension with other possibilities, other available stories."[18] Indeed, Christopher Fox convincingly argues that John Locke first articulated the modern individual psychological self, and that the problems of this articulation endlessly fascinated the Scriblerians.[19] So while Benjamin criticizes the limited and limiting version of "normal" masculinity suggested by classic psychoanalysis, Barash and Fox demonstrate that those very norms had not yet been fully installed in the early eighteenth century. This instability itself perhaps explains the intensity of the sexualized and gendered conflict between Pope and Cibber, for neither could depend upon an undisputed norm to be either aligned with or defined against.

While Pope and Cibber both succeeded as professional writers, their conflict invoked the terms of class as well as gender. Pope articulated his hostility to Cibber's violation of the aesthetic, a philosophical configuration enabled by changing structures of authority in general. "Aesthetics is born," Terry Eagleton has argued, "of the recognition that the world of perception and experience cannot simply be derived from abstract universal laws, but demands its own appropriate discourse and displays its own inner, if inferior, logic."[20] Further,

> once absolutist power had been overturned, each subject must function as its own seat of self-government. An erstwhile centralized authority must be parcellized and localized: absolved from continuous political supervision, the bourgeois subject must assume the burden of its own internalized governance. . . . Like the work of art as defined by the discourse of aesthetics, the bourgeois subject is autonomous and self-determining, acknowledges no merely extrinsic law but instead, in some mysterious fashion, gives the law to itself.[21]

Full articulation of the aesthetic, Eagleton suggests, becomes possible only with the decline of centralized, absolutist authority, for the aesthetic depends so profoundly on Enlightenment individuality. Pope represented Colley Cibber as the opposite of an autonomous individual who comprehends the aesthetic from within: he appears in Pope's writing as indistinct, Protean, oblivious to borders of the self, and even nonexistent. He is less consistently feminized—if by that we mean aligned with or resembling women—in *The Dunciad* than used to represent the failure to achieve masculine individuality.[22] Yet by citing Eagleton here I do not mean to suggest that Cibber adhered to an aristocratic mode outside of a bourgeois aesthetic that we should somehow prefer, for Cibber was nothing if not the consummate professional. In fact, one of Pope's central points about the dunces was their commercial dependence and thus class inferiority. Nevertheless, Cibber's foppish excess, the "effeminacy" that he performed and that had come to be associated with aristocratic masculinity, his cavalier disregard for Augustan order in his writing, all *recalled as they parodied* an earlier model of masculinity.[23] His particular style of professionalism, conversely, disturbed both configurations, for he exposed rather than mystified the financial motivations of his artistic accomplishment. Either way, Cibber stood outside of the bourgeois aesthetic that Pope helped to develop.

Perhaps the most extreme attack on Cibber's selfhood in *The Dunciad* appears not in the poem but in Warburton's preface. Here "Richardus Aristarchus" addresses the potential objection to locating Cibber as a hero while he "still existeth, and hath not yet finished his earthly course" (264). "Richardus Aristarchus" claims that Cibber has already taken care of this objection himself by promising never to change or amend, and having "publickly declared himself *incorrigible*, he is become *dead in law*, . . . and descendeth to the Poet as his property: who may take him, and deal with him, as if he had been dead as long as an old Egyptian hero; that is to say, *embowel* and *embalm him for posterity*" (265). The declaration of the living Cibber as truly dead represents, more than just about any other imaginable trope, the annihilation of enemy's self: in this preface, Cibber comes no longer to exist. But Warburton did not stop there: with no life of his own, the dead Cibber descends to Pope as his possession. The preface transforms the laureate from a person to a text, which in turn becomes Pope's literary property. The accomplishment of *The Dunciad*, according to this preface, lies in its revelation of Cibber's lack of property in himself and complete imprisonment within the verses of the poem, for there remains no Cibber outside of the text.

The Dunciad itself, conversely, continually suggests the (nevertheless absent) possibility of constructing an autonomous masculine self by revealing the (effeminate, anti-aesthetic) incapacity of other men to do so. Warburton represented Cibber as dead or nonexistent; *The Dunciad*, in contrast, accuses Cibber of plagiarism—of filling the void left by his empty subjectivity with words stolen from other men. Rather than not existing at all, the Cibber of the poem transgresses by recognizing no boundaries between self and other. In the earlier *Dunciad*, Pope represented Theobald as mired in textual excess, confusion, and despair:

> Studious he sate, with all his books around,
> Sinking from thought to thought, a vast profound!
> Plung'd for his sense, but found no bottom there;
> Then writ, and founder'd on, in mere despair.
> He roll'd his eyes that witness'd huge dismay,
> Where yet unpawn'd, much learned lumber lay,
> Volumes, whose size the space exactly fill'd:
> Or which fond authors were so good to gild;
> Or where, by sculpture made for ever known,
> The page admires new beauties, not its own. (A.1.110–20)

Theobald has no idea what to do with all the unpawned learned lumber he has collected. In the revised version, however, Cibber plagiarizes it:

> Next, o'er his Books his eyes began to roll,
> In pleasing memory of all he stole,
> How here he sipp'd, how there he plunder'd snug
> And suck'd all o'er, like an industrious Bug.
> Here lay poor Fletcher's half-eat scenes, and here
> The Frippery of crucify'd Molière;
> There hapless Shakespear, yet of Tibbald sore,
> Wish'd he had blotted for himself before. (B.1.127–34)

Cibber not only steals texts from other playwrights, but he actually *eats* them in Pope's imagination. Cibber literally has no integrity here, blurring all distinction between a self and another. Pope insisted on Cibber's indistinct self throughout the 1743 *Dunciad*, surrounding his hero with images of intertextuality, blurring, fog, and failed separation.[24]

Cibber took the charge of plagiarism seriously in his *Letter from Mr. Cibber, to Mr. Pope,* quoting Pope's couplet that "A patch'd, vamp'd, future, old, reviv'd, New piece, / 'Twixt Plautus, Fletcher, Shakespear, and Corneille, / Can make a Cibber, Johnson, or Ozell."[25] Cibber insisted that "this Libel was below you!" (33) and devoted considerable space to refuting it. No one else, he argued, would have recognized him in this "Scurvy Picture," "nor can I easily believe that you yourself do" (18). (Cibber, however, had endured this charge from a variety of sources during his entire career.) Evidently, Cibber recognized the importance of clearing himself of this charge, but at the same time did not deny his borrowing so much as defend the practice itself. He first compared himself to Dryden, who took "the same Liberty" with Shakespeare's *Tempest* and *Troilus and Cressida* and argued that the plays themselves "had been dead to the Stage out of all Memory, [and] have since been in a constant course of Acting above these thirty or forty Years" (32). Further, he insisted that reviving old plays did not diminish his originality elsewhere: "Is a Tailor, that can make a new Coat well, the worse Workman, because he can mend an old one?" (32–33). Ultimately, then, Cibber truly did seem to hold a more fluid understanding of literary property—an understanding that, as the comparison to Dryden suggests, once again looked back rather than forward. Less interested in policing the boundaries between self and other, Cibber saw little wrong with what others might call plagiarism.

But Pope not only represented Cibber as a violator of textual borders, but as a Protean creature—another version of the indistinct self. He reminded his readers of Cibber's long career as an actor: "Bays, form'd by nature Stage and Town to bless, / And act, and be, a Coxcomb with success" (B.1.109–10). An actor necessarily makes his living by performing different selves. Joseph R. Roach, in fact, argues that early modern theories of acting understood the body itself as subject to change, for invoking different emotions transformed one's physiology. For this reason, contemporaries understood acting as downright dangerous, since the performer could lose control of these transformations.[26] *The Dunciad* not only characterizes Cibber as Proteus, but first introduces all writers who escape from the cave of "Poverty and Poetry" as like the mythical shape-shifter: "Keen, hollow winds howl thro' the bleak recess, / Emblem of Music caus'd by Emptiness. / Hence Bards, like Proteus long in vain ty'd down, / Escape in Monsters, and amaze the town" (B.1.35–38). In a note praised by Pope, Warburton informatively elaborated:

> If I be not deceived in a part of learning which has so long exercised my pen, by *Proteus* must certainly be meant a hacknied Town scribler; and by his Transformations, the various disguises such a one assumes, to elude the pursuit of his irreconcilable enemy, the Bailiff. Proteus is represented as one bred of the mud and slime of Ægypt, the original soil of Arts and Letters: And what is a Town-scribler, but a creature made up of the excrements of luxurious Science? (*TE* 5.272, n.37)

In his practice of self-transformation for the sake of pleasing others, the "hack" by definition remains outside of aesthetic accomplishment and dominant masculinity. *The Dunciad* further characterizes Cibber as playing the Protean fop off-stage as well:

> Did on the stage my Fops appear confin'd?
> My Life gave ampler lessons to mankind. (1.191–92)

Fascination with clothing and new fashions make the fop an ever-transforming creature, with an elaborate, ever-updated exterior and no core being. Like their author, Cibber's works have no distinctiveness either. In the words of the chief dunce,

> Some Daemon stole my pen (forgive th' offence)
> And once betray'd me into common sense:
> Else all my Prose and Verse were much the same;
> This, prose on stilts; that, poetry fall'n lame. (1.187–90)

The Goddess Dulness likes exactly this kind of writing the best:

> Here to her Chosen all her works she shews;
> Prose swell'd to verse, verse loit'ring into prose:
> How random thoughts now meaning chance to find,
> Now leave all memory of sense behind:
> How Prologues into Prefaces decay
> And these to Notes are fritter'd quite away. (1.274–78)

Thus lack of distinctiveness becomes a primary quality of not just the laureate but of "dunces" in general. Their writing blurs all borders between genres and issues signifiers with no apparent destination. The detachment of signifier to signified or the charging of one signifier with a jumble of meanings threatens not only literature but reason and "the public world of art and politics."[27]

The ultimate image for nonindividuality, however, appears in the second book: the dunces' self-defining borders have so eroded that nothing at all remains. Dulness teases the booksellers with a contest over a nonexistent poet: "And now the victor stretch'd his eager hand / Where the tall Nothing stood, or seem'd to stand; / A shapeless shade, it melted from his sight, / Like forms in clouds, or visions in the night" (2.109–12). She tricks the booksellers by dressing up her hacks like "Congreve, Addison, and Prior"; once caught, they change back to their insubstantial selves: "So Proteus, hunted in a nobler shape, / Became, when seiz'd, a puppy, or an ape" (2.129–30). The Goddess Dulness is the biggest "nothing" in the poem, consistently described in terms of the destruction of all boundaries. As the daughter of "Chaos and eternal Night," Dulness rules the mind "in native Anarchy" (1.16). She appears in "clouded Majesty" (1.45) and watches over her many sons through self-generated fog: "Her ample presence fills up all the place; / A veil of fogs dilates her awful face: / Great in her charms!" (1.261–63). In her final triumph:

> *Religion* blushing veils her sacred fires,
> And unawares *Morality* expires.
> Nor *public* Flame, nor *private*, dares to shine;
> Nor *human* Spark is left, nor Glimpse *divine*!
> Lo! thy dread Empire, CHAOS! is restor'd;
> Light dies before thy uncreating word:
> Thy hand, great Anarch! lets the curtain fall;
> And Universal Darkness buries All. (4.649–56)

By the end of the poem, the great nothing of Dulness has spread to every corner of the earth. This borderless nothing not only articulates the spreading, rather than the containment, of the feminine, but also imagines the encroaching of Dulness as horrifically (and triumphantly, from her point of view) refusing maternal separation. Pope thus represents the eighteenth-century culture wars as the unfortunate triumph of female "nothing" over masculine struggles for selfhood. To be engulfed, like Cibber, in the fog of Dulness is to remain only half-born, choked and surrounded by a torrent of "nothing." Cibber's flaws emerge as grotesque, bodily ones, and masculinity emerges as a physical state of impenetrable boundaries.

Thus Dulness is not just a woman; she is a "Mighty Mother"(1.1).[28] In *The Dunciad*, birth becomes grotesque in its representation of the incapacity to establish an independent identity and fully to achieve masculine subjectivity.[29] When the Goddess arrives,

> Here she beholds the Chaos dark and deep,
> Where nameless Somethings in their causes sleep,
> 'Till genial Jacob, or a warm Third day,
> Call forth each mass, a Poem, or a Play:
> How hints, like spawn, scarce quick in embryo lie,
> How new-born nonsense first is taught to cry,
> Maggots half-form'd in rhyme exactly meet,
> And learn to crawl upon poetic feet. (1.55–62)

At the same time that the poem attacks the dunces by name, they nevertheless remain "nameless Somethings" with no distinct identity; their writing appears as an undifferentiated mass of text. The slimy process of birth, however, remains incomplete: hints lie scarce quick in embryo, nonsense can barely cry, maggots remain half-formed. Dulness marks her own image in her sons, but "chief in BAYS's monster-breeding breast" (1.108). Bays himself remains grotesquely and erotically attached to his mother, nursing from his position on her lap. In turn, Cibber becomes a mother as well, breeding more monsters:

> [Cibber] gnaw'd his pen, then dash'd it on the ground,
> Sinking from thought to thought, a vast profound!
> Plung'd for his sense, but found no bottom there,
> Yet wrote and flounder'd on, in mere despair.
> Round him much Embryo, much Abortion lay,
> Much future Ode, and abdicated Play;

Nonsense precipitate, like running Lead,
That slip'd thro' Cracks and Zig-zags of the Head;
All that on Folly Frenzy could beget,
Fruits of dull Heat, and Sooterkins of Wit. (1.117–26)

Cibber gestates but the birth remains incomplete, for he produces
abortions, embryos, and "Sooterkins" instead of children. Folly
and Frenzy copulate inside him, giving birth, with their inade-
quate heat, to these little monsters instead of respectable offspring. In *The Dunciad*, then, Cibber is both grotesquely
dependent on Mother Dulness and a grotesque mother himself.

Attachment to a nursing mother characterizes not just Cibber
in *The Dunciad*, but the proliferation of Dulness. The Goddess
defines herself not just as a "Mighty Mother" but specifically as
a nursing mother:

"O! when shall rise a Monarch all our own,
And I, a Nursing-mother, rock the throne,
'Twixt Prince and People close the Curtain draw,
Shade him from Light, and cover him from Law;
Fatten the Courtier, starve the learned band,
And suckle Armies, and dry-nurse the land:
'Till Senates nod to Lullabies divine,
And all be sleep, as at an Ode of thine." (1.311–18)

In this image of topsy-turvy authority, the powerful nursing
mother Dulness controls not just literature but politics as well,
asserting herself by feeding some and starving others. In Book 2,
Eliza Haywood appears not just as a mother with "Two babes of
love close clinging to her waist" (2.158), but, like Dulness herself,
as a *nursing* mother of "majestic size" (2.163) with "cow-like udders" (2.164). Perhaps the most grotesque "maternal" image of
all, however, appears in the "anal birth," as Richard Nash describes it, of the collector Annius's coins. Annius had swallowed
the coins to protect them, and now stuffs himself with food to re-
fund them with the help of James Douglas's "soft obstetric hand"
(4.394). The name of the physician points to another monstrous
birth, for Douglas earned his place in the poem through his
involvement in the infamous case of Mary Toft, who claimed to
have given birth to seventeen rabbits.[30]

The Dunciad may articulate hostility toward birth or mothers
in general, but it also obsessively rehearses instances of failed or
incomplete reproduction; there is always, as we have seen, something weird, grotesque, or monstrous about the relationship be-

tween mothers and their offspring in this poem. The poem uses the figure of Mother Dulness to represent, among other things, the threat of nonindividualization. Birth is never quite fully accomplished; the sons, rather than becoming their own men, remain nursing children in their adulthood. Dulness is not a mother who releases her sons to their own destinies, but rather a mother who imprisons her sons, who in turn express no desire to distinguish themselves from her. "Dunces" by definition, then, cannot grasp the aesthetic "dream of reconciliation—of individuals woven into intimate unity with no detriment to their specificity, of an abstract totality suffused with all the flesh-and-blood reality of the individual being."[31] The possibility of Pope's anxiety over a usurping mother is not my point here;[32] rather, by constructing the binary versions of selfhood as *either* the defeat of Mother Dulness *or* a grotesque, anti-aesthetic blurring of boundaries, Pope disavowed the possibility of intersubjectivity, in which entanglement with and even dependence on the other does not threaten the integrity (however illusory) of the self.

One strong element of the work of *The Dunciad* lies in the hope of suggesting an autonomous masculine self outside the poem by revealing the failures of so many men within it. Ultimately, however, the poem defers rather than produces this possibility, for nothing can escape the long arms of Dulness. Even if full separation, completed birth, and a dignified independence might in theory be feasible somewhere, they make no appearance in the world of professional authorship that Pope represented. The satirized permeability of boundaries emerges in *The Dunciad* as the only viable possibility. *The Dunciad*, then, on one hand parallels the oppositions of aesthetic/carnivalesque to masculine individuation/incomplete birth, where the figure of incomplete birth takes on a network of gendered associations, including plagiarism, in which the boundaries between self and other are not maintained. Yet, to end there would belie the complexity of *The Dunciad*, which, on the other hand, offers an exploration of the carnivalesque as among its greatest pleasures. Further, the poem records its own endless fascination with the "other," so much so that all other considerations become eclipsed in the end. What ultimately emerges, then, is a strange and intense dependence on the King of Dunces by a fellow professional author who wanted to absent himself from the disorderly marketplace but could not avoid his debt to it. There can be no professional who appears to rise above the marketplace without other professionals who remain mired in its muck and dependent on the popular gaze—a position that Colley Cibber delighted to fill.

Let us return, then, to a previously unanswered question: Why *Cibber*? While Pope first elected Lewis Theobald as King of Dunces, many scholars have noticed that the revised version of *The Dunciad* appears less trivial, less personal, and more philosophical.[33] If indeed the second *Dunciad* has less to do with petty squabbles, then what does Cibber represent? Colley Cibber began his career and earned much of his notoriety as an actor. He negotiated this position with panache, and even used it as a place from which to attack Pope: in one performance of *The Rehearsal*, Cibber ad-libbed a mocking reference to *Three Hours after Marriage* that apparently outraged the poet and has been credited (by Cibber himself, among others) with inciting Pope to give Cibber a starring role in *The Dunciad*. Cibber seems to have reveled in his specularization, becoming famous for his gigantic wigs and sartorial excess, especially when he played the fop. But as much as this kind of performance brought Cibber fame, fortune, and attention, it also brought its indignities. As Kristina Straub argues, the eighteenth century saw the emergence of a binary opposition between the empowered (masculine) spectator and the (feminized) player as a disempowered object of the gaze.[34] While all players occupied a socially ambiguous space, Cibber became particularly renowned for his equivocal position. His self-construction as fop and thus specular object even disturbed, Straub observes, the emergent gendered opposition between subject and object. Cibber's self-location as specular object becomes significant, as we have seen, in his dispute with Pope, for it certainly gave Pope grounds on which to challenge his rival. But if Cibber had remained only a gender-bending actor, Pope probably would have dispensed with him in one neat couplet instead of placing him so prominently in the lap of Dulness.

The revised *Dunciad*, of course, clearly promoted Cibber to the chief of dunces as a response, at least in part, to Cibber's own scandalous *Letter to Mr. Pope*, a text to which I will return.[35] I think it is also worth considering, however, the impact and significance on the hostility evident in Pope's poetry of not just Cibber's performance and his *Letter*, but of his *Apology for the Life of Colley Cibber*. In the preface to the 1743 version, "Richardus Aristarchus" preemptively defended *The Dunciad* against the charge of triviality by listing its hero's qualifications, the first and foremost being egotism. A true hero is wise, and

[i]t is the character of true *Wisdom*, to seek its chief support and confidence within itself; and to place that support in the resources which proceed from a conscious rectitude of Will.—And are the advantages of *Vanity*, when arising to the heroic standard, at all short of this self-complacence? Nay, are they not, in the opinion of the enamoured owner, far beyond it? "Let the world (will such an one say) impute to me what Folly or weakness they please; but till *Wisdom* can give me something that will make me more heartily happy, I am content to be GAZED AT." This we see is *Vanity* according to the *heroic* gage or measure. (256-7)

By quoting from the *Apology*, "Richardus Aristarchus" satirized Cibber for positioning himself as the object of the gaze. The more specific objection, however, and the evidence that truly reveals the heroic proportions of Cibber's vanity, was that he wrote and published a whole book positioning himself as the *subject* of readerly interest. The vanity we most literally "see" in this passage is textual: Cibber's body drew the gaze in the theater, but Cibber's words and voice draw our gaze when "Richardus Aristarchus" quotes them. Cibber's crime was not just configuring himself as a specular object, but *writing about* and *publishing* reports of his specularization.[36]

J. Paul Hunter describes Cibber's *Apology* as a landmark in the transition from the cultural dominance of the stage, with its public nature, to the dominance of reading, with its private nature. Thus Hunter sees Cibber's own career as a kind of microcosm of a larger transition: "it is not so much [Cibber's] official place in his culture that makes him a perfect monarch for a poem about taste as his uncanny ability to read the taste of his contemporaries."[37] Elsewhere, Hunter notes the simultaneous emergence of the novel and the autobiography as popular forms in the eighteenth century, arguing that both evidence a new kind of interest in the self, the individual.[38] Cibber may have described himself as a visual object in the *Apology*—"I am content to be gazed at"— but in the very act of doing so he became a speaking, imprinted subject.[39] Pope satirized Cibber as a *mock* hero at least in part because Cibber already had located himself as an actual hero of his novelistic narrative. But while Cibber's audacious *Apology* may establish a self in print, it is not the version of selfhood that *The Dunciad* implicitly idealizes.

The movement that Hunter sees in eighteenth-century culture from theater to reading and thus from public to private appears as part of the promise of the *Apology*, but within its pages something entirely different happens. Cibber did not so much capitulate to print culture as theatricalize it; he provided one of many enduring sites of resistance to print's apparent tendency to promote interiorization. Cibber recognized that as an actor he "may have naturally excited the Curiosity of his Spectators to know what he really was, when in no body's Shape but his own."[40] The *Apology* itself, however, offers hardly any personal information. In fact, the *Apology* has found its most eager audience in theater historians, who value the book for its description of other performers by an eyewitness. Observing that Cibber "never gives us any real insights into his character," Leonard R. N. Ashley suggests that "it was not the fashion of the period."[41] Yet fashion was changing. Cibber's own friend Laetitia Pilkington, to note just one prominent example, offered quite a bit of intimate detail in her autobiography.[42] After suggesting that this narrative will move us from the stage to a setting more intimate, the *Apology* deflects those expectations that other autobiographies fulfill by maintaining theatricality throughout. Cibber represented the *Apology* as a delightful opportunity for a "Coxcomb" to talk about himself—in itself a performative rather than a contemplative image. Most of the *Apology* consists of stories about other people, and even those stories generally concern the exterior rather than the interior, including detailed descriptions of performers' bodies and their acting techniques. Cibber's experience of attending Lady Churchill at dinner can serve as one of many possible examples of the volume's orientation:

> Being so near the Table, you may naturally ask me, what I might have heard to have pass'd in Conversation at it? which I should certainly tell you, had I attended to above two Words that were utter'd there, and those were, *Some Wine and Water*. These, I remember, came distinguish'd, and observ'd to my Ear, because they came from the fair Guest, whom I took such pleasure to wait on: Except at that single Sound, all my Senses were collected into my Eyes, which during the whole Entertainment wanted no better Amusement, then of stealing now and then the delight of gazing on the fair Object so near me.[43]

The *Apology* teases the reader with the possibility of revealing some intimate information about Lady Churchill, but instead reports the writer's utter oblivion to any conversation except the Lady's commands. Cibber created a scene suggesting theatricality and the fascinations of appearances alone, with himself as the audience and the Lady as a beautiful, admired actress.

Rather than repudiating or even compensating for the stage, then, the *Apology* extends theatricality to print. And rather than trying to recuperate the literal integrity that *The Dunciad* finds so distressingly lacking, the *Apology* instead delights in the world as an extended staging of exteriors for the benefit and pleasure of an audience. In describing Mrs. Oldfield's performance of Lady Betty Modish, for example, Cibber insisted that

> Had her Birth plac'd her in a higher Rank of Life, she had certainly appear'd, in reality, what in this Play she only, excellently, acted, an agreeably gay Woman of Quality, a little too conscious of her natural Attractions. I have often seen her, in private Societies, where Women of the best Rank might have borrow'd some part of her Behaviour, without the least Diminution of their Sense, or Dignity.[44]

Through her acting skills, then, Mrs. Oldfield actually performed quality better than the quality themselves. The actress did not mimic her betters, for they did not necessarily perform quality as well; the ladies, in fact, would have been well served to imitate the actress. Here the *Apology* characterizes the social world as a series of performances with no original but a proliferation of copies.

Cibber's performative vision assumed an intersubjective conception of selfhood, for here and throughout the *Apology*, the self has no meaning without its other, the audience. The talking coxcomb must talk *to* someone, and the *Apology* itself consistently invokes the "you" of the reader. Cibber's famed egotism can be understood in this context: he reported that his first applause "made my Heart leap with a higher Joy, than may be necessary to describe"[45] and confessed that the attacks against him only made him vain, "[f]or I consider, if I were quite good for nothing, these Pidlers in Wit would not be concern'd to take me to pieces, or (not to be quite so vain) when they moderately charge me with only Ignorance, or Dulness, I see nothing in That which an honest Man need be asham'd of" since essentially these "Retailers of Wit" make their living from attacking the famous.[46] Here Cibber brilliantly turned all attacks into the flattery of recognition, a strategy he repeated elsewhere:

> Let them enjoy the Jest, with Laugh incessant!
> For True, or False, or Right, or Wrong, 'tis pleasant!
> Mixt, in the wisest Heads, we find some Folly;
> Yet I find few such happy Fools—as Colley!
> So long t'have liv'd the daily Satire's Stroke,
> Unmov'd by Blows, that might have fell'd an Oak. (57)[47]

This is not simply to argue that Pope revealed the truth about Cibber's hollowness. Yet the dependence that Pope rendered grotesque as failed separation and incomplete birth may indeed identify an intersubjectivity that Cibber not only failed to deny, but theatricalized, delighted in, and (to some, frustratingly) "performed" in his autobiography—a genre that others were beginning to use for expressions of interior selfhood. This self-performance in some ways borrowed from an earlier, aristocratic mode of masculine self-display, but could not be repeated by the professional, middle-class Cibber without some dissonance and distance.[48] It was neither simply nostalgia nor a parody of aristocratic masculinity, but rather an exposure of the abjected, effeminate masculinity with ambiguous boundaries that *The Dunciad* attacks and that Cibber's audiences, at the same time, found endlessly fascinating. The *Apology* not only insists on its author's dependence on recognition, but suggests the performative nature of subjectivity itself.

For this reason, Cibber basked in the charge of vanity as the desire for others to look at him: "Vanity may be sometimes as necessary to an Author," he writes, "as Courage to a Soldier."[49] In his resistance to bourgeois interiority on one hand, *and* to the aristocratic (and also increasingly bourgeois) veiling of literature's entanglement with the marketplace on the other, Cibber emerged as a self-fashioned fop, both on stage and off. In *The Egoist*, "Frankley" comments on Cibber's performance of the fop, suggesting

> You may keep most of your Follies without being star'd at.
>
> *Auth.* Let 'em be star'd at! it would be hard if I could not stand that, after having been star'd at by so many Thousands for near fifty Years together.
>
> *Fran.* Nay! that's no Consequence neither; because, in a Play, you were never supposed to be yourself.
>
> *Auth.* You are right—but that was only one of my wanton ways of expressing myself.[50]

A reader may hope for a complex interior underneath the masque of the fop, but will only, Cibber insisted, find more of the fop. The fop shares the aristocratic pleasure of display, but at the same time—at least in Cibber's case—locates this display in a public, *commercial* space of performance. Cibber understood, and even more disturbingly, *exposed*, his dependence on others as a financial as well as emotional relationship. Perhaps unsurprisingly, then, the *Apology* develops an extended metaphor of theatrical production as a form of prostitution. Cibber argued that while, on one hand, instead of only producing operas, pantomimes, and other spectacles— "these Gin-shops of the Stage"—his company "still had a due Respect to several select Plays, that were able to be their own Support; and in which we found our constant Account, without painting, and patching them out, like Prostitutes, with these Follies, in fashion," on the other hand, in a competitive market he "had not virtue enough to starve."[51] In his declared refusal to retain his "virtue" in the face of financial temptation, Cibber aligned not just his productions but himself with eighteenth-century stereotypes of prostitution. Thus Cibber characterized his relationship with the audience as not just financial and emotional, but also as erotic. This erotic dimension appears in the dedication "To A Certain Gentleman" (identified by B. R. S. Fone as Henry Pelham) as well, although perhaps less explicitly than in the image of prostitution: "When I see you lay aside the Advantages of Superiority," Cibber wrote, "and by your own Cheerfulness of Spirits, call out all that Nature has given me to meet them; then 'tis I taste you! Then Life runs high! I desire! I possess you!"[52]

While Pope mocked Cibber in *The Dunciad* with the scope of a poet engaged in, as much scholarship has demonstrated, social, moral, educational, and aesthetic controversies, Cibber's wittily crude missives, on the contrary, were overwhelmingly physical and sexual. *The Dunciad*, of course, makes suggestions about the sexuality of the poet's rivals as well. Cibber's particular strategy, however, was to violate Pope by exposing and imagining his sexuality as *public*. Cibber himself, as suggested above, remained less vulnerable in this arena, for his self-construction already depended in part on a public, erotic relationship with an audience. In his *Letter from Mr. Cibber to Mr. Pope,* the laureate declared himself unequal to the task of responding to Pope's first *Dunciad*; the contest "seems but to put me upon a level with a famous Boxer at the *Bear-Garden,* called *Rugged and Tough,* who would stand being drubb'd for Hours together, 'till wearying out his Antagonist by the repeated Labour of laying him on, and by keeping his own Wind . . . honest *Rugged* sometimes came off victorious."[53] If Cibber appeared to grant to Pope the superior wit, he nevertheless claimed for himself the superior masculine body—a theme carried throughout the entire *Letter*—implicitly comparing his robust body to Pope's puny one.[54] Even in his literary aspirations, Cibber declared his body as the issue: Pope could not truly hurt his rival because "I wrote more to be Fed, than be Famous, and since my Writings still give me a Dinner, do you rhyme me out of my Stomach if you can" (9). Cibber compared his own immediate and pleasurable relationship with performance to Pope's overly intellectualized one; while usually playing the role himself, Cibber here cast Pope as the self-absorbed fop:

> though I grant [*The Dunciad*] a better Poem of its Kind, than ever was writ; yet when I read it, with those vain-glorious encumbrances of Notes, and Remarks, upon almost every Line of it, I find myself in the uneasy Condition I was once in at an Opera, where sitting with a silent Desire to hear a favourite Air, by a famous Performer, a Coxcombly Connoisseur, at my Elbow, was so fond of shewing his own Taste, that by his continual Remarks, and prating in Praise of every Grace and Cadence, my Attention and Pleasure in the Song was quite lost and confounded. (9–10)

Instead of battling Pope on the poet's own terms of print, Cibber used print to refer to his own authority on the stage. In fact, he attributed Pope's fury to the poet's relative helplessness in comparison to the actor's power to ridicule him in a more immediate public forum: "I once as publickly offended him, before a thousand Spectators" (17). Cibber then told the anecdote of his ad-libbing a satiric reference to *Three Hours after Marriage,* "[u]pon which, I doubt, the Audience by the Roar of their Applause shew'd their proportionable Contempt of the Play" (18). Cibber dragged Pope into the position that would otherwise be reserved for *him*: as the specular object of ridicule. Further, Cibber represented himself as able to turn the audience's gaze from himself, in the position of the absurd Mr. Bayes from *The Rehearsal*, to Pope, who did not take it nearly as well: "after the Play was over, [Pope] came behind the Scenes, with his Lips pale and his Voice trembling, to call me to account for the Insult: And accordingly fell upon me with all the foul Language, that a Wit out of his Senses could be capable of. . . . Now let the Reader judge by this Concern, who was the true Mother of the Child!" (18–19). In Cibber's description, Pope became the irrational, ranting, feminized (even maternal), specular object, "almost choked with the foam of his Passion," while Cibber remained the speaking subject, controlling the audience's vision with his words. In this anecdote, Cibber gloated over the theater's triumph over print; he saw himself as gaining the upper hand by embracing the embodiment that *The Dunciad* presents as a sign of corruption.

The most memorable attack on Pope's masculinity in the *Letter,* however, appears in response to Pope's accusation in his *Epistle to Dr Arbuthnot*, "And has not Colley too his Lord, and Whore?" Cibber insisted that he would have the better of Pope on this one, for "I know more of *your* whoring than you do of *mine*" (46). Cibber's anecdote articulated his own superior masculinity in both sexual and public terms:

> He may remember, then (or if he won't I will) when *Button*'s Coffeehouse was in vogue, and so long ago, as when he had not translated above two or three Books of *Homer*; there was a late young Nobleman (as much his *Lord* as mine) who had a good deal of wicked Humour, and who, though he was fond of having Wits in his Company, was not so restrained by his Conscience, but that he lov'd to laugh at any merry Mischief he could do them: This noble Wag, I say, in his usual *Gayetè de Coeur*, with another Gentleman still in Being, one Evening slily seduced the celebrated Mr. *Pope* as a Wit, and myself as a Laugher, to a certain House of Carnal Recreation, near the *Hay-Market*; where his Lordship's Frolick propos'd was to slip his little *Homer*, as he call'd him, at a Girl of the Game, that he might see what sort of Figure a Man of his Size, Sobriety, and Vigour (in Verse) would make, when the frail Fit of Love got into him. (47–48)

Soon a "smirking Damsel" appeared with sufficient charms to "tempt the little-tiny Manhood of Mr. *Pope* into the next Room with her." At this, "his Lordship was in as much Joy, as what might happen within, as our small Friend could probably be in Possession of it" (48). Cibber, on the other had, began to grow concerned for the poet's health and

> threw open the Door upon him, where I found this little hasty Hero, like a terrible *Tom Tit*, pertly perching upon the Mount of Love! But such was my Surprize, that I fairly laid hold of his Heels, and actually drew him down safe and sound from his Danger. My Lord, who staid tittering without, in hopes the sweet Mischief he came for would have been compleated, upon my giving an Account of the Action within, began to curse, and call me an hundred silly Puppies, for my impertinently spoiling the Sport; to which with great Gravity I reply'd; pray, my Lord, consider what I have done was, in regard to the Honour of our Nation! For would you have had so glorious a Work as that of making *Homer* speak elegant *English*, cut short by laying up our little Gentleman of a Malady, which his thin Body might never have been cured of? No, my Lord! *Homer* would have been too serious a Sacrifice to our Evening Merriment. Now as his *Homer* has since been so happily compleated, who can say, that the World may not have been

obliged to the kindly Care of *Colley* that so great a Work ever came to
Perfection? (48–49)

The laureate missed no opportunity to observe the size of Pope's
body and, by insinuation, the size of his penis. This kind of attack
on Pope was not unique to Cibber and overdetermined by the
poet's deformity;[55] Kristina Straub is clearly right to call this a
"passive-aggressive act of castration with a vengeance. If Pope
[had] the phallus that his literary sharpness would seem to ac-
cord him, Cibber [suggested it was] a pitiful little thing, not
worth having."[56] While I also agree with Straub that "the Cibber
who gleefully narrates this scurrilous and cruel story about the
physically ill and sexually insecure Pope is rather more of a
prick" than an upholder of the law of the father,[57] I would like to
focus on Cibber's particular strategy of narrating Pope's engagement in *public* sex.

The comparison between the two male bodies stands out as the
most visceral and vicious image in this anecdote; nevertheless, it
may not be the most revealing aspect of this story for discovering
the dynamic between these two writers. Cibber constructed this
scene as a homosocial scenario that was, in Cibber's narrative,
itself orchestrated by the Lord, who "slily seduced" both Cibber
and Pope to the whorehouse. In the classic homosocial arrangement that Eve Kosofsky Sedgwick describes, two men articulate
desire for each other through the mediation of a woman.[58] Cibber,
however, configured a triangulation in which all three significant
participants are men, for Pope's sexuality replaces the woman's
as the conduit of pleasure for Cibber and the Lord. *The Letter* positions *Pope*'s sexuality and not the prostitute's as the source of
amusement: the Lord selected Pope as a wit, but Cibber as a
"Laugher," as a man with whom to enjoy the spectacle of Pope's
"little-tiny Manhood." In the process of becoming objectified
himself, Pope in this anecdote utterly failed to objectify the
woman. The Lord and Cibber shuttled Pope (not the prostitute)
between them, for the Lord coaxed Pope into the bedroom and
Cibber pulled him out. The very thought of Pope's sexuality gave
the Lord, according to Cibber, as much delight as it offered the
poet himself. *The Letter* not only diminishes Pope through his
"little-tiny Manhood," but creates an image of this tiny Manhood
overwhelmed by a (comparatively) gigantic Mount of Love—the
difference being so great that Pope could "perch" on it. Was Pope
about to penetrate this woman or fall into her abyss?

Cibber's revenge consisted not just in his overdetermined

mockery of Pope's body, but in moving this body from the poet's (relatively) disembodied realm of print into the actor's embodied world of public exposure. It was not simply sex at stake here, but *public* sex. Cibber and his Lordship set up Pope's encounter with a prostitute as a semipublic form of entertainment; Cibber's publication of the story increased its circulation into an even wider public. While this *Letter* used the medium of print to battle Pope, the anecdote itself reads like a theatrical farce, highly dependent on visual and physical comedy. One can almost picture the climactic scene on stage when the self-parodic Cibber swings open the bedroom door, fully intent on rescuing the frustrated poet from his great mistake. Interrupted sex, after all, remains a staple of theatrical comedy. Further, the stage fop in plays of this era, including Cibber's own, tended to function as a "third wheel" between lovers trying to get together, even if he married at the end. The *Letter* played on this convention and turned it into the farce of the poet and the whore. Intuiting the visual significance of this anecdote, contemporaries even more devastatingly circulated humiliating graphics of this scene that apparently caused the poet great consternation.

At the same time Cibber used this story to report his homosocial bonding with a Lord, he also used it to satirize Pope's claim to distance from the marketplace: against the Lord's wishes, Cibber "rescued" Pope from commercial sex. While this gesture, as Straub points out, may "castrate" Pope, it also suggests Cibber's equal footing with and independence from the patronizing—in both senses—aristocrat in the context of Pope's dependence *and* immersion in the most scandalous market of all. While *The Letter* makes an analogy between Pope's tiny wit and his tiny manhood, this particular anecdote ends with an even more aggressive undermining of Pope's authorship through an appropriation of his crowning achievement, for perhaps the most powerful attack in this passage lies in Cibber's satire of Pope's claim of superiority to market-driven professionals by usurping control over Pope's translation of Homer. Through the rescue of Pope's "thin body," Cibber claimed responsibility for production of his Homer, putting *himself* in the position of patron, guardian, and enabler, claiming that the world retained an obligation to *him* for the final product. In rescuing Pope's "Homer" from infection by the market-driven prostitute, Cibber comically claimed responsibility for Pope's aesthetic and bodily purity. Cibber represented Pope as profoundly dependent on aristocratic approval and the rational

guidance of his friend, without whom he surely would have ruined his "Homer" through infection by the (sexual) marketplace.

The last *Dunciad,* however, seemed to shake Cibber in a way
the other attacks did not, for his assault became even more virulent and crude in *Another Letter,* promising to "answer your
Challenge, and come to a Trial of Manhood with you"[59] and drop-
ping the artfulness of the first letter. This trial proceeded without
subtlety: "whenever I observe your *Grimalkin* Spirit shew but
the least grinning Gasp of Life, I shall take the honest Liberty of
old Towser the House-Dog, and merrily lift up my Leg to have
a little more Game with you" (7). Cibber turned himself into a
urinating Towser, but Pope metamorphosed into more dependent
creatures: "why so immoderately jealous of your Fame, that like
my Lady's Lap-Dog you must snap at the Nose of every Mortal,
that meddles with it?" (12); Pope had "[j]ust the very Wanton-
ness of a Lady's merry Monkey in Favour, never more delighted,
than in doing a mischief" (14). In summing up Pope's "incurable
Nature," Cibber combined bestial with sadistic images of helplessness:

> for tho' in my first Letter, without regard to your Quality, I had hon-
> estly taken the Whip and Bell to you, and (as every Body tells me)
> make you as uneasy as a Rat in a hot Kettle for a Twelvemonth to-
> gether, I still find that bitter Pug is at his old Tricks again, and as
> silly a Devil as ever; but at your Peril be it, little Gentleman, for I
> shall have t'other Frisk with you, and don't despair that the very No-
> tice I am now taking of you, will once more make your Fame fly, like
> a yelping Cur with a Bottle at his Tail. (15)

Recalling the image of domination from the first letter, the laureate also charged that "[i]f therefore you think you have the Right
to lay your satyrical Tail at my Door, whenever your Muse has a
Looseness, have not I an equal Right to rub your Nose in it?" (16).
This literary diarrhea crudely imaged Pope as lacking bodily control in an infantile way; the lapdog, the merry monkey, and the
bitter pug are infantilized dependents on an indulgent lady. Despite some similar themes, however, this letter lacked the confidence of the first, which breezily praised the poet before exposing
its devastating anecdote. Its crude vehemence suggests that
Pope's estimation truly may have held some meaning for Cibber.

In both *The Dunciad* and in Cibber's letters, the most important rival is not Mother Dulness, women writers, or the indulgent
patron or patroness, but rather the other man (or men) whose

particular claim to selfhood exposes the vulnerability of emergent forms of masculinity. Dulness can offer little threat without her devotees. By parading himself on stage and then extending theatricality into his *Apology*, Cibber embarrassed masculinity itself—a gesture that gave rise, as I have suggested, to the virulence of Pope's attack. Yet Pope, as many scholars have noticed, constructed his persona no less diligently: "the independent, patronless, author," as Catherine Gallagher observes, "became the poet-hero of the age, an image that reached grandiose proportions in Pope's self-representation."[60] In perhaps more subtle ways, this grandiosity embarrassed masculinity as well. Starting from positions of compromised masculinity but from different vantage points—Pope's mastery of print compared to Cibber's mastery of theatricality—they entered this contest with particular vigor. In doing so, they became each other's "other."

Pope's "Girl of the Game": The Prostitution of the Author and the Business of Culture

ERIC V. CHANDLER

> So, Thee and I may make a Pother,
> And closely press, in *Print*, each other,
> The more we rail, the more bespatter,
> Twill make our *Pamphlets* sell the better,
> Write *Satire*, then, for *Daily*-bread;
> Do you *Dunce* me, I'll *Tom-Tit* you—
> —*Sawney and Colley, A Poetical Dialogue* (1742)

WITH THE DISCOURSE OF PROSTITUTION USEFULLY ESTABLISHED IN recent feminist re-examinations of the history of women's writing,[1] the more general association between prostitution and the literary industry—an association that could make anyone engaged in the business of books, male or female, a whore or a whore's consort—now seems to demand study. As Shannon Bell warns against essentializing the meaning of the female prostitute body and historically shows how that body "signified differently in different discourses,"[2] we can take her insight further by stressing the need to resist naturalizing the label "whore" as only a woman writer's burden to resist, manipulate, or even embrace. Although, with the image of the monstrous "fecund female," the figure of the prostitute fits into a larger pattern of "misogyny that becomes encoded in English culture in an attempt to exorcise anxieties regarding desire, power, and chaos,"[3] the identification of the pattern should not blind us to the variety of nuances with which the figure was used. Within the established discursive lines of the early eighteenth century, we must recover these nuances and the subject positions they imply.

When we look for the broader use of the label "prostitute" in eighteenth-century writing, we find it seemingly ubiquitous.[4] In a moment of self-pity in *A Trip to Jamaica* (1698), Edward Ward complains that

The condition of an Author, is much like that of a Strumpet, . . . and if the Reason be requir'd, Why we betake our selves to so Scandalous a Profession as Whoring or Pamphleteering, the same Answer will serve us both, viz. That the unhappy circumstances of a Narrow Fortune, hath forc'd us to do that for our Subsistence, which we are much asham'd of.[5]

Smarting from Edmund Curll's key to *A Tale of the Tub*, Jonathan Swift accuses Curll in a postscript to the fifth edition (1710) of being a "prostitute bookseller."[6] In *A Vindication of the Press* (1718), Defoe acknowledges that authors, "who are reduc'd to a Necessity of constant writing for a Subsistence," produce "numerous Performances" that "cannot possibly be so correct as they might be, could more Time be afforded in the Composure." Despite their "Inclinations," "these Gentlemen . . . are entirely oblig'd to prostrate their Pens to the Town, as Ladies of Pleasure do their Bodies," in doing what they can to survive.[7] And in an epigram for *The Grub Street Journal* (2 July 1730), that satirical organ designed as an ongoing assault on the literary industry, Alexander Pope compares James Moore Smythe's alleged plagiarism to a "Cinder Whore['s]" theft of a "gold watch."[8] As these examples suggest, the recurrence to the prostitute appears in discussions about various aspects of the growing commercialization of literary and publishing practice and the central issue of financially motivated authorship. In all these responses lie fundamental questions about the direction of literary culture—what is the significance of literary commercialization for English culture and should such commercialization be thwarted, excused, or promoted?

In this context, Colley Cibber's charge against Alexander Pope in immediate response to the poet's attack in *The New Dunciad* (1742)—that, as a young man, Pope unsuccessfully attempted to have sex with a prostitute—becomes much more than the malicious scandal-mongering that scholars too easily dismiss as both a cost of doing authorial business in the early eighteenth century and a particular plight of Pope's. If we examine the satirical logic of the charge in relation to the texts that both motivated and followed it, especially the *Dunciads*, we find that the figure of the prostitute fits into a larger debate about literary commercialization, definitions of high and low culture, and authorial self-representation. Pope seeks to divide culture between the categories of the commercially motivated or prostituted (Cibber, Grub Street, and the dunces) and the intellectually and aesthetically inspired

(Pope and his Scriblerian friends). Cibber, however, denies Pope this opposition. For Cibber, commercial motivation is unjustly stigmatized because on some level all cultural production is and must be commercial; literary success requires not merely intellectual genius, but necessarily entrepreneurial astuteness. Cibber's image of Pope impotent in the lap of a whore collapses both the poet's cultural scheme and his self-representation. It iconically insinuates that, behind the scenes and in his own way, Pope himself is every bit the whore and ultimately no different from anyone else, except perhaps in his inability, his feebleness or impotence, in admitting his actual role in the marketplace.

A "Frail Fit of Love": Cibber's Tale

In 1742 Colley Cibber published *A Letter from Mr. Cibber to Mr. Pope*, a dull piece in its plodding, point-by-point refutations of Pope's attacks on the poet laureate in various pieces. It inadvertently tends to confirm Cibber as a "dunce," except for one extraordinary moment when Cibber narrates a harshly comical episode about Pope, which occurred twenty-seven years earlier while the poet was translating his immensely profitable *Iliad*. According to Cibber, a mutual friend, the Earl of Warwick, wanted to "slip his little *Homer*, as he call'd him, at a Girl of the Game, that he might see what sort of Figure a Man of [Pope's] Size, Sobriety, and Vigour (in Verse) would make, when the frail Fit of Love had got into him."[9] This lord, with Cibber as a sidekick, "seduced the celebrated Mr. *Pope* . . . to a certain House of Carnal Recreation" (47) where a "smirking Damsel . . . happen'd to have Charms sufficient to tempt the little-tiny Manhood of Mr. *Pope* into the next Room with her" (48). Cibber, observing that Pope "had staid as long as, without Hazard of his Health he might," barged into the room and "found this little hasty Hero, like a terrible *Tom Tit*, pertly perching upon the Mount of Love!" (48). Warwick "began to curse, and call me an hundred silly Puppies, for my impertinently spoiling the Sport" (48–49). With "great Gravity," Cibber replies

> Pray, my Lord, consider what I have done, was in regard to the Honour of our Nation! For would you have had so glorious a Work as that of making *Homer* speak elegant *English*, cut short by laying up our little Gentleman of a Malady, which his thin Body might never have

been cured of? No, my Lord! *Homer* would have been too serious a Sacrifice to our Evening's Merriment. (49)

Cibber conclusively reflects "Now, as his *Homer* has since been so happily compleated, who can say, that the World may not have been obliged to the kindly Care of *Colley*, that so great a Work ever came to Perfection?" (49).

In this story, we see Cibber's honed skills as a comic actor and playwright. The story's awkward style is that of orality; it is a comfortable and homespun story to be told in a pub or coffee-house, which has been translated into written text. It progresses through imagistic hyperbole and lewd insinuation, centered on the conventional male-club preoccupations with sexual prowess and impotency. A well-crafted dirty joke, complete with a series of punch lines, its memorability guarantees the story's popularity. It takes Pope from the sublimity of Virgilian poetics to the bathos of the body. This joke subsequently exploded on the publishing scene with several pamphlets and newspaper articles immediately appearing, some siding with Pope, many others with Cibber, and still others attempting neutrality.[10] Most, however, acknowledged at the very least the joke's humor. The reviewer for *The Universal Spectator*, whose piece ran in three parts and was reprinted in *The Gentleman's Magazine*, observes that the story is "very extraordinary, and has rais'd such [a] Variety of Conversation in Town."[11] He proceeds to quote it entirely and provides the standard conclusion: the "amorous Tale of *Pope's* Gallantry, and the Merit which *Cibber* claims from saving him . . . , has such ludicrous Humour in the Narration, that I believe it generally raises a Smile in most Readers: This is the chief Battery, and he plays it off with all the Art and Strength he is Master of."[12] As is evident in this multipartite review and its reprinting, the world of publishing exploited the joke's success and gave it further currency. Everyone came to know Cibber's joke, and it seemed that most were compelled to laugh with the laureate even in spite of themselves.

In one of the few serious studies of Cibber's account and the events surrounding it, Norman Ault concludes that since Cibber had to go twenty-seven years into the past to find a scandalous and perhaps factually dubious story about Pope, the laureate inadvertently tends to confirm, if nothing else, Pope's long life of virtue.[13] This defensive assessment implicitly underscores that the story's value lies not in its revelation of biographical detail, but in its satirical effectiveness as partially measured by its im-

And has not Sawney too his Lord and Whore?, engraved
frontispiece for *A Letter from Mr. Cibber to Mr. Pope* (London:
Lewis, 1742), London, British Museum, Satires, no. 2574.

mense popularity. For example, Isaac Disraeli strikingly speculates about the frontispiece for Cibber's *Letter* based on a larger
print depicting the young Pope lying prone with his whore, "[it]
was seen by more persons, probably, than read the *Dunciad*."[14]
The huge canonical presence of the sustained Scriblerian attack
on Grub Street, which belittles individual "Dunces" and their satirical efforts as little more than insignificant yet unpleasant irri-
tants, causes us to miss the implications of the story's popularity.
The implicit assumption seems to be that prurient interest was
the natural and unfortunate tendency of mindless popular culture into which the pop-performer and entertainment entrepreneur Cibber knew all too well how to tap. To understand the
importance and lure of the story of the whore, we must get beyond the impression that it is merely an example of kiss-and-tell
tabloid celebrity deflation common in the eighteenth century's
culture wars, which Pope's *Dunciad*s had helped spawn. We must
examine the nameless whore not as a participant in a historical

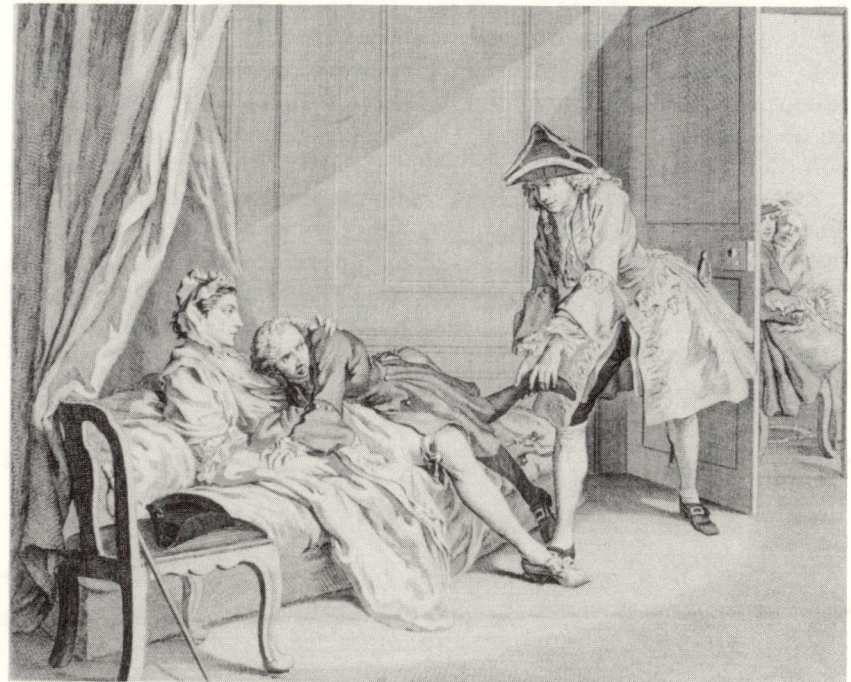

Hubert François Gravelot, *And has not Sawney too his Lord and
Whore?*, line engraving (1742), London, British Museum, Prints and
Drawings, Satires, no. 2573.

scandal, but as a satirical symbol embedded and signifying in a culturally specific semiotic topography.

In *Sexual Suspects*, Kristina Straub suggests this cultural-studies approach in her sensitive analysis of the figure of the schoolboy and its relationship to homophobic eighteenth-century anxieties about pederasty in the Pope–Cibber controversy. The schoolboy trope signifies the "subjected," sexually ambiguous, and vulnerable; he is the object of transgressive pederast desire and traditional educational discipline centered on corporal punishment. In struggles over cultural authority, the establishment of the manly and sexually normative self in explicit contradistinction to the schoolboy other is a standard rhetorical formulation. According to Straub, Pope conventionally employs this construction in his *Dunciad*s, but Cibber partially reverses it in his *Letter*: he identifies himself with the schoolboy in a process of "making a spectacle out of his faults" and "claim[ing] a kind of control over his self-display."[15] Straub is right as far as she takes this important observation, but the dynamic of reversal in identification is true for many of the tropes that Cibber deploys, and in his *Letter* it is not the image of the schoolboy that generates such a "Variety of Conversation in Town," but the image of the whore, an image with which Cibber also, although more subtly, identifies. In the semiotic topography, the presence of the prostitute becomes a critical touchstone or evaluative anchor. The whore draws our gaze and makes us focus on the activity around her; she is a silent but compelling center. Cibber's story is well told, but its force comes, in part, from the whore's very presence.[16] She has a peculiar but definite associative value, and through her Cibber insists on the all-encompassing reality of the economic conditions of cultural production, conditions that Pope ascribes to others, but denies for himself.

Having One's "Lord and Whore": The Context of the Original Insult

The concept of prostitution and the specific image of the whore are particularly powerful tropes for commercially motivated cultural production. The whore fundamentally represents ultimate commercial (self-)abjection—the *quid pro quo* of money for sexual use of a female body. The development of capitalism was associated by Pope and the Scriblerians with the feminization and morbidity of culture. Capitalism's paradigmatic foil was civic humanism that assumes financial disinterestedness, philosophical objectivity, and healthy communal engagement on the part of the culture-producing male subject because of his seeming economic independence—he is already in possession of wealth (ideally old, inherited, and landed), not in the process of capitalistically acquiring it.[17] Prostitution stands as a negative general equivalent—a privilege point of abjection to which everything else is compared to determine its relative wretchedness—for a complex of commercial taboos, at the heart of which is the commodification of that which should not be commodified: sexual bodies, culture, and literature. Because commercialism seems motivated by the ethos that finding innovative ways of making money—especially in those areas of cultural life that have yet to be capitalized upon—is the business of the world, it becomes characterized as prostitution. And the whore is the privileged point of reference to which all commercial servility can be compared.[18] When the prostitute appears, she taints all that is associated with her; her presence conventionally creates the perceptual frame within which all is seen as wrongfully driven by corrupt and mercenary motives.

Cibber's *Letter* is a response to previous attacks by Pope that associated first the "dunces" in general and later Cibber in particular with prostitution. In *The Dunciad Variorum* (1729), the tickling contest becomes a homosexual prostitutional competition in successfully masturbating the patron for his gold. The phrase "nobler palms" used to introduce the contest quickly degenerates into a brutal pun: from the "laurels" of authorial victory to the "hands" of pen-gripping, gold-holding, and penis-stroking (2.183). At one point the verse seems to want to confuse syntactically the hand of the tickling author with that of the money-possessing patron, thus suggesting an image of ineptly furious masturbatory effort: "Unlucky Oldmixon! thy lordly master / The more thou ticklest, gripes his fist the faster" (2.201–2). This image of the author prostituting himself in the pursuit of patronage functions in the larger suggestive pattern of whores and bodies. Cloacina, the goddess of sewers, "ministers to Jove with purest hands" and in the process aids Curll because "he [had] fish'd her nether realms for wit" (2.90, 93). The euphemism confuses hygienic assistance with a sexual act: Curll services (wipes or excites) Cloacina who services Jove. Later Eliza Haywood, whose "cow-like udders" (2.156) were originally described in the 1728 *Dunciad* as "fore-buttocks to the navel bare" (5:120n. 152) is the prostitute prize won by Curll in the pissing contest, which conflates scatological and sexual display. The *Dunciad*s, especially in the second books, produce a world of corporeal chaos: of sexual, excretory, and reproductive bodies massed together in the frenzied production of bad culture.

In the *Epistle to Dr Arbuthnot* (1735), Pope discusses the reformational inefficacy of his satires as a justification of their reputed cruelty. The poet asks "Whom have I hurt? has Poet yet, or Peer, / Lost the arch'd eye-brow, or *Parnassian* sneer? / And has not *Colley* still his Lord, and Whore?" (95–97). In other words, despite Pope's mockery, Cibber still has his patrons and still makes enough money to frequent brothels. The pairing of "Lord and Whore" has an additional cunning in that it not only associates Cibber with prostitutes, but it also implicitly turns him into one, at least in his pursuit of patronage. In this brief mention of Cibber, Pope economically implies the impurity of the laureate's cultural production. It is a striking line, one that Cibber himself comes back to in one of his punch lines: "And now again, gentle Reader, let it be judged, whether the *Lord* and the *Whore* abovemention'd might not with equal Justice, have been apply'd to sober *Sawney* the Satyrist, as to *Colley* the Criminal?" (49).

In *The New Dunciad* (1742), Pope turns the meretricious association into a monumental emblem:

> Then rose [Dulness] the Seed of Chaos, and of Night,
> To blot out Order, and extinguish Light,
> Of dull and venal a new World to mold,
> And bring Saturnian days of Lead and Gold.
>   She mounts the Throne, her head a Cloud conceal'd,
> In broad Effulgence all below reveal'd,
> ('Tis thus aspiring Dulness ever shines,)
> Soft on her lap her Laureat son reclines. (4.13–20)

With her head hidden in a "Cloud" and her reproductive and excretory organs "all below reveal'd," Dulness is the ultimate cultural whore, for her creation is a "dull and venal" "new World." "Venal" suggests the ultimate criterion for the dull—the motivating economic corruption. Thus Dulness is a whore goddess, and her court is peopled by both figurative and literal whores: the "phantom represent[ing] the nature and the genius of the *Italian* Opera" is called a "harlot" (4.45), and to underscore the fact that the "Stews and Palace equally [were] explor'd" (4.315), the "pupil" fresh from his Grand Tour forms a threesome with his "Governor" and "whore" (4.272). At the poem's opening, Pope provocatively places Cibber "soft on" Dulness's "lap." While this phrasing infantilizes the laureate, it also hints at surrealistic incest; Cibber is not only born of Dulness, but with Dulness may engender more dulness. "Soft" implies either Cibber's post-coital swoon or his pre-coital struggle to achieve an erection. It does not matter if Cibber is copulating or impotent, for either way, Dulness's new world must be sterile in its self-proliferation.

Thus, on the most superficial level, Cibber's whore story turns the tables on Pope and makes him out to be a hypocrite; if the *"Lord* and *Whore"* line applies to Cibber, then it equally does so to Pope. As Pope does to Cibber in *The New Dunciad*, the laureate's story both places the poet in a whore's lap and infantilizes him (he is childlike in his tinyness and position). The tale further implies that Pope's self-prostitution in courting patronage allowed a "noble Wag" to exploit him for a joke. Moreover, as *The New Dunciad* suggests that Cibber, although weak, nevertheless may be the progenitor of a future line of dulness, Cibber's story of the prostitute associates Pope's poetic "Vigour" and his whole cultural position with pitiful sexual impotence compounded by the threat of venereal disease. His vision of a culture clearly divided between the high and the low (with himself as high culture's defender positioned on the line of demarcation to turn back cultural pretenders and parvenus) will not be reproduced. On top of these Popeian refashionings, Cibber asserts a twisted proprietary claim—because he saved Pope's body from syphilitic ravages, Cibber is ultimately responsible for Pope's works and especially his popular *Iliad* (1715–20). At a time when copyright provided a new legal order to the literary marketplace and when Pope stood out as an author who uniquely realized the implications of this order by inventively exercising his copyright, Cibber's mock claim, with the added insinuation that Pope's production, his *Homer*, had something necessarily to do with Cibberian salvation from his libidinous but frail and probably impotent body, must have reverberated with particular irony.[19] As Carolyn Williams explains, Pope had intended the publication of his *Iliad* and *Odyssey* (1725–6) to serve as a fulfillment of "his quest for a masculine role in society."[20] Cibber's tale provides a context for this publication and mocks any Popiean pretense to conventional, classical, or even libertine virility. Furthermore, it ultimately hints that even Pope's cherished Homerian achievement, however acclaimed, could also be read as a form of prostitution—the poet's own exploitation and commercialization of the classics.

But in pointing to Pope's own association with lords and

whores, Cibber is not denying Pope's original charge. In fact, the laureate seems to welcome it. Cibber asks, "By the Way, gentle Reader, don't you think, to say only, *a Man has his Whore*, without some particular Circumstance to aggravate the Vice, is the flattest Piece of Satyr that ever fell from the formidable Pen of Mr. *Pope*?" The laureate continues: "take the first ten thousand Men you meet, and I believe, you would be no Loser if you betted ten to one that every single Sinner of them, one with another, had Been guilty of the same Frailty" (*Letter*, 48). This embrace of the whore, on behalf of not only himself but all sexually capable men, suggests the more profound implications of Cibber's story as a response to Pope's cultural vision. As the poignant coupling of "dull and venal" implies at the beginning of *The New Dunciad*, Pope's main criticism of the dunces is that they represent a low cultural production distinguished by inherently corrupt commercial motives. They produce neither out of disinterestedness nor from a need to propagate useful truths. Their production is born out of both the necessity to make a subsistence living and, once survival is assured, the desire eventually to profit. In other words, they are first desperately driven by hunger and cold, by the vulnerability of their own bodies, and not the strength of their minds, to produce whatever will sell. And thus, for Pope, their production is dreadfully wrong. Cibber, conversely, repeatedly underscores the opposite view. For him, the making of money is a perfectly natural aspect of all cultural activity—and one that should not be denied, but indeed better understood.

In his *An Apology for the Life of Mr. Colley Cibber* (1740), Cibber frankly discusses the economic motives that influence the management of a theater: "when one Company is too hard for another, the lower in Reputation, has always been forc'd to exhibit some new fangled Foppery, to draw the Multitude after them."[21] This exposition partly seems a measured response to Pope's attack in the earlier *Dunciad*s, in which Pope insinuates that by becoming "New wizards" in popular stage spectacle (3.262), Cibber and his partner in the management of the Drury Lane Theatre, Barton Booth, abjectly followed the example of John Rich, the successful manager of the Lincoln's Inn Fields Theatre who had introduced, among other things, pantomime to the English stage. After making this observation about the adoption of "new fangled Foppery," Cibber explains how dance with elaborate scenery was introduced to his stage and that of the competing theater: "[thus] sprung forth that Succession of monstrous Medlies, that have so long infested the Stage, and which arose upon one another alternately, at both Houses outvying, in Expense, like contending Bribes on both sides at an Election, to secure a Majority of the Multitude." Cibber concludes that "I . . . had not Virtue enough to starve, by opposing a Multitude" (*Apology*, 279, 280). His comment illustrates that the practical consequences of competition in a limited theater market is artistic degeneration. Implicitly, the theater manager, Cibber, is not finally culpable. By the licensing of one theater rather than two, the government can ensure the quality of stage performances. This insight, however, requires the understanding that art will be sacrificed for survival and that there are no heroes or martyrs in the cultural marketplace.

Cibber brings this perception of economic rule to his understanding of his unfriendly relations with Pope:

> When I therefore find my Name at length, in the Satyrical Works of our most celebrated living Author, I never look upon those Lines as Malice meant to me, . . . but Profit to himself: One of his Points must be, to have many Readers: . . . a Lick at the *Laureat* will always be a sure bait . . . to catch him little Readers[.] (25)

In a mixture of tonal amiability and rhetorical pointedness, Cibber here makes Pope's motives no better than those of the dunces, as defined eleven years earlier in his 1729 *Dunciad Variorum*. In the introductory "Letter to the Publisher," the speaker Cleland accuses Pope's victims of being "the first Aggressors: they had try'd till they were weary, what was to be got by railing at each other; no body was either concern'd, or surpriz'd, if this or that Scribler was prov'd a Dunce: but every one was curious to read what could be said to prove Mr. Pope one, and was ready to pay something for such a discovery" (5:12). According to Cibber in his *Apology*, Pope attacks him because his prominence as laureate makes such attacks profitable. Thus Pope in his poetry resembles both Cibber in his theater and the dunces in the literary marketplace: all are motivated to attract consumers, to make a profit, and therefore all are seduced by money or the need to make a living to compromise art for spectacle. But Cibber, who acknowledges that he is as much a creature of economy as anyone else, articulates his willingness to overlook apparent "Malice" and to forgive the attacks. Pope, however, using the language of class superiority and cultural vigilantism that associates the dunces with "assassinates [sic], popular insurrections, the insolence of the rabble without doors and of domesticks within," ad-

vocates in the *Variorum* a "publick punishment" that only "a
good writer inflicts" (5:14). The implication, therefore, of Cibber's statement is that Pope is not only ill natured, but hypocritically so. This same theme gets taken up two years after the
Apology in Cibber's *Letter*. To Pope's general charge that Cibber
is a bad poet, Cibber responds, "I wrote [more] to be Fed, than be
Famous, and since my Writings still give me a Dinner, do you
rhyme me out of my Stomach if you can" (*Letter*, 5). This point is
repeated even more forcefully after Pope's 1743 *Dunciad* in Cibber's *Another Occasional Letter* (1744): "But in the honest use,
you Sir, have made of your Talent, how far is this High-spirited
Poetical Courage more excusable, than that of a Highway-man?
Who takes but our Mony from us, as you would our more valuable
good Name, to supply your equally craving Wants of Food, or of
Fame?"[22] According to Cibber, Pope not only employs market-
place-oriented strategies in his poetry, but engages in commercial
cruelty and perhaps even illegality: he attempts to crush the competition and render them unable to support or feed themselves.
And for Cibber, so consciously engaged in the marketplace himself, this cruelty is a crime; it is a theft of property, of the means
to make a living.

Meditations on "Fame and Money": Subsequent Reactions

The most famous response to Cibber's *Letter* was, of course,
Pope's 1743 *Dunciad*, which includes a revised *New Dunciad* as
the fourth and last book and Cibber as the new king of the dunces
to replace "a certain Pretender, Pseudo-Poet, or Phantom, of the
name of Tibbald" (5:252). The introductory matter places this
Dunciad fully in the context not merely of Cibber's pamphlet, but
of his tale about Pope. The "Advertisement to the Reader,"
signed with Warburton's initials but most likely authored by
Pope,[23] cavalierly explains that the laureate's "ridiculous book
against [Pope], full of Personal Reflections," only "furnished"
the poet "with a lucky opportunity of improving *This Poem*, by
giving it the only thing it wanted, a *more considerable Hero*"
(5:251). "Personal Reflections" euphemistically refers only to the
story of the whore. In "Richardus Aristarchus of the Hero of the
Poem," Pope's collaborator Warburton tries to counter, on the
poet's behalf, Cibber's tale by directing attention to the laureate's
own septuagenarian sex life.[24] In defining the qualities of a mock

or "lesser" epic hero, Warburton lists *"Vanity, Impudence,* and *Debauchery,"* and in a longish section about *"Gentle Love,"* he makes a joke out of the longevity of Cibber's seemingly transgressive libido (5:256). Ordinarily love "evaporates in the heat of *Youth,"* but in Cibber, "it acquireth strength by *Old age*; and becometh a standing ornament to the little Epic" (5: 258). This coyly suggests that the laureate's erection serves *The Dunciad* as a central signifier for dulness. Through convoluted sarcasm, Warburton attacks Cibber's defense that all men, or "the first ten thousand . . . you meet," have at one time or another whored (5:258). Warburton implies that this claim only makes Cibber *"common,"* or socially inferior, and therefore perhaps unfit for even mock epic. But from this low note, the speaker rallies, for in fact he finds something in Cibber's sexuality yet extraordinary: "The man is sure enough a Hero, who has his Lady [whore] at fourscore. How doth his Modesty herein lessen the merit of a *whole well-spent* Life" of whore-mongering (5:258).

> But let us farther remark, that the calling *his* whore, implieth she was *his own,* and not his *neighbour*'s. Truly a commendable Continence! . . . For how much Self-denial was necessary not to covet his Neighbour's whore? and what disorders must the coveting her have occasion'd, in that Society, where (according to this Political Calculator) *nine* in *ten* of all ages have their *concubines.* (5:259)

Warburton portrays Cibber as an old man suffering from a kind of juvenile satyriasis that makes him find all whores irresistibly desirable and from the delusion that he can possess a whore (call her "his") when the very identity of the prostitute body depends not on possession (as a man possesses his wife), but on its fluid purchasability. And in his (theater/whorehouse) "Society," in which all men's women are whores, he must practice a "Continence," which is physiologically detrimental, for as his various productions manifest (especially such things as his self-indulgent *Apology* and his *Letter*), the laureate is fundamentally incontinent—a squirter of bad text as well as bad seed, and thus a perfect king of the dunces.[25]

Several of the pro-Cibberian pamphlets following the *Letter* seize on Cibber's economic theme. For example, *A Letter to Mr. C—b—r,* probably by John Hervey,[26] compares the laureate and Pope: "both of you came into the World to make that Fortune you were not born to. You chose to be an Actor on the Stage, he a Performer in the Press. You wrote Plays for Fame and Money, he wrote Poems from the same Motives."[27] In *The Difference between Verbal and Practical Virtue*, also attributed to Hervey, Pope is placed in a long line of poets who "tho' they scourge the vicious" fail to "shun the Vice" and thus "lash the Times as Swimmers do the Tide, / And kick and cuff the Stream on which they ride." Pope "rails at Lies, and yet for half a Crown / Coins and disperses Lies thro' all the Town";[28] the tide he beats at but rides is cultural commercialism, the actual order of his day and the future.[29] And in *Sawney and Colley, A Poetical Dialogue*, Colley enthusiastically urges Sawney:

> So, Thee and I may make a Pother,
> And closely press, in *Print*, each other,
> The more we rail, the more bespatter,
> Twill make our *Pamphlets* sell the better,
> Write *Satire*, then, for *Daily*-bread;
> Do you *Dunce* me, I'll *Tom-Tit* you.[30]

This pamphlet suggests the possibility that Pope and Cibber's satirical battles are cultural quackery motivated by the common need to make a living; here Colley and Sawney become co-conspirators or collaborators in a text-proliferating, business-promoting event. Furthermore, the language implies that their pamphlet-war "Pother" is a kind of homosexual and sadomasochistic but still (re)productive intercourse. The phrase "closely press . . . each other" with the intentional clumsiness of the qualifying parenthetical "in Print" urges us to imagine a physical embrace with "bespatter" now becoming mutual ejaculation. The line "Do you *Dunce* me, I'll *Tom-Tit* you," which in itself suggests that Cibber's insult is at least as good as Pope's (despite the poet's cultural pretensions), becomes in this context a sexual proposition, and *"Tom-Tit"* slips in and out of various registers of significance. In his original story, Cibber uses the image of a tiny, delicate bird, the tom-tit or titmouse, to emphasize Pope's own absurd and unmanly smallness especially in relation to the whore, "the Mount of Love." But in the passage from *Sawney and Colley*, "Tit" stands out with possible sexual implication—as slang, it can either mean a "girl or young woman," thus a whore for Cibber, or, even more to the point, female genitals,[31] the counterpart to Cibber's erection that will become the implied emblem of Dulness in the introduction to the 1743 *Dunciad*.[32] "Tom," the shortened form of the obviously male first name Thomas, and "tit" together make a hermaphroditic compound and further suggest Pope's own sexual monstrousness: possessing a penis, but not virile enough to wield it properly. But the line also transmogrifies the couple into components of the hand-press. They "press" against "each other" in the production of their attacks like a platen against an inked form to produce a printed sheet. They bespatter each other with their texts, and in this sense with ink. Texts, the mechanical means for producing them, and copulating bodies become chaotically mixed up in a profitable pamphlet war.

Each of these pro-Cibber pamphlets portrays Pope as motivated by the need to make a living—just like everyone in the literary marketplace. Therefore, his cultural production is no higher than anyone else's. In all this, Cibber comes across perhaps as a bit of a fool, but a self-acknowledged and sincere fool. He is weak, but in his writings he acknowledges his weakness and even finds strength in the acknowledgment. This admission of weakness occurs on several levels. He confirms that his poetry is mediocre, especially when compared to Pope's—so mediocre, in fact, that he admits he can only respond to Pope's "Sharpness of Verse" with the "blunt and weak Weapon of Prose." Cibber identifies with beaten and violated schoolboys but also with soldiers, and even the "famous Boxer, at the *Bear-Garden*, called *Rugged and Tough*," who lacks the skill to ward off his opponent's blows, yet has the endurance to take a beating and does, until the attacker is so worn out by his efforts that he can be knocked out easily (*Letter*, 4). But Cibber even provocatively goes beyond these self-identifications by equating himself not simply with the whore's customer, but with a feminized subject position and ultimately with the whore herself.

In a prefatory epistle, "Mr. C—b—r to Mr. P.," for "*The Difference between Verbal and Practical Virtue*," Cibber states that

> since you thought most unrighteously and unjustly to fall upon me and crush me, only because you imagin'd your Self strong and me weak, as *France* fell upon the Queen of *Hungary*, if I like her . . . have encouraged such a Friend to me, as *England* has been to her, to espouse my Cause, and turn all the Weight of the War upon you . . . ; with what reasonable and equitable Pleasure may I not pursue my Blow till I make you repent, by laying you on your Back, the ungrateful Returns you have made me for saving you from Destruction when you laid yourself on your Belly.[33]

This passage refers to the beginning of the War of Austrian Succession, when, to press dubious territorial claims, an alliance of

France, Spain, Bavaria, Saxony, and Prussia initiated hostilities against the Habsburg Empress Maria Theresa. Out of its habitual antagonism toward France, Britain allied itself with the empress. The historical details are not particularly important, but of interest are the images in several prints, dated February 1741/42 (a little before publication of the pamphlet containing Cibber's prefatory letter), that the outbreak of the war engendered. The most common show a woman, the empress, being stripped and sexually molested; her clothes represent her territorial possessions and the gang rapists the alliance against her. Another version, which exploits contemporary anxieties about the sexual proclivities of the medical profession, has the empress convulsed on a closestool and vomiting into a pan while a panel of male physicians, the alliance, gazes on. In this print, rather than seizing her clothes, her violators, emblematized by the huge phallic clyster in the foreground, brutalize and violate her with false cures. In all these prints a figure dressed as a Catholic priest, representing Cardinal Fleury and France, is next to the victim in the process of grabbing her in some way. In two of the prints, he reaches for

The Queen of Hungary Stript, line engraving (1742), London, British Museum, Prints and Drawings, Satires, no. 2513.2.

Vanlot, **F----H Pacification of the Q---n of H-----y Stript,** line engraving (1741/2), London, British Museum, Prints and Drawings, Satires, no. 2515.

her genitalia; in the medical piece, he holds her wrist with one hand to check her pulse as he writes with the other "Lower the Pulse with Clyster," but his knowing expression directed at the viewer reveals his lascivious intentions. When Cibber compares himself to the "Queen of Hungary," the image of the stripped and sexually violated woman being molested by a papist priest (a common pornographic, anti-Catholic, and Francophobic motif) is necessarily evoked as a jab, among other things, at Pope's Catholicism.

This association plays into Cibber's seemingly sincere representation of poetic weakness. Cibber's England is Lord Hervey, the pamphlet's coauthor and an ally who can offer necessary poetic assistance against Pope the Catholic. Cibber's identification becomes provocatively confused when, later in the passage, he boasts that he will lay Pope "on your Back," the posture of an opponent defeated in battle, but also the conventional female po-

Vanlot, *The Consultation of Physicians, on the Case of the Queen of Hungary*, line engraving (1741/2), London, British Museum, Prints and Drawings, Satires, no. 2514.

sition in intercourse and the position of the whore in the prints illustrating Cibber's story. This latter reading becomes authorized later in the sentence when Cibber refers to Pope's ingratitude for Cibber's saving him when Pope was "on his belly." The verbal play turns Pope into his own sexual complement: he is both on his belly and on his back, or as Iago says, the beast with two backs, except more monstrous because the backs are notably deformed and the figure self-contained. But this is just one implication of the wordplay. If Cibber is the Queen of Hungary, then Pope is Cibber's stripper and abuser, both sexual and proprietary. The poet is also a kind of charlatan offering and administering false cultural cures—his satire—while veiling his actual intentions (wealth and fame) and drives (ill nature and even homosexual obsession). So if Pope was at one time on his belly, he screwed not only his whore, but somehow Cibber as well. Cibber thus analogically becomes Pope's "tit," his girl, his whore, his orifice. But when Cibber lays Pope on his back, he screws Pope and turns Pope into his own little "tom-*tit*."

The "Privilege of Denying" the Body

In discussing university teaching, bell hooks recently commented that only those with power have "the privilege of denying their body."[34] Pope did not deny his body, at least not completely. His deformity was an undeniable aspect of his life, so when his satirical antagonists made harsh reference to it, he responded with his own more gentle allusions to "this long Disease, my Life" (4:105.132). Cibber, too, represents this Popeian body, making it tiny, fragile, and, most important, impotent. But the image of an impotent Pope contains more than cruelty and insult. Cibber's point is that bodies have an undeniable economic existence; they have natural drives and appetites and thus must be fed and supported. The force of Cibber's argument, extended over several texts, is not that Pope's body is diseased and crooked, but that Pope seems to be in a state of corporeal denial. And what he denies is not so much his body's disease and pathological uniqueness, but its commonality with the bodies of other men and women all participating in the business of books. Both Cibber and Pope were effective literary businessmen. But while Cibber "speaks far more openly of the opportunities and disappointments occasioned by the economic individualism of his times," Pope not only conceals his own entrepreneurial efforts with a "carefully stage-managed public image of virtue and propriety";[35] he relentlessly and very publicly defines himself in contradistinction to the marketplace order. For Cibber, Pope is impotent because in attacking dunces and their bodies with his excremental visions of a surreal Grub Street characterized by commercial corruption, he manifests a troubling lack of any real appreciation for the basic and common conditions of cultural production; as Colley explains in *Sawney and Colley*, "But thus thy *Satire's* guiltless grown, / Who slanders *all* Men, slanders *none*; / As impotent in *Spite* as *Love*, / *Contempt* [for humanity] alone by each you move" (7). At times Pope may feign an almost Cibberian sympathy or understanding, but even then he does so only, unlike Cibber, to deny his commonality. In his *Epistle to Dr Arbuthnot*, for example, although Gildon drew "his venal quill" to abuse Pope, the poet did not take the attack personally, but instead charitably— and condescendingly—"wished the man a dinner" (151–52), implicitly belittling the possible basic needs that made Gildon's pen "venal" in the first place. Pope's civic humanistic paradigm of cultural producers free from material influence and thus able to realize a purer aesthetic and philosophical excellence is a reification. In his crude way, Cibber makes concrete the centrality of the body in the relations of cultural production. Thus Cibber not only has (by his own account) a normal sexual appetite that finds whores an outlet, but he is a whore and so is Pope. And nothing is wrong with their prostitution except, according to Cibber, Pope's aggressive denial of it.

Certainly Cibber's view of Pope is not without either the spite of a Popeian victim or the designs of a player in the literary marketplace. As Joseph Guerinot and Thomas Gilmore point out, Cibber's counterattacks on Pope fit very well into a pattern of "dunce" charges: that the poet was venal, that he ridiculed poverty, that he made money, and that he was wealthy. The identification of the pattern, however, seems only to diminish its significance. In the generality of dunce attacks, Guerinot mostly sees a measure of the "calumny, detraction, and critical misunderstanding Pope endured."[36] This attitude seems like a latter-day version of Pope's own in which the poet's detractors are likened to little more than an irritating swarm of insignificant but occasionally biting insects. As Pat Rogers perceptively explains, "the Augustans learnt to portray folly as a collectivity," and in such a portrayal individual "folly" becomes trivialized as merely part of a trend seized upon by the dull crowd. For Rogers, the "shabby purlieus" of collective Grub Street serve only as a "drab and joyless" backdrop that sets off the brilliant "gaiety of vision that belongs to Pope, Swift and their friends."[37] Rogers's study, like Guerinot's bibliography, brings "Grub Street" into focus, only to silence its authors and booksellers by establishing their collectivity. Just as Jerome McGann demonstrates that there is a "Romantic ideology" that scholars have tended to embrace uncritically,[38] we can say that an Augustan ideology has been similarly embraced. The Scriblerians and their admirers produced, as Kathy MacDermott phrases it, "a mythology of Grub Street" that scholarship has tended to reproduce and extend.[39] This mythology (complete with such dismissive qualifiers as "dunce" and "hack") creates historical blind spots and removes literary products from the context of those culture wars (Modern versus Ancient, Dunce versus Scriblerian) taking place during the first half of the eighteenth century.

While wary of the distortions and exaggerations of satire (employed, of course, by all sides), we must see in those patterns of pamphlet attacks discursive clues to real cultural preoccupations. Why should anyone care if Pope made money, was commercially motivated, or unsympathetic to impoverished authors? Guerinot's useful listing of each pamphlet's charges tends to make them appear ridiculous and trite from our removed twentieth-century standpoint. But the pamphleteers must have thought that these charges would strike a chord with some readership, and as we saw so evident in the spin-off prints and pamphlets, Cibber's *Letter* did just that. Perhaps what Cibber and the other "dunces" knew was simply that a profit could be made in scurrility and scandal. But to dismiss their efforts as merely so motivated would be reductive; the relationship between literary culture and commerce was a compelling contemporary issue, and considerations of the relative wealth or impecuniousness of cultural producers in relationship especially to both their implicit and explicit self-representations and entrepreneurial practices was a natural aspect of the issue. The scurrilousness and scandalmongering were just a few of the strategies used to confront it. Pope and Cibber—both celebrities and both vying for a position at the head of culture as some kind of "laureate"—represented antithetical positions (and in some ways practices). The image of the prostitute was deployed by both to define and enhance one position partially through the undermining of the other.

In his *Dunciads*, Pope uses the figure of the whore with other images to stigmatize the economic wretchedness of his cultural foes. Cibber complicates the use of the image in a doubling-back gesture that combines confession, accusation, and libertine display. Both Pope and Cibber work around the popular concern about culture and commerce and tap into a well-established prostitutional discourse. While innovative in other ways, Pope's performance is brilliantly conventional in using the prostitute as a figure of abjection. Cibber's crude tale in the context of his own self-representations offers some unexpected spins: the acceptance of commerce, which leads to his and Pope's identification with the prostitute.

Not "The Only Trifler in the Nation":
Pope and the Man of Leisure in *The Dunciad*

I<small>N HER</small> *VINDICATION OF THE RIGHTS OF WOMAN* (1792), M<small>ARY</small> W<small>OLL</small>-stonecraft repeatedly quotes from Pope's *Of the Characters of Women*, agreeing with the poet that women's love of pleasure and sexual power determines the course of their lives: forbidden by men to direct their energies toward an important social purpose, women of the middle and upper classes immerse themselves in gallantry, ornamentation, and other pursuits that extensive leisure makes possible. Wollstonecraft goes on to declare that "people of rank and fortune" resemble leisured women not only in being preoccupied with self-display and amusements but also in being exempt from the need to exert themselves in productive, character-building employments. A third category of effeminate, useless citizens, however, includes male writers like Pope himself: "A king is always a king, and a woman always a woman. His authority and her sex ever stand between them and rational converse. . . . And a wit [is] always a wit, might be added, for the vain fooleries of wits and beauties to obtain attention, and make conquests, are much upon a par."[1] To Wollstonecraft, wits have much in common with women: lacking any better function, they exist to amuse the idle hours of an audience whose judgment determines their worth.

Writing a decade earlier in 1782, Vicesimus Knox also compares men of wit (and specifically poets) to beauties:

> [T]he admirers of English poetry are divided into two parties. The objects of their love are, perhaps, of equal beauty, though they greatly differ in their air, their dress, the turn of their features, and their complexion. On one side, are the lovers and imitators of Spenser and Milton; and on the other, those of Dryden, Boileau, and Pope.[2]

Knox's trope here places poets in the subordinate role of women whose attractive charms are observed and evaluated by male readers; the characteristics of the poets' verse—what earlier critics might have referred to as genius, fancy, and style—have become the products of female invention ("air," "dress," "complexion") created at the toilette. Although Knox's metaphor of wits as love objects lacks the satiric tone of Wollstonecraft's remarks, the representations of both writers arise from a single source: controversies in the early eighteenth century debating the social usefulness and cultural importance of men composing verse for a living. And these controversies were formulated and argued in a rhetoric of gender-based tropes, traces of which appear in the comments of Wollstonecraft and Knox. A review of writings by and about Alexander Pope reveals his centrality to debates over the nature of literary labor and the class and gender status it conferred upon professional writers. I argue here that Book 4 of the 1743 *Dunciad* illustrates Pope's final repudiation of concepts of masculine conduct that excluded the poet. By challenging his culture's idealization of the aristocrat and the literary authority afforded to rank and birth, his verses make way for the new, emerging connection between manliness and bourgeois professionalism that Pope had come to support during the course of his career.

The frequency of contemporary attacks on Pope's masculinity can be gauged through Richard Savage's defense of Pope: *"what Evidence* will you produce, in a Point you hint at (doubtless of great Importance to the Commonwealth of Learning) *Whether* Mr. Pope *be, or be not, a Woman's Man?* Since he has no *Wife* of his own to appeal to, can any of *your Wives* or *Daughters* bear Testimony in it?"[3] Savage was replying to pieces like the anonymous critique of Pope entitled "The Poet finish'd in Prose" (one of Edmund Curll's publications), which reduced Pope's "Fondness for Retirement"—his celebrated retreat from the corruption of urban life and letters—to a fear of rape by Lady Mary Wortley Montagu and a preference for masturbation over intercourse with women ("no doubt he has found out some other Amusement, equally entertaining to him in his Solitude, and which makes him less sollicitous about losing the Favour of the Ladies").[4] The open questioning of Pope's masculinity occurred frequently throughout his life: as Claudia Thomas notes, Pope's enemies often derided him as "the Ladies' Play-Thing," charging him with effeminacy for the sweetness or smoothness of his verse, his fragile body, and his inclusion of women as the audience for his work.[5] In fact, according to Colley Cibber, Pope's success as a poet required abstention from the sexual activity common to young men about town; he claimed that he interrupted Pope's dalliance with a "Girl of the Game" to preserve the Homer translation.[6] Cibber implied that Pope's infirm body propelled him toward insignificant literary production ("making *Homer* speak elegant *English*") instead of the traditional sport of youths—fornication. But to the author of "The Poet finish'd in Prose," what really lowered Pope's position on the hierarchies of both class and gender was his role as a purveyor of entertainment for the public:

[A]ll *Poets* are Tradesmen, from *Stephen Duck* down to Dr. *Young*; they are a sort of *Haberdashers of small Ware*; and *Poetry* is a *Trade*, and the most insignificant of all others. I believe it would be no difficult Matter to prove, that the most inconsiderable *Tinker* in *Great-Britain*, who can mend your Kettle, is a better Subject, and more valuable Citizen, than either *Farinelli* or *Pope*, tho' the two last are so great Masters in the Art of *tickling your Ears*, and the former is sure to set your Teeth on edge. How little Reason has a Man to grow insolent upon excelling in Trifles! (27–28)

On the scale of occupations, poets, like opera singers, rank low—certainly below kettle menders and corn cutters—for their usefulness to the state. Aligning Pope with the castrato Farinelli was a popular method of discrediting the poet's work by implying its deviation from a rough, manly, English literary style. The figure of the castrato featured prominently in eighteenth-century critiques of popular amusements: aside from its associations with foreign luxury, Catholicism, and physical deformation, the trope also underscores the loss of masculinity that accompanies the entertainer's status in a consumer culture.[7] Attacks on Swift and Pope's *Miscellanies* also show the contemporary association of entertainment with effeminacy; the poets are characterized as indulgent mothers (not fathers, since frivolity is a trait foreign to mature manhood) spoiling the moral fiber of their audience:

'Tis too well known, that the Generality of Readers had rather be amus'd than instructed. . . . But for Authors to tell frivolous Tales, purely for telling-sake, to collect Trifles by Volumes, to deal by their Readers as fond Mothers do by their Children, and give them Toys and Gewgaws, instead of Lessons useful for Life, is wicked, if done with Design to corrupt their Understandings; and if done with no Design, idle and impertinent, unbecoming the Character of a Man.[8]

By pleasing the "Generality of Readers" rather than an elite male group, and by neglecting instruction in favor of turning a profit, writers like Pope supposedly forsake the character appropriate to their gender. Other critics continued this censure of Pope, arguing that the popularity of his verse compromised its masculine qualities. The antagonistic Giles Jacob asks whether "there [is] in his Poems any Thing but sinewless Versification, and sonorous Nonsense?,"implying that Pope's verse is flaccid and effeminate, or "sinewless," because its supposedly easy rhythms and lack of moral message violate the complex formal structure and lucid expression of sense that educated men were trained to value in poetry.[9] Even a text as classical as the Homer translation came under censure, because it provided pleasure to groups of readers who would otherwise remain ignorant of the original poem; in search of profits from subscribers, Pope has emasculated Homer by putting him in "tawd'ry, Tinsel, fashionable Dress": "He smoothes him o'er, and gives him grace and ease, / And makes him *fine*,—the *Beaus* and *Belles* to please."[10] Such criticism continued even after Pope's death. Joseph Warton claims that Pope's ethical verse is a lesser variety of poetry because it "lies more level to the general capacities of men, than the higher flights of more genuine poetry,"[11] while William Cowper maintains that Pope's very strengths—his "nice" ear and "delicate" touch—"Made poetry a mere mechanic art" subject to imitation by "ev'ry warbler" who rhymes.[12]

Pope's own writings show the extent of his concern about poets increasingly being defined as purveyors of pleasure in a commercial culture.[13] Barred by his religion and political sympathies from positions of influence in the church and state, Pope had a difficult time placing himself within the traditional boundaries of elite masculine activity. The preface to the first collected volume of Pope's *Works* (1717) reveals his adoption of the indolent, insouciant attitude that aristocratic poets like Rochester had affected a generation before: "Poetry and Criticism [are] by no means the universal concern of the world, but only the affair of idle men who write in their closets, and of idle men who read there."[14] Pope's words here may sound like the pose of a gentleman poet eschewing any commercial motive for his work; he represents the leisured male as composing for the enjoyment of companions of his own class and gender, and portrays poetry as the private "affair" of a learned elite. Yet Pope also appears ambivalent about the retreat from "all the reasonable aims of life" (xxvi) that writing poetry requires, and articulates a sense of the poet's estrangement from important masculine concerns: "One may be ashamed to consume half one's days in bringing sense and rhyme together" (xxviii). Moreover, the choice of poetry as a vocation at a time when verse was being sold and circulated to a large audience of consumers places the poet in an illusory state similar to that of royalty and attractive women, whose self-image—based upon the opinions of others—bears no relation to reality: "If he is made to hope he may please the world, he falls under very unlucky circumstances; for from the moment he prints, he must expect to hear no more truth, than if he were a Prince, or a Beauty" (xxvi). Like princes or beauties, poets are the objects of public envy and admiration, both of which contribute to an exaggerated assessment of their qualities, whether good or bad; by contrast, "truth" is located in privacy—in the time before print, or before the poet's indulgence in self-display ranks him among other victims of false consciousness.

Like the 1717 preface, the correspondence written in the early years of Pope's career reveals tensions over poetry's compatibility with masculine conduct and pursuits. Writing to his friend Henry Cromwell in 1710, Pope defends the seriousness of his labor by distinguishing himself from the gentleman amateur Richard Crashaw:

> I take this Poet to have writ like a Gentleman, that is, at leisure hours, and more to keep out of idleness, than to establish a reputation: so that nothing regular or just can be expected from him. . . . only pretty conceptions, fine metaphors, glitt'ring expressions, and something of a neat cast of Verse, (which are properly the dress, gems, or loose ornaments of Poetry) may be found in these verses. This is indeed the case of most other Poetical Writers of *Miscellanies*; nor can it well be otherwise, since no man can be a true Poet, who writes for diversion only.[15]

Written to display its author's genteel accomplishments, Crashaw's verse disregards the "Soul of Poetry"—elements such as "Design, Form, [and] Fable"—and concentrates instead on its surface qualities: the poems' "pretty," "fine," and "glitt'ring" features thus indicate the writer's fundamental triviality. Pope's metaphors also portray Crashaw's work as explicitly feminine in nature: composed of dress, gems, and ornaments, the poems, like the items on Belinda's toilette (or like Belinda herself) are constructed to "strike the sight" of their intended audience. Finally, using the language of painting, Pope compares Crashaw's poetic technique to the weaker, less masculine elements of visual art: "their *Colouring* entertains the sight, but the *Lines* and *Life* of the Picture are not to be inspected too narrowly" (*Corr.*, 1:110). Like women, the poems of this amateur (to borrow Pope's later expression) are "best distinguish'd by black, brown, or fair," for only a masculine style of expression confers individuality, or character, upon an author.

Yet however much Pope desired to contrast his commitment to "establish a reputation," or earn the esteem of the learned, with Crashaw's contributions to leisure-hour miscellanies, he remained disturbed by contemporary critiques of poetry as an occupation removed from matters of importance. For instance, while translating the *Iliad* in 1715—the year of the Scots' uprising—Pope reveals his vexation and impotence at being compelled to recount ancient wars instead of participating in modern ones: "I never had so much cause as now to complain of my poetical star, that fixes me at this tumultuous time, to attend the gingling of rymes and the measuring of syllables: To be almost the only trifler in the nation; and as ridiculous as the Poet in *Petronius*, who while all the rest in the ship were either labouring or praying for life, was scratching his head in a little room, to write a fine description of the tempest" (*Corr.*, 1:324). The sense of isolation that Pope describes here indicates the marginal position to which he believed himself confined. But Pope's simile also suggests the uselessness of poets in general (not only those who are Catholic, Tory, or physically deformed) in a crisis that calls for exertion rather than contemplation. Throughout the volumes of his early correspondence, Pope repeatedly selects the metaphor of a horse and bells to describe the denigration he feels at employing himself for the amusement of others. In writing to the devout John Caryll, Pope excuses his attention to verse, maintaining that it does not occupy his whole life: "I really make no other use of poetry now, than horses do of the bells that gingle about their ears (tho' now and then they toss their heads as if they were proud of 'em), only to travel on a little more merrily" (*Corr.*, 1:191). Always conscious of his audience, Pope may have sought to emphasize his moral gravity, yet the image of the poet as a horse shaking its bells expresses his anxieties about being treated like a menial by those who request his work: "To say truth, the Lives of those we call Great & Happy are divided between those two States; & in each of them, we Poetical Fidlers make but part of their Pleasure, or of their Equipage" (*Corr.*, 2:195). Here Pope borrows the language of his detractors in envisioning himself as a retainer in the aristocratic households of his audience; occupying a place "next to some *Italian* Chymists, Fidlers, Bricklayers, and Opera-makers" (*Corr.*, 1: 347),the poet is transformed into an "Instrument" of diversion for his patron's idle hours. Yet Pope himself was never subject to such patrons, and with the fame and the profits of the *Iliad* translation supporting him (profits that amounted to more than 4,000 pounds), he did not depend upon pleasing the great for his livelihood. Rather, written in 1723, Pope's remarks refer to his work on the *Odyssey*, and to the pressure he felt to satisfy the friends who were awaiting the text's completion. Although Bernard Lintot's financing of the Homer translation made Pope financially independent of patrons, the rhetoric of Pope's correspondence suggests the limits of this independence: his letters reveal the subordination that accompanied poets' occupational identity, regardless of the source of their income.

Over the years, Pope began to imagine and construct a new economic and sexual ideal of authorship through his attacks upon a prominent critic of his professional career—John, Lord Hervey. Hervey conveniently provided a kind of focal point for Pope's self-definition: a dilettante writer, aristocrat, and courtier, Hervey symbolized the structure of power that relegated Pope, the writer by trade, to the margins of respectability. Hervey himself used his rank, and the authority it conferred, as a weapon against Pope. Their quarrel, initiated by their allegiance to opposing political parties, escalated in the early 1730s when Pope repeatedly criticized Hervey as "Lord *Fanny*," a spinner of weak couplets ("The First Satire of the Second Book of Horace Imitated") and as Fannius, the impudent flatterer of patrons ("The Fourth Satire of Dr. John Donne . . . Versifyed"). In response, Hervey anonymously published *An Epistle from a Nobleman to a Doctor of Divinity* (1733), verses that denigrate Pope's talent and satirize his pretensions to the upper-class privilege of using the classics as cultural capital.[16] Hervey found especially impertinent Pope's translation of the *Iliad* and *Odyssey* into English for a profit. According to Hervey, Pope's sterile invention and schoolboy verse render void "This Jingler's Claim / Or to an Author's, or a Poet's Name"; only boys and girls (the least discriminating consumers of literature) appreciate Pope's *Homer*.[17] The motive for Hervey's attack on Pope, though, was not so much a desire to preserve the classics from modern translators and a popular readership as a distaste for what Hervey considered the poet's desire to climb above his rank and aspire to the company of gentlemen:

I own I have an aversion to those wits by profession, who think it incumbent upon them always to reflect and express themselves differently from the rest of the world; they are a sort of mental poster-masters in company who think they must distort themselves to entertain you, and often give me pain, but never give me pleasure. Pope is the head of this sect. If he had never talked, one should have thought he had more wit than any man that ever lived, and if he had never written he would have talked much better; but the endeavouring to raise his character as a companion up to the point it stands as an author, has sunk it as much below its natural pitch as he has endeavoured to put it above it. But this is a rock many have split upon as well as him.[18]

To Hervey, the profession of writing was incompatible with the genteel social status that Pope seemingly affected; the poet's "character as a companion"to men of rank suffers from his compulsion to advertise or display his talents (to be a "mental poster-master"). As Hervey sees it, Pope's aspirations to politeness are at odds with his role as an entertainer, a role Hervey believed Pope internalized to the point where it determined his conduct. By contrast, Hervey's social superiority and secure class standing enabled him to mock both his own poetic efforts and Pope's satiric appraisal of them:

> Guiltless of Thought, each Blockhead may compose
> This nothing-meaning Verse, as fast as Prose.
> And P—e with Justice of such Lines may say,
> *His Lordship spins a thousand in a Day.* (*Epistle,* 6–7)

Pope, "who at *Crambo* plays with Pen and Ink" (7), lacks the confidence and sense of play that characterize the aristocratic writer, and the poet's labored, self-conscious attention to his craft makes him akin to mechanics or laborers whose livelihood depends on catering to the needs and pleasures of others.[19]

Pope responded to this attack on his work in his unpublished "Letter to a Noble Lord, On occasion of some Libels written and propagated at Court" (1733), and the rhetorical strategies he employed in his own defense represented the professional poet, rather than the aristocrat, as the upholder of a masculine ideal. Moreover, the bourgeois quality of this ideal shows its significant break from previous conventions of male sexual and literary authority. Rather than ignoring Hervey's status and its privileges, Pope emphasizes them, but only to attack the nobleman's pretensions that birth gives him the license to write: "When I consider the *great difference* betwixt the rank your *Lordship* holds in the *World*, and the rank which your *writings* are like to hold in the *learned world,* I presume that distinction of style is but necessary, which you will see observ'd thro' this letter. When I speak of *you,* my Lord, it will be with all the deference due to the inequality which Fortune has made between you and myself: but when I speak of your *writings,* my Lord, I must, I can do nothing but trifle."[20] Stooping beneath his class, Hervey has "modestly" chosen a pen instead of a sword for his attack upon Pope, yet his choice of this weapon places him at a disadvantage, since Pope's literary skill more than compensates for the accidental benefits bestowed upon Hervey by Fortune: the switch from violence to wit as a means of establishing dominance enables the rise of a new elite who, like Pope, exhibit their masculine superiority by displaying their considerable talents.

The implications of this disparity between amateur and professional production are examined by Baudrillard, who describes the shift toward a "constraint of leisure" or a suspicion of "non-instrumentality as the source of [aesthetic and symbolic] values" that accompanied the development of a capitalist economy: "the current status of the everyday object results from the conflict, or rather, compromise, between two opposed moralities: an aristocratic morality of *'otium'* and a puritan work ethic."[21] Accompanying this change in the nature of the object, including poetry, is an increased emphasis on labor rather than leisure as the basis of social status for men: "everywhere *homo faber* is the double of *homo otiosus.*"[22] Pope himself articulates the superiority of *homo faber* throughout his work. As early as 1717, in a poem entitled "Sandys's Ghost: Or a Proper New Ballad on the New Ovid's Metamorphosis, As It Was Intended To Be Translated By Persons Of Quality," Pope had warned aristocratic writers that membership in an elite social class does not always result in "Verses Sterling":

> For not the Desk with silver Nails,
>   Nor *Bureau* of Expence,
> Nor Standish well japan'd, avails
>   To writing of good Sense. (9–12)

Despite the beauty of their expensive writing implements, the "quality" ultimately translate Ovid into "Waste-Paper." Yet while the "Lords and Lordings" described in "Sandys's Ghost" appear bumbling and incompetent, their masculinity still remains unquestioned. By contrast, Pope argues years later that Hervey's incapacity as a poet embarrasses his audience because it reveals his intellectual (and, by implication, sexual) immaturity. Poetry—imaged in the "Letter to a Noble Lord" as Pegasus— requires reserves of ability and manliness that make it a task too difficult for an effete aristocrat to master: "should your Lordship be only like a *Boy* that is *run away with*; and run away with by a *Very Foal*; really common charity, as well as respect for a noble family, would oblige me to stop your career, and to *help you down* from *this Pegasus*" (2:443). Pope goes on to assert that Hervey's status as the son of an earl, which gave him countless advantages in his upbringing, education, and career advancement, actually hinders the writing of verse, which demands the sturdy middle-class virtues of incessant study, labor, and perseverance:

> Surely the little praise of a *Writer* should be a thing below your ambition: You, who were no sooner born, but in the lap of the Graces; no sooner at school, but in the arms of the Muses; no sooner in the World, but you practic'd all the skill of it; no sooner in the Court, but you possess'd all the art of it! Unrivall'd as you are, in making a figure, and in making a speech, methinks, my Lord, you may well give up the poor talent of turning a Distich. (2:443)

Coddled and encouraged by female approval, Hervey learns a kind of assurance that feminizes him: like women, he acquires the highly artificial manners that enable him to survive and thrive in the complex, hostile society of the court. The "Letter" 's catalog of Hervey's strengths includes delivering sycophantic speeches in support of Walpole's government and "making a figure," or parading his body for public admiration and applause—an act that led contemporaries to designate him "Lady of the Lords." Adam Smith's *Theory of Moral Sentiments* (1759) analyzes the purpose of this display, and concludes that the aristocrat's pride in his appearance, by commanding the respect, envy, and awe of spectators, serves as a means of retaining his control over the populace: "His air, his manner, his deportment, all mark that elegant and graceful sense of his own superiority, which those who are born to inferior stations can hardly ever arrive at. These are the arts by which he proposes to make mankind more easily submit to his authority, and to govern their inclinations according to his own pleasure: and in this he is seldom disappointed."[23] (Smith to a great extent shares Pope's contempt for this form of social dominance: "To figure at a ball is [the aristocrat's] great triumph, and to succeed in an intrigue of gallantry, his highest exploit" [*Theory*, 55].) While acknowledging the physical defects for which Hervey and Lady Mary Wortley Montagu lampooned him ("Verses Address'd to the Imitator of the First Satire of the Second Book of Horace," 1733), Pope undermines the connection between masculine authority and aristocratic self-display:

> It is true, my Lord, I am short, not well shap'd, generally ill-dress'd, if not sometimes dirty. Your Lordship and Ladyship are still in bloom; your Figures such, as rival the *Apollo* of *Belvedere*, and the *Venus* of *Medicis*; and your faces so finish'd, that neither sickness nor passion can deprive them of *Colour*; I will allow your own in particular to be the finest that ever *Man* was blest with: preserve it, my Lord, and reflect, that to be a Critic, would cost it too many *frowns*, and to be a Statesman, too many *wrinkles*! (2:445)

Pope here employs a tactic that is common in his work: comparing his deformity to the "finish'd" appearance of his two antagonists enables him to contrast his sincerity and moral health with their duplicity and moral decay.[24] This passage, however, goes even further in its indictment of Hervey, for it implies that his handsome face—the "finest that ever *Man* was blest with"—indicates his unfitness for the traditional masculine occupations of criticism and statesmanship. Using one's judgment for the evaluation of literature or for the management of the nation renders one unsuitable as an object of admiring glances; the physical signs of masculine intellectual activity like frowns and wrinkles conflict with the exercise of authority through parading the body—an exercise that noblemen like Hervey and coquettes like Lady Mary enjoy. Mental labor, Pope implies, is deforming, but like the deliberate ugliness of Pope's satire—whose "filthy Simile[s]" and "beastly Line[s]" expose abuses of power in high places—his body, made ugly through the hard work of thinking, guarantees the integrity of his character. By this logic, the ill-shaped, slovenly, tradesman-like Pope is more compatible with manly endeavors like verse and criticism than the aristocrat whose self-conscious attention to appearance makes him a spectacle.

Although much of Pope's verse satirizes the moral and intellectual shortcomings of the upper classes, his challenge to the cultural authority of aristocratic males receives its most sustained articulation in *The Dunciad*'s fourth book.[25] Once the focus of Pope's attacks, Hervey receives only a brief mention here; rather, the systems of power that sustain the dominance of peers like

Hervey come under scrutiny for their encouragement of a danger-ous effeminacy in ruling-class men—an effeminacy that eventu-ally infects and weakens the entire nation. One of these systems, patronage, lies at the root of aristocratic influence, and Pope dis-plays patrons' corrupting force through their support of Italian opera:

> . . . a Harlot form soft sliding by,
> With mincing step, small voice, and languid eye;
> Foreign her air, her robe's discordant pride
> In patch-work flutt'ring, and her head aside.
> By singing Peers up-held on either hand,
> She tripp'd and laugh'd, too pretty much to stand;
> Cast on the prostrate Nine a scornful look. (4.45–51)

Aficionados of opera and amateur performers themselves, the "singing Peers" encourage opera through subscriptions, since its frivolity prohibits it from standing on its own, or facing rejection from the general, ticket-buying public. Pope's note to this passage emphasizes the threat of sexual indeterminacy that accompanies opera. Although he assigns it female pronouns in his verses, his commentary censures its "affected airs" and "effeminate sounds" (n.45), terms that imply an exaggerated or simulated femininity and that perhaps allude to the presence of castrati on the stage.[26] The performance of opera erases other distinctions as well: "Chromatic tortures soon shall drive them [the muses] hence, / Break all their nerves, and fritter all their sense: / One Trill shall harmonize joy, grief, and rage" (4.55–57). As Pope's note indicates, this chaos of sound appeals only to effete nobles: "that harmony which conforms to the Sense, and applies to the Passions"—a harmony exemplified in the music of "Giant Han-del"—"proved . . . too manly for the fine Gentlemen of his age" (n.54). The masculine understanding that would appreciate sense in music and bold, martial sounds has disappeared, and Handel's attempts to revive it lead to his banishment by Dulness:

> "To stir, to rouze, to shake the Soul he comes,
> And Jove's own Thunders follow Mars's Drums.
> Arrest him, Empress; or you sleep no more"—
> She heard, and drove him to th' Hibernian shore. (4.67–70)

Years earlier, critics had compared Pope to Farinelli and im-plied that those who provide entertainment for the public jeopar-dize their masculinity; here Pope reverses this criticism, for

Handel, the paid performer, attempts to preserve a manly spirit in music while the peers introduce and protect art forms that promote effeminacy. Patronage, or the network of relationships between benefactors and dependents that maintains aristocratic influence over the church, the state, and the arts, cooperates with Dulness in Pope's verses ("There march'd the bard and blockhead, side by side, / Who rhym'd for hire, and patroniz'd for pride" [4.101–2]). This exchange of patrons' financial support for influence over their clients not only erodes the integrity of both parties, but also infects English culture at large with the degraded tastes of the ruling elite.

Like patronage, education also reproduced ruling-class masculine power, most explicitly through university training. Pope himself, we have seen, faced criticism from Hervey and others for a kind of intellectual poaching—that is, his translations of Homer appropriated the classics in a manner presumptuous for someone who had never studied at Oxford or Cambridge. *The Dunciad*, however, reveals that life at school, instead of guiding noblemen into mental and physical maturity, actually emasculates them. Book 4's portrayal of aristocratic education and its crippling effects begins with a speech by the ghost of Dr. Busby, past headmaster of Westminster School, regarding classical translation:

> We ply the Memory, we load the brain,
> Bind rebel Wit, and double chain on chain,
> Confine the thought, to exercise the breath;
> And keep them in the pale of Words till death.
> Whate'er the talents, or howe'er design'd,
> We hang one jingling padlock on the mind:
> A Poet the first day, he dips his quill;
> And what the last? a very Poet still. (4.157–64)

The students' confinement to verse translation without a chance to exercise the "quick springs of Sense" (4.156) in understanding and criticism leaves them intellectually stunted.[27] Moreover, Busby's methods—teaching languages through flogging—produces generations of mentally cowed men. Upon hearing Busby's voice, "The pale Boy-Senator yet tingling stands, / And holds his breeches close with both his hands" (4.147–48); Pope's note details the political consequences of such fear: "let it not be imagined the author would insinuate these youthful Senators (tho' so lately come from school) to be under the undue influence of any *Master*" (n.148). Of course, Pope is insinuating the subjugation of the young lords to Walpole, their "Master" in Parliament. Busby's teaching, both in content (rote repetition) and in method (physical punishment) ensures that his boys will be boys forever.[28]

The perpetual adolescence of aristocrats remains unchallenged through their European travels; in fact, the Continental tour, supposed to add cosmopolitan sophistication to the English gentleman (and prepare him for his future role in governing the state), instead guarantees his immaturity ("he ne'er was Boy, nor Man" [4.288]). A member of the "gay embroider'd race" (4.275), the "young Aeneas" passes undistinguished through school and college, but makes a spectacle of himself abroad:

> Intrepid then, o'er seas and lands he flew:
> Europe he saw, and Europe saw him too.
> There all thy gifts and graces we display,
> Thou [Dulness], only thou, directing all our way! (4.293–96)

Being the object of the gaze and attracting admiration through display of one's graces are usually functions performed by women; here, the noble youth engages in feminine conduct, which the tour only encourages. He learns to act obsequiously from the "silken sons" of France (4.298); to be contentedly oppressed from "lands of singing, or of dancing slaves" (4.305); and to prefer effeminate (and perhaps homoerotic) pleasure over martial rigor and commerce from Venice: "Where, eas'd of Fleets, the Adriatic main / Wafts the smooth Eunuch and enamour'd swain" (4.309–10). The tour degenerates into an orgy of consumption, as the passive youth is led by his governor from vice to vice; Pope's ironic adverbial phrases—"with spirit whored," "Judicious drank," "greatly-daring din'd"—emphasize the pupil's disturbing lack of spirit, judgment, and daring. Finally, the aristocrat exchanges "Classic learning"—the "dull lumber of the Latin store" (4.319), which legitimizes his cultural and sexual superiority—for familiar knowledge of the opera. This exchange effectively nullifies his claims to manhood:

> See now, half-cur'd, and perfectly well-bred,
> With nothing but a Solo in his head;
> As much Estate, and Principle, and Wit,
> As Jansen, Fleetwood, Cibber shall think fit. (4.323–26)

As Pope observes, the now complete English gentleman remains incapable of handling his patrimony and exercising his moral character; although mature in years, he lives dependent upon the guardianship of showmen and gamblers like Jansen, Fleetwood, and Cibber, "who, tho' not Governors by profession, had, . . . concern'd themselves in the Education of Youth; and regulated their Wits, their Morals, or their Finances, at that period of their age which is the most important, their entrance into the polite world" (n.326). In the political rhetoric of Pope's time, careful management of one's paternal estate signified a measure of self-control, or the subordination of individual desire for the good of the nation; from this perspective, the youth and the race he represents are unfit for the ruling-class privileges their birth and gender assign to them.

In *The Dunciad*'s final lines, Pope investigates the concept of aristocratic leisure, or the freedom from the need to spend one's life in production of pleasure for others. Pope's upper-class detractors (and critics who adopted the rhetoric of their betters) maintained that the poet's commercial sale of his verse demoted him to the level of a mechanic; moreover, as one whose livelihood involved providing amusement for vacant hours—an act perceived as feminine in his culture—Pope found his gender identity threatened, too. Yet *The Dunciad* challenges this criticism by portraying the masculine elite engaged in leisure pursuits that are a parody of work. Notably, the peers do not (or cannot) compose verse; rather, inspired by Dulness, they play at a kind of labor that levels them with the lowest of commoners:

> The Cap and Switch be sacred to his Grace;
> With Staff and Pumps the Marquis lead the Race;
> From Stage to Stage the licens'd Earl may run,
> Pair'd with his Fellow-Charioteer the Sun;
> The learned Baron Butterflies design,
> Or draw to silk Arachne's subtile line; (4.585–90)

In an effort to while away unproductive time, a duke turns jockey, a marquis becomes a footman, an earl drives a stagecoach, and a baron tries his hand at weaving spider webs. To contemporary readers, the aristocrats' engagement in manual labor would indicate their negligible talents and degraded sensibilities: imitating a worker not only meant adopting an inferior social status, but also a subordinate sexual position, for in Pope's day, masculinity was gauged in terms of class distinctions among men. Those on the bottom of the hierarchy, including laborers, found themselves lowered to the ranks of boys for their lack of economic

clout and social influence.[29] In *The Dunciad*, then, the gentlemen's déclassé pastimes demean them to the level of their subor-
dinates, whose menial occupations conferred the stigma of
immaturity. These trivial pursuits, though, grow more serious
and more damaging when they engage the nation's rulers: "Others import yet nobler arts from France, / Teach Kings to fiddle,
and make Senates dance" (4.597–98). In his note to this couplet,
Pope describes fiddling as "an ancient amusement of Sovereign
Princes, (viz.) Achilles, Alexander, Nero," and explains that senates dance "either after their Prince, or to Pontoise, or Siberia"
(n.598); this list of warlords and tyrants who called the tunes for
legislators suggests that indulgence in pleasure is a sign of their
destructive willfulness, while the enforced performance of the
people's representatives signifies their subservience. In the worst
scenario, amusement becomes a privilege of the powerful who
seek their satisfaction at the cost of the nation as a whole. The
"Unfinish'd Treaties," "Chiefless Armies," and yawning navies
depicted in *The Dunciad*'s final lines reveal the collapse that occurs when masculine activity gets diverted from its proper chan-
nels. Yet poets like Pope are not responsible for such diversions;
rather, the text suggests that the fault lies with ruling-class men
who cannot fulfill the expectations for their status and gender,
and instead, through boredom generated by incapacity, become
poor imitators of the mechanics (including fiddlers, singers, and
dancers) whom they vilify. Pope's depiction of male aristocrats
demeaning themselves in pursuits of pleasure indicates a growing
cultural disdain for *homo otiosus*, and a corresponding elevation
of professionals like himself, whose engagement in difficult intellectual labor—including the work of poetry—testifies to their superior manhood.

As part of Pope's response to the devaluation of his work, *The
Dunciad* hit its mark. The comments of his posthumous biogra-
phers reveal how his indictment of aristocratic masculinity, and
the institutions that preserved its authority, helped to revise popular perceptions of the poet's own status and vocation. In his *Life
of Alexander Pope* (1769), Owen Ruffhead celebrates Pope's independence from his aristocratic supporters ("though he lived
among the great and wealthy, he lived with them upon the easy
terms of reciprocal amity, and social familiarity"[30]), but gives
even more praise to his commitment to productive intellectual
work. Ruffhead extols his "persevering industry" in study and
verse writing as well as his abstention from "the violent agita-
tions of licentious pleasures" (1:20) and gluttony that tainted the

elite households where he visited. Pope, Ruffhead notes with approval, found satisfaction in his writing alone rather than with women or at table. Johnson in his "Life of Pope" was more skeptical about the poet's abstemious nature ("He was too indulgent to his appetite"[31]), and located other signs of aristocratic frailty in Pope's preoccupation with his health: "The indulgence and accommodation which his sickness required had taught him all the unpleasing and unsocial qualities of a valetudinary man. He expected that every thing should give way to his humour, as a child whose parents will not hear her cry has an unresisted dominion in the nursery" (*Lives*, 3:198). While critical of Pope's occasional lapses into effeminacy and even childishness, the tenor of Johnson's remarks indicates how much he took for granted the bourgeois ideal of manhood that Pope struggled to legitimize. With approval rather than apology, Johnson foregrounds Pope's involvement in the literary market; Pope, he observes, "considered poetry as the business of his life; and, however he might seem to lament his occupation, he followed it with constancy" (*Lives*, 3:218). And whereas Pope could only try to mitigate the dangers of defining himself as a producer of texts for the amusement of audiences, Johnson argues that Pope's claim to notice lies solely in his works and in the pleasure they give: "One of his favourite topicks is contempt of his own poetry. For this, it if had been real, he would deserve no commendation, and in this he certainly was not sincere; for his high value of himself was sufficiently observed, and of what could he be proud but of his poetry?" (*Lives*, 3:208). Yet Johnson's annoyance with Pope is a testament to Pope's ultimate success rather than to his failure. The affectation and insecurity that Johnson criticizes in Pope arose from tensions about charges of triviality that accompanied his participation in commercial print culture—tensions that Johnson, writing in 1779, no longer had to face. Although Pope himself remained uncertain about whether a consumer economy made possible the poet's masculine independence, he effectively questioned the cultural hegemony of gentlemen amateurs: in *The Dunciad*, the systems of patronage, education, and consumption that legitimize aristocratic power are shown to encourage the very effeminacy ascribed to entertainers like Pope. As Johnson points out, Pope's attachment to aristocratic systems of value compromised his claims to independence ("His admiration of the Great seems to have increased in the advance of life" [*Lives*, 3:205]). Yet while Pope himself did not completely embody the

bourgeois model of authorship and manhood, he helped inaugu-
rate this model. The remarks by Wollstonecraft and Knox that
began this essay, then, are residual reminders of sentiments that
faded away under the challenge, and eventual dominance, of
Pope's alternative constructions.

Dissecting the Authorial Body: Pope, Curll, and the Portrait of a "Hack Writer"

CATHERINE INGRASSIA

POPE'S CONSTRUCTION IN *THE DUNCIAD* OF THE WORLD OF GRUB Street and its denizens continues to cast a long shadow over discussions of eighteenth-century literary production. Much of the critical discourse on *The Dunciad* has been a product of the consistent reading of the poem as a text that, despite its heteroglossia, concludes rather than initiates a broader cultural conversation. Though a dynamic site of diverse activity, Grub Street was represented in a monolithic (and fundamentally antagonistic) vision. The production of complex and varied texts and genres that characterized this literary milieu was erased or obscured under the damning rubric of "bad" writing.[1] In *The Dunciad*, Pope represents a literary world marked by fundamentally opposed forces. The frantic and mercenary hacks with their ephemeral, devalued products stand in stark contrast to the privileged and "classical" gentleman-author who writes for a place in literary history.

Pope's ordering of eighteenth-century cultural production and the construction of a dominant hierarchy influenced the writing of literary history, which, until recently, silently acceded to his model and maintained a relatively dunce versus poet, hack versus anti-hack mentality. While the characterization of Alexander Pope as an active participant in the commercialized literary marketplace has gained increasing acceptance following the work of scholars like David Foxon, when discussing the environment of literary production in the early eighteenth century, scholars often continue to cast Pope as the last outpost of high literary production in a marketplace increasingly shaped by successful businessmen like bookseller Edmund Curll. Curll and Pope metonymically function as opposing forces of high and low culture—"true literature" and "crass commercialism."

Models of cultural relations perpetuate this binarism in an attempt to discuss the complex literary configurations. Ronald Paulson, Pat Rogers and, in a different context, Mikhail Bakhtin, each have theorized the practices of and relationship between disparate social formations and cultural categories as oppositional. Paulson classifies eighteenth-century literary texts as "popular" and "polite."[2] Rogers labels Grub Street a literary "subculture," presumably in opposition to the dominant "culture" of Augustan literary production.[3] And Bakhtin, in his discussion of folk culture, identifies divergent cultural impulses as "classical" and "carnivalesque."[4] Certainly, these models provide the scholar a vocabulary with which to discuss complex cultural relations. Indeed, the literary production of Grub Street strikingly invokes the cultural dynamics of the carnivalesque: its irreverence, its suspension of hierarchical distinctions, its preoccupation with the body, and its invigorating energy all capture the carnivalesque impulse. As such, the products of Grub Street symbolically oppose the ordered, polite, and rational—"classical"—activity of high cultural production. Yet, however illuminating these terms are (and I employ notions of the carnivalesque below), they risk replicating (in some form) the antagonistic and irreconcilable model Pope depicts in *The Dunciad*. The period is characterized not by boundaries but by transgressions, by the seepage of categories. The sites of cultural activity are mutually informing, indeed symbiotic. The intersection rather than the opposition of constructed distinctions such as Paulson's popular and polite, Pat Rogers's culture and subculture, or Bakhtin's classical and carnivalesque more accurately captures the cultural dynamic. As Peter Stallybrass and Allon White note in their discussion of the nature of symbolic hierarchies, high discourse with its "lofty style, exalted aim and sublime ends" is informed by "the debasements and degradations of low discourse." The two cannot be read apart but must be relationally configured.[5]

In part, the intersection or invasion of categories was inevitable because of all writers' dependence on the new financial mechanisms that inform the production and consumption of literary commodities. By worshipping Dulness and the marketplace, the hack writer, as envisaged by Pope, subjected literature to the economic laws of supply and demand. "They were manufacturing to order," writes Pat Rogers, "a product—literature—which in the past had largely been the preserve of the learned, the leisured, and the secure."[6] The commercial preoccupation altered the figure of the author and his text. Lady Mary Wortley Montagu complained that the vocation of authorship had degenerated into a "trade." The mercenary attitude of authors, coupled with a lack of originality (exacerbated in part by the relentless need to produce), damaged the quality and status of "writing": "The Press is loaded by the servile Flock of Imitators. . . . The Greatest Virtue, Justice, and the most distinguishing prerogative of Mankind, writeing [sic], when duly executed does Honor to Human nature, but when degenerated into Trades are the most contemptible ways of getting Bread."[7] The function of writing as a trade and a writer as a professional comparable to a "money-jobber" was increasingly accepted, if not celebrated, by those who operated in that capacity. In essence, then, the commercial writer was dependent on the imaginative forces that enabled his profession as well as on the economic laws of the marketplace. Though Pope attempted to obscure his own financial preoccupations, he manipulated his early literary career to achieve the financial security that enabled him to write seemingly free of immediate material concerns. As he later wrote, "(Thanks to Homer) . . . I live and thrive / Indebted to no Prince or Peer alive."[8] The constructed hierarchy of the Augustan literary landscape quickly blurs in light of the phenomenal economic success Pope realized, his ongoing symbolic and material appropriation of Grub Street, and the confluence of commercial and literary activity. The self-revealing hybridity within the poem suggests the contradictions inherent in Pope's career and marks the uneasy relationship between what Mark Rose, in another context, describes as "the traditional world of the author as gentleman and scholar and the emergent world of the author as professional."[9] Popularity, frequency of publication, and profit were not only the concerns of authors writing to make a living wage, but of a self-styled artist like Pope.

The intersection of popular and polite, manifested by common economic interests, also extended to Pope's appropriation of the metaphor and imagery of Grub Street in an attempt to contain and thus control those forces. Although Pope professed an aversion to the carnivalesque literary milieu of the dunces, *The Dunciad* vividly illustrates his intimate knowledge of, if not fascination with, its subversive energy ultimately essential to his work. As Stallybrass and White observe, "the mitigating fact of Pope's superior poetic ability [and I would add superior control over the production of his texts] could not save him from being immersed in the very process of grotesque debasement which he scorned in others" (117). *The Dunciad* draws on Pope's understanding of the situation of a commercial author and yokes the classical and the carnivalesque as an epic poem about the denizens of Grub Street. Pope used the images, ideas, and impulses of the commercial literary marketplace to increase his poetic power—he controlled those images within his own discursive configuration while benefiting from their cultural resonance. He planned for the poem to demonstrate his mastery in an ongoing struggle for literary authority and control.

Yet his level of involvement went much further than just verbal appropriation. During the period surrounding the publication of *The Dunciad*, Pope quite consciously exploited the emerging vehicles of literary commercialization to increase his own marketability. Pope arguably calculated *The Dunciad* as a vehicle for a protracted paper war (what Richard Savage called the "Dunce Wars") that would increase his literary stock and his economic gain. *The Dunciad* initially appears to be Pope's exclusionary attempt to silence the feminized and female opposition he believed was eroding culture as well as encroaching on his stature as an artist. But he paradoxically attempted to silence the same voices he wanted to engage in a profitable dialogue. *The Dunciad*, with its radical ambivalence, is marked by a tension that underlies Pope's efforts to deny his associations with a world to which he was unavoidably and inextricably linked. In some ways, Pope's contemporaries more accurately recognized the commercial nature of Pope's relationship with Grub Street. James Boswell recorded Samuel Johnson's claim that Pope "wrote his *Dunciad* for fame. That was his primary motive."[10] Johnson's comment draws upon the adversarial and commercial relationship between Pope and the professional writers of Grub Street, a competitive rivalry upon the playing field of print culture. Indeed, *The Dunciad* plunged Pope into a protracted Grub Street exchange that forces us to reconsider the relationship between the poet and his alleged nemesis Edmund Curll and, perhaps, to view it as did Pope's contemporaries. The paper war inaugurated by the publication of *The Dunciad* indicates that Pope's relationship with Curll, though born of animosity, was fundamentally symbiotic. Each man invigorated the other's career in profound and important ways. Pope's financial success and his manipulation of Curll suggest that Pope, largely in control of the production and sale of his works after 1727, benefited from the proliferation of pamphlets that kept his name in the marketplace and justified his subsequent publications. While Pope professed a lack of concern with financial rewards, claiming, "I can be content with a bare saving game" (*Corr.*, 1:236), he stood to gain a great deal from the succession of pamphlets from Curll's stable of hack writers that kept his name and *The Dunciad* in the marketplace. Not only could he cultivate the position of the besieged and morally superior author and potentially enhance his cultural currency, he could also represent himself as compelled to issue subsequent editions of the poem to correct or respond to the words of his literary enemies.[11] The extended discursive exercise enabled Pope to refine his poem further and gain additional material for his work.

However, the terms of the exchange were not limited to the textual production of each man. As competitors in the literary marketplace, the two men struggled for control of Pope's socio-poetic persona and offered competing versions of "Pope." As has been well documented, Pope carefully constructed the pose of the gentleman poet, removed from the concerns and pressures of the literary marketplace. For Pope, poetry played a compensatory role, both publicly and privately, that, to a certain extent, assuaged his social and sexual insecurities, and increased his sense of limited personal power. Pope occupied a cultural position that might be read as "feminized" in contrast to the normative performance of masculinity dominant in a patriarchal culture. He was denied access to the public activities that authenticated masculine power. He lived a marginalized life constrained by circumstances largely beyond his control: his religion denied him the opportunity for a formal classical education, political involvement, or the possession of property within London; his physical infirmities limited his social and geographic mobility; and his elaborate process of "putting himself together" every morning made him dependent daily on personal servants.[12] Pope recognized his inability to fulfill what his culture understood as the standards defining masculinity—an ideology he aggressively defended in his poetry. Pope's self-perceived feminization caused him to use poetry and textual production in a complicated compensatory strategy to overcome his fears of social and sexual inadequacy and to fulfill (if only discursively) his culture's construction of masculinity. Pope repeatedly suggested that writing good poetry is a vigorous, "manly" activity; literary authority contributes to sexual identity. In *An Essay on Criticism*, for example, in contrast to the "Patriarch-Wits" of the "Golden Age" (479), current writers "In the fat Age of Pleasure" (532), "Rhyme with all the Rage of Impotence" (609). Writing marked by "Dulness with Obscenity" is as "Shameful sure as Impotence in Love" (532–33). Rival poets or critics who "cannot write" burn with "an Eunuch's spite" (30–31). The images of feminized dunces as symbolically emasculated illustrates Pope's representation of the writing of good poetry as a powerful, authorizing, and culturally "masculine" activity.

At the same time, Pope was acutely aware that, as a poet, he relied on those cultural forces, such as imagination and fancy, he defined as feminized. As his description of the "Cave of Spleen" in Canto 4 of *The Rape of the Lock* makes clear, Pope had an uneasy understanding that the sensibility that creates female maladies was closely connected to the imaginative forces that enable literary production, "th' Hysteric or Poetic fit" (60): "On various Tempers act by various ways, / Make some take Physick, others scribble Plays" (*TE* 2:186, 4.60–61). The fundamentally ambivalent (and perhaps androgynous) nature of the literary enterprise made Pope all the more vigilant in protecting—indeed cultivating—his poetic capital, and representing poetry as a rational, masculine pursuit. Of course, Pope also recognized that his carefully constructed socio-poetic persona, like his poetry, existed only through discursive representations that depended on a symbolic, rather than tangible, economy. A mutually reinforcing relationship emerged between the symbolic and material economy. The more closely Pope could control the production, dissemination, and interpretation of his works, the more he profited from those texts in material and symbolic ways.

The categories Pope established for himself were deeply contested within his own personal and professional existence. The series of pamphlets following the 1728 publication of *The Dunciad*, orchestrated by bookseller Edmund Curll, highlights those contradictions. The texts do not so much subvert the hierarchies constructed by Pope (although they retain a carnivalesque and decidedly transgressive impulse) as dissolve them in an attempt to represent Grub Street as an egalitarian site of literary production. Curll, in a sense, reconfigures the relationship between Pope, and the marketplace and the other professional writers and booksellers. The responses to the 1728 *Dunciad*, published by Curll and including responses by the women writers Pope attacked, highlight the precarious control Pope had over his literary texts, his cultural persona, and his discursive performance of masculinity. The exchange between the two men illustrates their competing negotiation of cultural authority, literary space, and Pope's construction of self. Curll's publications complicated and ultimately fragmented the stable persona Pope carefully created and cultivated. Curll constructed, and placed into circulation, unauthorized "versions" of the author that actively competed with the persona constructed by Pope.

Curll and Pope's relationship suggests a literary manifestation of the homosocial desire Eve Sedgwick identifies as central to the male power relations present in any patriarchal society. Sedgwick describes male homosocial relations, conducted through the exchange of an erotic object, a woman, as a way to maintain and transmit patriarchal power. "The bond that links the two rivals is as intense and potent as the bond that links either of the rivals to his beloved: that the bonds of 'rivalry' and 'love,' differently as they are experienced, are equally powerful and in many senses equivalent."[13] While Sedgwick speaks primarily in terms of rivals in a romantic context, the homosocial relationship she details resembles other male–male relationships in eighteenth-century England: financial, mercantile, and literary. In the literary marketplace, the rivalry between Pope and Curll analogously defined their commercial and textual relationship. While competing for cultural space, literary authority, and multiple forms of paper credit, their rivalry also focused quite specifically on mastery and control over Pope's poetic construction of self. Though literary or textual rather than sexual rivals, the two men struggled over what, for Pope, amounted to an "erotic" object—certainly the compensatory, gendered, and slightly sexualized role Pope accorded to his poetry made it the object of a considerable amount of emotional energy. Just as superiority within a romantic triangle validated the masculinity and cultural potency of the victor, control over Pope's discursive body of work, and the socio-poetic persona constructed within, was integral to his sense of authenticity within eighteenth-century society. That, coupled with the connection between literary and sexual authority, and Pope's apparent inability to engage in a conventional sexual rivalry for a woman, heightens the affinities with homosocial relationships as described by Sedgwick. Pope certainly demonstrated a lifelong commitment to the verbally constructed object of the men's rivalry—his discursive construction of self and the accompanying "body" of work.

Curll, in a sequence of pamphlets responding to *The Dunciad*, constructed an equally potent alternative persona of Pope to compete with the poet in terms of the market and cultural authority. Curll transcoded Pope and his work with the imagery and associations of the carnivalesque to locate Pope in the commercialized marketplace, and to negate or reveal as counterfeit the poet's carefully constructed public image. Curll's technique revealed Pope's reliance on paper credit and his affinities with the feminized world of hack writers. Curll's gesture was not necessarily subversive (although the impulse is definitely transgressive); rather he wanted to locate Pope within the cultural space of Grub Street and to reveal the commercial motivation (both symbolic and material) that drove both men.

Using three basic strategies, Curll's publications attempted to destabilize Pope's position within the implicit hierarchy of the print trade as he positioned Pope's texts as simultaneous utterances within a larger cultural discourse. First, Curll demonstrated the intertextuality between Pope's work and Grub Street publications and denied the dominance of either. Curll's pamphlets intimated (correctly) that *The Dunciad* could not have existed without Pope's construction of Grub Street as its foil, and that understanding this poem required an intimate knowledge of the commercial literary environment.[14] Second, Curll expropriated Pope's texts, public and private, and radically altered the context of Pope's work. Pope's youthful letters to Henry Cromwell, the allegedly scandalous sections of his poetry, and his responses to Grub Street attacks, coupled with Curll's commentary on the same, complicated and in some ways diminished Pope's socio-poetic persona. Finally, Curll focused on Pope's physical body, which the poet worked hard to ignore or obscure, and made it another contested construction within their exchange. Verbal and visual images of Pope's body circulated in the texts following *The Dunciad*. Curll metaphorically (re)presented Pope's physical body in a manner that invokes Bakhtin's concept of "grotesque realism" with its emphasis on "degradation, that is the lowering of all that is high, spiritual, ideal, abstract" and thus "a transfer to the material level, to the sphere of earth and body."[15] It renders the body as incomplete, with orifices emphasized and "its lower regions given priority over its upper regions."[16] As such, the carnivalesque figure starkly opposes the classical image of the complete, finished man, an image Pope tried to construct poetically, and failed to achieve personally. Though we now read these attacks on Pope's physical disabilities as unfair or cruel, Curll's preoccupation with the body indicates his recognition of Pope's compensatory strategy, which necessarily privileges the power of the poetic and the cerebral and denies his own physical limitations. "Reconstructing" Pope in those terms and thus dissecting the authorial body, Curll cast the author as the symbolic manifestation of these contradictory forces of high and low, classical and carnivalesque, the lofty mind and the base body. Thus Pope becomes a hybrid, the physical embodiment of the violation of the very cultural categories he casts as central.[17]

Curll's *Compleat Key to the Dunciad*, published 28 May 1728, immediately constructed the illusion of textual and critical interdependence between Curll and Pope, an intimacy that allows Curll to "coauthor" *The Dunciad*. The epigram on the first page of the key establishes the men's connection and casts them as literary equals: "How easily two Wits agree? / One finds the Poem, one the Key."[18] Though the "key" actually depends upon *The Dunciad*, Curll reverses the power relationship and makes readers of *The Dunciad* depend on the key to get the fullest meaning of the poem. By revealing the names Pope omitted and assuming the role of the translator, Curll heightens the poem's satiric sting and preempts Pope's voice (and arguably prompts the subsequent reading apparatus Pope himself provided with *The Dunciad Variorum*). Curll continues this ploy in *The Curliad* when he expresses gratitude that "Mr. Pope has corrected two small faults in my key" (12); in return, Curll lists the faults he detected in Pope's work. Pope's later textual reference to Curll demonstrates how Curll penetrated his text, causing him to react, rethink, or revise his words.

In the following year, Curll further exploited the mutually constructed sense of intertextuality and used his attacks on Pope as a vehicle to advertise more anti-Pope publications and to exploit the marketability of Pope's name. In these pamphlets, Curll strategically placed advertisements for other anti-Pope materials that had been "lately published," and he tried to lure readers into his shop "where may be had, *The Progress of Dulness. The Popiad. And A Key to the Dunciad.*"[19] In the attacks, Curll also furnished scholarly footnotes that referred the reader to the growing Curll library of Pope material: "See Pope's Familiar Letters to Henry Cromwell, Esq.; pg. 28, vol. 1"[20] or "See the Remarks on Mr. Pope's Temple of Fame subjoined to the Progress of Dulness."[21] In essence, Curll offered what Terry Eagleton, discussing Samuel Richardson's addenda to *Clarissa*, terms a "kit" for reading. A "great unwieldly container," writes Eagleton, the kit is "crammed with spare parts and agreeable extras, for which the manufacturer never ceases to churn out new streamlined improvements, ingenious additions and revised instruction sheets. . . . One text ceaselessly spawns another."[22] Curll and Pope both acted as manufacturers, "spawning" successive editions of their respective works. By making frequent reference to an extensive array of Pope-related publications, Curll invites the reader to construct his own collection. Taking Curll's invitation to heart, Pope himself assembled a Grub Street "kit" with perfect copies of the pamphlets bound in three volumes for his library at Twickenham.[23] Samuel Johnson recounts Jonathan Richardson's visit to Pope, where he discovered the poet reading the bound pamphlets. Looking up, he reportedly exclaimed, "these thing are my diversion . . . such things are sport to me."[24] As Pope read, the painter observed "his features writhen in anguish" (188), revealing the conflict Pope experienced between reading the texts as pieces in a larger game—a sport or diversion—and seeing them as stains on his literary reputation.

Even as Curll's publishing strategy exposed Pope's material connections with Grub Street, Curll highlighted Pope's symbolic connection with the expropriation of Pope's texts and the "reconstruction" of his body—often simultaneously—which evidenced the carnivalesque aspects of Pope's life and work. Among the sources Curll exploited most heavily were letters Pope had written to Henry Cromwell between approximately 1706 and 1712. Written in what James Winn terms Pope's "rake period," the letters recount Pope's various experiences with women and include the now-famous Rondeau and his parody of the First Psalm. While these youthful letters did not necessarily damage his literary reputation, they did deflate his moral reputation because they diminished his image as a morally superior man, which in many ways was the linchpin of Pope's socio-poetic persona. As Pope remarked to Aaron Hill in a moment of uncharacteristic (and perhaps feigned) humility, "I vow to God, I never thought any great matters of my poetical capacity. . . . But, I do know certainly, my moral Life is superior to that of most of the wits of these days" (*Corr.*, 3:166).[25] In the Cromwell letters, however, Curll discovered "a vicious Scene" as "painted by the profligate and profane Pen of Alexander Pope of Twickenham, Esq." (vii).

In *The Female Dunciad*, published 8 August 1728, Curll supplements these letters with commentary by a "female critic" who describes them as "sufficient testimonies of Mr. Pope's Immorality, Profaness and Obscenity."[26] Her comments, which create another type of intertextual dialogue between Pope and the Grub Street critic, highlight the portions of the letters that express interest more appropriate to a hack than to the "morally superior" master of Twickenham. One of the more damning letters is that of 21 December 1711, in which Pope discusses his desire for the Blount sisters, "two such ladies, that in good faith 'tis all I'm able to do, to keep myself in my skin" (8). Affecting a libertine attitude, Pope wishfully comments:

Let me but have the Reputation of these [ladies] in my keeping, and
as for my own, let the Devil, or Dennis, take it for ever! How gladly
wou'd I give all I am worth, that is to say, my Pastorals, for one of
their Maiden heads, and my Essay, for the other ? I wou'd lay out all
my Poetry in Love, an Original for a Lady, and a translation for a
Waiting Maid! (9)

The letter makes explicit the compensatory role poetry played for
Pope—"all I am worth"—and the discrepancy between Pope's
verbal fantasies and physical realities. Read in economic terms,
the exchange posed in the letter—pastoral for maidenhead—
reveals Pope's recognition that a shrewd investment of his high
cultural status and his poetic material (his capital or paper credit)
could potentially yield interest in the form of physical (i.e., sexual) satisfaction. Pope wants to use the business of poetry as a
means to gain (if only imaginatively) the pleasure of sexual intimacy. Pope does not conflate the high and the low but rather attempts to play one against the other, because he wants to
exchange the products of the high for the pleasures of the low
(with literary and social hierarchy intact). Though intentionally
amusing, the letter reveals Pope's discomfort with the complicated situation he had created for himself with his use of poetry
and language as a compensatory tool.

Curll heightened the incongruity of Pope's sentiments by publishing the Cromwell letters with a novel by Eliza Haywood, *The
History of Clarina*. Given the realities of eighteenth-century literary production, it is possible that Haywood did not write *The History of Clarina* specifically for *The Female Dunciad*. Nonetheless,
it effectively complements the portrait of Pope Curll attempted to
construct, and comments on the role of the satirist in its opening
section. It also constructs another type of dialogue between Haywood and Pope, an interaction underscored by the epistolary form
of the novel. The opening paragraphs of the text praise the un-
named gentleman recipient, a satirist, for the "sweetness" of his
"Disposition, and that Tenderness with which you consider the
Errors of your Fellow Creatures" (17–18) in his "endeavour for a
Reformation of Manners" (17). She remarks that should she find
"in the Course of your Papers, all the little Inadvertencies of my
own Life recorded, I am sensible it will be done in such a Manner
as I cannot but approve" (18). Though not a specific reference to
The Dunciad or Pope's scurrilous representation of Haywood
(which certainly alludes to real or imagined "inadvertencies" in
her life), the comment resonates with the potent images of that

portrait. The novel itself offers a depiction of the "deformities of vice" that might on some level be read as metaphorically descriptive of Pope's relationship with women and his literary colleagues. The lovely Clarina, too closely influenced by her maid Aglaura, is entranced by a letter from Merovius (actually the son of Aglaura) who describes his attempted suicide motivated by his unrequited love for her. Merovius, with the aid of Aglaura, persuades Clarina to marry him secretly, then abandons her, pregnant, after spending all her money. Alone, estranged from her family, and "destitute of all the Necessaries of Life" (38), Clarina subsequently lives "the Life of a kept Mistress" (40), her reputation and life ruined. Merovius's metamorphosis from devoted suitor to vindictive spouse parallels the shifting representation of Pope in *The Female Dunciad* and the final metamorphosis described in the poem of the same name at the end of the text. "The New Metamorphosis. Being a Familiar Letter from a Gentleman in Town to a Lady . . . Occasion'd by the Dunciad" asks why "a Poet renown'd for Politeness, and Fire, / Has stain'd all his Laurels in Puddles and Mire"; "What Merit so bright, can encourage a Poet / To attack all the World, with his Jingle and Low-Wit!" (43). Just as *The Dunciad* has ruined the reputations of various authors, male and female, so too, the poem suggests, has the text—and the metamorphosis it marks—ruined Pope's reputation as well: "Could not the great Wit, the prime Bard of the Nation, / Be content to enjoy such a vast Reputation." Rather than "admiring" his poetry, readers are now "forc[ed] . . . to dread them." Haywood's contribution to the text highlights Pope's (new) reputation for viciously representing women; like Clarina, she has had her reputation destroyed by a faithless man.

The combination of discourses (which in many ways more accurately replicates the multiple discourses that comprise literary culture) also implies that Pope's letters would be of sufficient interest to the readers of the female novelist, a titillation Pope certainly would resist. The maneuver attempts to ally Pope with the feminizing force he despised, a force emphasized by the female critics' salacious commentary. *The Female Dunciad* juxtaposes Pope and Haywood, letters and commentary, Twickenham and Grub Street to show how their intersection more accurately represents the multivalent discourse of Pope. Curll later assures his customers, "As to Mr. Pope's Letters, every impartial Reader" will find Pope's "Judgement both of Men and Books, is exactly conformable to present Sentiments of the Author of the *Dunciad*" (*Curliad*, 23).

In addition to the Cromwell letters, Curll captured by textual means any responses his work elicited from Pope—such as his denial of *A Popp upon Pope*. Often attributed to Lady Mary Wortley Montagu, the pamphlet, which appeared on 1 June 1728, recounts the alleged beating of Pope "by two evil disposed persons out of spite and revenge for a harmless lampoon [*The Dunciad*] which the said poet had writ."[27] Though the piece begins with a pious admonishment against brutalizing papists, it quickly concentrates on graphically describing Pope's beating. Hoisted over the back of one man, "poor master Pope" is beaten with a rod by another who "did, with great violence and an unmerciful Hand, strike Mr. Pope so hard upon his naked Posteriors, that he voided large Quantities of Blood, which being yellow . . . had a great Proportion of Gall mixed with it, which occasioned the said color." The description diminished Pope to the level of a schoolboy beaten for a minor infraction, "a harmless lampoon." As Kristina Straub reminds us, "the spectacle of the schoolboy's bent knees or his bared ass before the corrective birch constitutes a semiotic terrain upon which are continually being inscribed masculinities defined in power relation to each other" (69). While the identity of the two assailants remains unknown, Pope's masculinity, through Curll's rendering of the event, is not only subordinant but contested. Left "weltring in his own blood," with the lower half of his body naked, Pope is reduced to a base physical level. The physical displaces the cerebral, leaving Pope disordered, raving "for Pen, Ink and Paper" no doubt in an attempt to regain textual control over a physical situation. The humiliation is heightened when Miss Blount arrives to carry Pope home in her apron. The verbal image of Pope being whipped by two men upon his "naked posteriors" capitalized on the sexual ambiguity implicit in Pope's marginalized body as well as his Catholicism, and the description subtly underscores the homoerotic implications of the scenario, and the relationship between the two men.

The pamphlet did not go unnoticed by Pope, who took out an advertisement in the 14 June *Daily Post* to denounce the piece. "Perhaps," suggests Maynard Mack, "he feared that, however fictional in this instance, the idea might catch on; more likely he found its patronizing tone toward Martha as well as himself too humiliating to go unchallenged."[28] In his denial, Pope declares,

Whereas there has been a scandalous Paper cried about the Streets under the title of A Popp upon Pope, insinuating that I was whipped

in Ham-walks on Thursday last. This is to give Notice that I did not
stir out of my House at Twickenham all that day.

Ironically, that brief notice only provided Curll with more material, for he reprinted it next to *A Popp upon Pope* in his longer
pamphlet, *The Popiad*.[29] The propinquity of these pieces traps
Pope within another Curll publication—literally binding him
(and his words) to Grub Street and again creating the illusion of
dialogue between the two men. And Pope's brief statement
(which in original form might actually have interested readers in
A Popp upon Pope) looks insignificant if not arrogant next to the
far more titillating and explicit essay.

Pamphlets like *The Popiad* depicted Pope—verbally and visually—with grotesque realism contrary to the classical images of
the "finished, complete man" he strove poetically to construct.[30]
Indeed the paper wars attempted to deny Pope any physical dignity or credibility, something he sought to create and maintain.
Pope's pursuit of the "classical status" as an author extended to
what William Wimsatt terms "the delineation and public projec-
tion of his own image." Pope's formal portraits—which only represented his head and shoulders—often evoked iconographic
features associated with Greco-Roman portraiture. A Roman toga
and a wreath of ivy leaves, a profile pose imitating a medallic representation, and use of the uroboros, the ancient symbol of eternity: all contributed to Pope's efforts to transcend visually his
temporal surroundings and to ignore his obvious physical differences.[31] Although we tend to remember Pope's sanctioned portraits, equally viable alternate portraits circulated with
competing authority. For example, the well-known frontispiece to
Pope Alexander's Supremacy (1729) had a composite of Pope's
head atop a monkey's body. In response to Pope's portrait of Ap-
pius in *An Essay on Criticism*, John Dennis had written of Pope,
"As there is no Creature in Nature so venomous, there is nothing
so stupid and so impotent as a hunch-backed toad." Curll's last
anti-Pope pamphlet of 1728, *Codrus: or The Dunciad Dissected*,
took Dennis's comment to a hyperbolic extreme with Elizabeth
Thomas's fable "Father Pope and his Son, or the Toad and the
Ox." "Father Pope" rewrites Pope's biography as an animal story
reminiscent of the broadsheet theme of the "World Upside
Down."[32] The fable describes Pope as a toad "deformed in shape,
of Pigmy stature: / A Proud, Conceited peevish Creature" (12)
who achieves great poetic success. The text inextricably links the
toad's grotesque physicality with its poetic ability, depicting the

poetry as almost a type of bodily discharge, an overflow of bad
humors. Pope's satires are "stinking venom" (18) and "nauseous
slaver" (18), and, in the case of *The Dunciad*:

> . . . Take away the filthy Part,
> Of T—d, and Spew, and Mud and Fart:
> (Words which no Gentleman could use,
> And e'en a Nightman would refuse.)
> There nought remain'd, save to the elf
> A Disemboguement of himself.

The toad's animosity and competitiveness ultimately cause him
to explode, revealing that he had neither "Limb, nor Bone, nor
flesh, nor Skin," and was nothing but a "splatch of squalid gore"
(21). This consistent yoking of the physical and the poetic echoes
Pope's representations in *The Dunciad*, where he depicts the
texts of women writers as grotesque or abnormal physicality:
Corinna's (Elizabeth Thomas) public urination; Eliza Haywood's
distended, udder-like breasts and her "two babes of love"; and
Dulness's amorphous body and uncontrollable fecundity, which
spawns countless dunces and "dull" texts. While Thomas's representation was designed to satirize Pope, it actually highlighted
perhaps the most serious and complicated issue for Pope, personally and professionally. Pope's poetry simultaneously sprang
from and denied his physical condition, what he called in *Epistle
to Arbuthnot* "this long disease, my life." Pope compensated for
his physical limitations and social and religious marginality
through the forceful use of poetry and language, which allowed
him to touch, influence, or affect a range of people, particularly
women. Yet that marginality and distance in part enabled Pope's
distinctive poetic voice. Curll seemingly recognized Pope's strategy and attempted to deflate his persona not only through a symbolic inversion, but also with a further feminization of Pope
within a literary hierarchy. The images of grotesque physicality
underscored Pope's compromised sexuality, an ambivalence Curll
exploited by making Pope's body the locus of attack. By emphasizing the connection between the body and the mind, Curll con-
flated the dichotomy seen as central to eighteenth-century
rational masculinity, and represented the poet's body as a (if not
the) source of the poetic.

In the summer of 1735, Curll went one step further: he made
"Pope's Head" his shop sign in Rose Street, Covent Garden, and
used a line engraving of the same image as the frontispiece in his

books. Curll described his intention "to hang him in effigy for a sign to all spectators of his falsehood and my own veracity."[33] The gesture captures the essence of the men's relationship. Curll's appropriation of Pope's physical image materially manifests the symbolic medium of their exchange. They were competing for control over Pope's persona and literary commodities, and the economic rewards of both. By using Pope's image to mark the site of commercial activity, Curll literally merged the tenuous oppositions that characterize this period: the literary and the commercial, the classic and the carnivalesque. Curll's shop sign, like *The Dunciad* itself, is a testimony to what Stallybrass and White term a "hybridization" of culture. A hybridization "produces new combinations and strange instabilities in a given semiotic system. It therefore generates the possibility of shifting the very terms of the system itself by erasing and interrogating the relationships which constitute it" (58). To have "Pope" in a sense advertise for Curll certainly shifted the terms of their relationship. Yet the iconic use of Pope in the geographic location of Grub Street symbolically enacted the reciprocal cultural activity that enabled the literary production of both men.

Curll's attacks on Pope stemmed from his own experience manipulating the power of language, print culture, and paper credit to elevate one's financial if not social situation. Curll notes that he and Pope began in similar social positions—"Mr. Pope is the son of a trader, and so is Mr. Curll,—par nobile"—and reached similar heights in their respective fields: "Mr. Pope is no more a gentleman than Mr. Curll, nor more eminent as a Poet than he as Bookseller."[34] *The Curliad, A Hypercritic upon the Dunciad Variorum* (1729) presents the men's relationship as one of competition, reciprocity, and dialogue within a shared discursive space. The Steele epigram on the title page, "Soon will that Die which adds thy name to mine / Let me then Live join'd to a Work of Thine," accurately articulates the symbiotic nature of the relationship.[35] Curll describes their verbal jostling as mutually beneficial, a sort of literary (and financial) quid pro quo: "Whatever mention Mr. Pope thinks fit to honour Me withal, in any of his Labours, I shall always take it in good part. . . . If I have done Him any service, he is, in our Shop-stile—heartily welcome" (19). The mention of his print shop's reply to a customer—"heartily welcome"— casts Pope as a consumer, and their relationship as commerce. Curll claims that he has "generously" printed Pope's material, albeit pirated, for twelve years, and that he "shall continue his Fame" (21) by printing editions in years to come. Just as *The Dunciad*, arguably Pope's most powerful poem, gained much of its force from Pope's appropriation of Grub Street, Curll similarly prospered by connecting himself to Pope. He observes that "A fitter Couple, sure, were never hatch'd / Some marri'd are, indeed, but we are match'd."[36]

The men's relationship continued after the 1728 *Dunciad* as the two men manipulated each other, prompting attacks, responses, and mutual notoriety. In a well-known example of his cunning, in 1735, Pope—using an anonymous middle-man—tricked Curll into buying a "collection" of his letters that contained his correspondence with peers. Curll advertised the impending publication of the letters and their peer-related contents, and was promptly arrested. Pope later used the self-generated publicity to sell his own authorized edition of the letters. Pope could be said to have "won" that round, since the appearance of Curll's five-volume edition provided Pope with the needed excuse to publish an authorized version of his own correspondence. Yet it remains equally potent that Pope needed the "unauthorized" version of his correspondence to justify his own self-congratulatory gesture of publication, another strategic discursive move to enhance his poetic persona. But Curll's representation of the two men's relationship within his edition provides an important postscript to the "dunce wars" and the men's respective effects on print culture. In *Volume Four of Mr. Pope's Literary Correspondence*, "An Essay on the Character of Mr. Curll," allegedly written by "A. Pope," claims Curll "carried his Trade many Lengths beyond what it ever before had arrived at, and that he was the Envy and Admiration of all his Profession."[37] To this passage Curll adds, "if he has carried the Art of Bookselling beyond all his Contemporaries, has not Mr. Pope done the same by the Art of Poetry" (149). The statement identifies the men as successful innovators who redefined their professions. In doing so, it elides the art of bookselling (commerce) and the art of poetry (literature). Booksellers, poets, publishers, and hack writers are, like bankers and stockjobbers, all tradesmen in a growing commercial space. Indeed James Ralph, in *The Case of Authors by Profession or Trade* (1758), defiantly asserts that the "writer who serves himself and the Public together, has as good a Right to the Product in Money of his Abilities, as the Landholder to his Rent, or the Money-Jobber to his Interest."[38]

Curll's publication of Pope's letters and the accompanying commentary support the traditional image of Curll as the opportunistic bookseller whose marketing savvy and unscrupulousness somehow made him a sort of parasite who profited from his consumption and reproduction of "real" literature. The "unspeakable Curll," as biographer Ralph Straus calls him, did manipulate or bribe the aristocracy and the clergy to lend their names and thus credibility to his publications. He exploited the hack writers by publishing their works for his financial gain while limiting their profits. He antagonized "elite" writers by pirating editions of their texts, composing keys to their popular works, or printing scandalous pamphlets attacking them personally or professionally. But this behavior, motivated primarily by a desire for fame and economic gain, allowed Curll to compete in and in a sense reshape the literary marketplace.

In many ways, however, Curll's actions replicated those of Pope, a man similarly interested in fame, status, and financial profit. Pope and Curll, each in his own way and for his own reasons, attempted to cast Grub Street and the more sweeping emergence of the print trade as a cultural site marked by oppositions, antagonism, and mutually exclusive categories. The more interesting and ultimately potent areas of that milieu exist in the margins, the seepage, the transgressions that define and empower the literary production of both men. Though Curll attempted to subvert the persona Pope so carefully constructed, he complicated rather than diminished it. He placed it more fully and accurately within the context and interactions of eighteenth-century literary production (a gesture comparable to that of modern literary scholars). While Pope's literary texts remain dominant, his sociopoetic persona and the modern subject lurking beneath grows ever more complex and unattainable. Does the poet himself become a subject of interest in this period because of that complexity, or is the complexity (which Pope to a certain degree attempted to obscure) revealed because of the interest? Does the cultural preoccupation with Pope prefigure the cult of celebrity with which we now live, or does his misshapen body, beautiful face, and marginalized social position cultivate a fascination that transcends the poetic? Certainly the culture in which Pope wrote was deeply figured by the contradictions and the social imbrications he explored.

Just as the tendency to read cultural relations with a hack/anti-hack mentality has dominated the literary history of the eighteenth century, a similarly binary reading of Pope as a subject emerges. A strain of scholarship sympathetic to Pope exists, as exemplified by someone like Maynard Mack: scholars who read Pope much in the way he presented himself in the *Epistle to*

Arbuthnot—as a besieged, morally superior poet writing for altruistic and often generous purposes. Others, like Pope's contemporary John Dennis or any number of modern scholars, read him as embittered, spiteful, and malicious—a poet whose work was fueled by personal vendetta as much as by a desire to produce "objective" social commentary. Obviously, neither "Pope" can accommodate the actual historical practice, motivation, and "intention" behind the poet (to which we will never have access). Did Pope resist those cultural forces he saw as threatening to his vision of literary and economic culture? Yes, as evidenced by his construction of those as corrupt, devalued, and feminized actions. Was he complicit in those cultural innovations, profiting from the apparatus of literary production and, in various ways, from the structures of the new financial order? Of course. And his marked and sustained involvement in the literary and financial spheres arguably fueled the compensatory antagonism with which he represented the dunces in both.

Ultimately, we must reconfigure the hierarchies and cultural relations that define eighteenth-century literary production. Pope, despite his association with the social and literary elite, suffered from his own marginality. His religion, his political beliefs, his physical condition, and of course his pen forced him into an uneasy situation where he, in a sense, continually had to earn his position, a position that could be terminated at any time (as demonstrated by his relationship with Lady Mary Wortley Montagu). Similarly, his relationships with colleagues like Swift were marked by a broader marginality, for both men battled the political and economic forces above them while resisting the competing energy of Grub Street below. Pope straddled the world of the elite and the popular, claiming the former as the rightful domain of the Virgilian model of his career, yet simultaneously exploiting the energy and opportunity of the latter.

"Consummatum Est": Alexander Pope's 1743 *Dunciad* and Mock-Apocalypse

THOMAS JEMIELITY

WHEN, AT THE CONCLUSION OF THE 1743 *DUNCIAD*, THE "GREAT Anarch . . . lets the curtain fall; / And Universal Darkness buries All" (4.655–56), Alexander Pope completes a formally designed mock-apocalypse that pervades the poem as a whole and that has been an integral informing principle of it even in its earliest versions in 1728 and 1729.[1] To my knowledge, however, Paul Korshin's *Typologies in England 1650–1820* (1982) is the only analysis to designate the form of Pope's poem as mock-apocalypse. After describing *The Dunciad* as "a shadowy prefiguration of a glorious antitype which . . . will arrive at some future time," Korshin, in a note, draws the reader's attention to Aubrey Williams's groundbreaking study of the poem, *Pope's Dunciad: A Study of Its Meaning* (1955). Apart from Williams, however, Korshin observes: "Most other studies of the poem virtually ignore Pope's apocalypse."[2] When I had earlier returned to that important, seminal, and now four-decades-old study of the poem, I had expected to find that my contribution in teaching *The Dunciad* as a mock-apocalypse was at best repetitive, however obscured over the years the point at which Williams ended and I began. Surprisingly, I discovered that while Williams is most certainly aware of many apocalyptic echoes in *The Dunciad* from Revelation, Daniel, and other biblical sources, he explicitly denies that Pope's religious inversions in *The Dunciad* embody some formal principle: "The inversions of Christian themes and situations in *The Dunciad*," he states, "cannot be said to function as a formal, precisely determinable 'structure.' " Even Paul Korshin, obviously sensitive to the mock-apocalyptic form of *The Dunciad*, describes "only the conclusion to Book 4" as "a parodic figural analogy to the Last Judgment."[3] Yet the dunces are summoned before the Throne of Dulness at the very start of Book 4 by "Fame's posterior Trumpet" (4.70), a ludicrous analogy to Gabriel's legendary summons, loud and, I assume, off-key.

166

In this essay I argue that Pope designed *The Dunciad* formally as a mock-apocalypse, that is, as an absurd mock-religious vision of the end of the world, and did so in a poem that, in any of its versions, anticipated and led up to the upside-down General Judgment finally achieved in Book 4. Like its principal biblical model, Pope's Book of Revelation presents the "salvation history" of the dunces in a Genesis-to-Revelation framework—first introduced in *The Dunciad* of 1728—that apes the same biblical panorama in the concluding book of the Christian scriptures. This mock-apocalyptic structure is not limited, consequently, to merely the end of Book 4 and its most explicitly absurd universal Judgment. The unresolved conclusion to Book 2, in every version of *The Dunciad*, for example, becomes a major parody of the conclusion Pope finally achieved in 1743. One parody prefigures a second. Astonishing indeed is the extent to which Pope captured so many features of the biblical picture of the dreaded *Dies Irae*, but here in a carnivalesque celebration of the finally triumphant forces of chaos. Like countless poets, composers, and painters, Alexander Pope was teased from even his earliest years with an imaginative vision of how the world would end. In all the versions of *The Dunciad*, indeed, with earlier hints in "On Silence" and "Messiah," Pope was teased by, flirted with, and expanded this theme, hilariously realized in the completed mock-apocalypse of *The Dunciad* of 1743. I am not unaware of the frequency with which "apocalyptic" and even "mock-apocalyptic" have been used adjectivally to describe at least some of Pope's final poem. But, in support of my central thesis, this essay provides a thorough, specific, and multifaceted answer to a basic question: What makes Pope's *Dunciad* formally a mock-apocalypse? This issue remains largely unexplored, despite the wealth of analysis about Pope's use of biblical typology in the poem.[4]

Let me pose the problem with two comparative examples. Pope's verse-letter on the use of riches, his *Epistle to Bathurst*, concludes with the witty, devastating, and very funny version of the Job story in the fortunes, misfortunes, and final damnation of Sir Balaam, a would-be success among the Cits. Yet no one would call Pope's sketch or the poem as a whole mock-apocalyptic. Mere use of biblical typology, however ludicrously done, does not constitute mock-apocalypse. To use a more general term I have found useful in denoting such use of religious and biblical material in satire, the sketch of Sir Balaam is mock-*biblical*.[5] So too is the mock-*prophetic* narrative John Dryden employs as the structure of *MacFlecknoe*. Providing an absurd correspondence among the Hebrew prophets, John the Baptist, and Jesus as Messiah, Dryden there gives us earlier bad writers as prophetic types, Richard Flecknoe as John, and, finally, Thomas Shadwell as the Messiah of Dulness—and this in a narrative that presents the Abbott-and-Costello team of this mock-biblical farce as Elisha receiving finally and impatiently the prophetic mantle of Elijah.[6] This is mock-prophetic narrative, certainly, studded with ludicrously used biblical typology, but it is hardly a mock-apocalypse. Again, mere ludicrous use of biblical typology does not create mock-apocalypse. What specifically then about Alexander Pope's *Dunciad* makes it a poem that not only relies extensively on our familiarity with satirically used religious and biblical material, but also makes that particular use not simply mock-biblical but, more specifically and generically, mock-apocalyptic?

Prophecy and Apocalypse

An important part of the answer to this question must begin with an awareness of the difference between prophecy and apocalypse as literary and biblical forms.[7] This awareness, however, becomes more complex when we realize that the common assumptions we bring to biblical texts as readers, and even as believers in the waning years of the twentieth century, often differ markedly from the assumptions Christian readers brought to those same texts in the eighteenth century. Typology in Pope's time was, as Korshin perceptively points out, "a method of decoding as well as a code, a science of exegesis as well as one of mysterious foreshadowing."[8] In this method and science of interpretation, the entirety of the Hebrew scriptures foreshadows and even predicts events in the Christian, and this foreshadowing is not limited to the canonical texts of the fifteen Hebrew prophets.[9] So, for example, while the prophet Isaiah's famous "A virgin shall conceive" (7:14) is believed to predict the birth of Jesus, so too Moses' forty-day-and-night fast with Yahweh in the desert, recorded in Exodus (34:28), a historical and legal text, foreshadows and predicts Jesus' forty-day stay in the desert prior to embarking on his public ministry (Matthew 4:1–2; Mark 1:12–13; Luke 4:1–2). The Hebrew scriptures as a whole and in endless detail promise fulfillment in the Christian scriptures. The Old predicts the New. Such a framework of interpretation allows any Hebrew text to be figurative and predictive regardless of form.

But in the Christian hermeneutic, among Catholics and Protestants alike, all that the Hebrew scriptures foreshadow and predict has not been fulfilled, of course. Christians still await the Second Coming of Christ as Judge to usher in a millennium that finally vindicates the elect. The Book of Revelation concludes the Christian scriptures with such a vindication, and assimilates to its purposes appropriate hints from the Book of Daniel, especially for the Son-of-Man figure and Jesus' discourses on the Last Days in the three synoptic gospels.[10] In the aftermath of the violent divisiveness engendered by the Protestant Reformation, the typology of what we now see as the apocalyptic writings in both scriptures is applied frequently, of course, to one's religious enemies. Those familiar with the abundant literature of post-Reformation polemic and millennial texts know that the Beast and the Whore of Babylon, to cite but two figures in John's Apocalypse, are very contemporary characters in the religious and religious-political controversies of the sixteenth and seventeenth centuries. As Paul Korshin points out:

> Of all the biblical prophecies the books of Daniel and Revelation affected views of secular history most profoundly. . . . The millennial prophecies would be intimately associated with contemporary eschatologies. With the assistance of impassioned pulpit oratory, the English public would be able to read Revelation in particular side by side with contemporary history. Events that boded ill could be seen as apocalyptic, as antitypes of the prefigurations in Scripture and, finally, as types themselves of a yet greater Millennium.[11]

When we turn, however, to the assumptions of contemporary biblical criticism, a strikingly different picture confronts us. Apart from schools of interpretation that insist on a literal reading of the biblical text—the contents of Bible mean exactly what a literal understanding would perceive them to mean— contemporary biblical scholarship admits considerable latitude in understanding these texts. Specifically, in the prophetic and apocalyptic texts important for understanding the rich dimensions of *The Dunciad*, present-day biblical scholars, apart from those literally inclined, deny any predictive element not only in the Hebrew scriptures as a whole but also in the texts of the fifteen canonical prophets. Indeed, on the few occasions when the canonical prophets do predict, their predictions frequently misfire badly.[12] In the case of apocalypse, the predictions are known to have been after the fact; apocalypse predicts accurately because the events it forecasts have already occurred.[13] The two most striking examples are the persecution of the Jews by Antiochus IV Epiphanes, the subject of the apocalyptic sections of Daniel, and the persecution of the Christians, perhaps under Domitian, which prompts the encouragement offered to Christians in the Book of Revelation.[14] So the text of Isaiah or the forty-day fast of Moses, at best, have liturgical and analogical appropriateness without any claim to their being predictive. Pope's use of apocalyptic features, consequently, as this essay notes in specific contexts, reflects both his perceptive, imaginative, and witty understanding of apocalypse in his own time, as well as the coincidental, uncanny, and presumably unconscious anticipations of apocalypse as modern biblical scholarship interprets it.

Very relevant, for example, to Alexander Pope's capturing of many features of apocalypse is his at least implicit awareness of the differing treatment of the future in prophecy and apocalypse. Succinctly, because its content is essentially criticism or judgment, Hebrew prophecy invariably presents the future as a consequence of present action, sometimes with uncanny perception. The prophetic position is basically, "This will happen so because of how you are acting now."[15] In apocalypse, the future is determined, not contingent. Something happens because God wills it so, and because God personally intervenes. The distresses of the elect are so severe that only irresistible divine intervention can remedy them. That intervention is determined and cannot be forestalled. Astonishing in Pope's *Dunciad* is the extent to which his poem has captured this feature, as well as many others, of biblical apocalypse, and in a manner that would satisfy the biblically aware of both his time and ours. In claiming generic identifiability for apocalypse, Bernard McGinn defines it so: " 'Apocalypse' is a genre of revelatory literature with a narrative framework, in which a revelation is mediated by an otherworldly being to a human recipient, disclosing a transcendent reality which is both temporal, in so far as it envisages eschatological salvation, and spatial, in so far as it involves another, supernatural world."[16]

The Dunciad as Mock-Apocalypse

What, then, are the apocalyptic features Pope introduced into *The Dunciad* so thoroughly and so well? I have no doubt that Pope consciously set out to use biblical apocalypse ludicrously in *The Dunciad*. First, although the basic situation of the last book—an assumed universal group of people assembled before a judge who determines their reward or punishment—has no parallel in classical literature, such a scene is not uncommon in Judeo-Christian apocalyptic: in Revelation, in Daniel, and in the discourses of Jesus on the end of time in gospels like Mark. In other words, Pope does not have available to him any paradigm except the Judeo-Christian for the scene he constructs in *Dunciad*, Book 4. Ovid's account of a destroying flood in the story of Baucis and Philemon, in the eighth book of the *Metamorphoses*, is more striking for its dissimilarities than for its likenesses. The catastrophe, first, is limited to a single town. The two elderly survivors are rewarded, not for a lifetime of virtue, but for an act of hospitality to disguised gods, whose inhospitable treatment from the other townspeople leads the divinities to destroy them with a flood. No universal, apocalyptic catastrophe here. Seneca's ridiculing treatment of the dead Emperor Claudius, refused entrance to Olympus by a pantheon embarrassed by this new claimant, shows little if any affinity with apocalypse.[17] *Dunciad*, Book 4 is filled with Pope's satiric inversions of this form of religious writing, the single most popular religious genre in the Near East for roughly two centuries on either side of the life of the historical Jesus, a genre that profoundly influenced the earliest Christian writings, canonical and otherwise. These writings in the Hebrew and Christian canon include not only Revelation and most of the last several chapters of Daniel (7–12), but also sections of the Hebrew prophets and the apocalyptic discourses of Jesus. Doubleday's 1983 publication, in the first volume of Old Testament pseudepigrapha, lists eighteen apocalypses and six testaments with apocalyptic sections, all noncanonical.[18]

Secondly, Pope fashioned a view of his late career that inadvertently captures and parallels a second feature of apocalypse: how it emerges in the third century B.C. in response to prophecy's failure to reinforce the hope that a call to ethically improved human action can advantageously influence the future. In Hebrew scriptures, apocalypse supplants prophecy. In Pope, apocalypse supplants satire. And if, as I have argued elsewhere, satire shares innumerable characteristics with prophecy because of their common content in criticism or judgment, then Pope, in biblical terms, abandons prophecy for apocalypse.[19] First, the biblical situation.

Canonical Hebrew prophecy spans roughly a four-century period, from the activity of Hosea and Amos in the mid-700s B.C. to that of the Deutero–Zechariah in the 300s B.C., at the latest. Its

most prolific and familiar period is from the mid-700s into the
mid-500s B.C., that is, from just before the fall of the Northern
kingdom (or Israel) in 721 B.C. to the fall of the Southern kingdom
(or Judah) in 587 B.C. and the Babylonian exile of two or three
generations that followed. The catastrophes that befell these divided remnants of the once-united kingdoms of David and Solo-
mon are interpreted by the prophets as punishments, collectively
suffered, for the sins of the Israelites and later of the Judahites.
The prophetic ethic necessarily assumes collective responsibility,
collective guilt, and, by implication, however feebly conveyed, the
possibility that a change in behavior can effect a change in God's
designs. Central to prophetic proclamation and judgment is the
conviction of a morally conditioned future: Such will happen because you are acting so now.

What weakens confidence in this prophetic assurance is, first,
the frequency of conflicting prophetic messages among the prophets of Yahweh. The encounter between Jeremiah and Hananiah,
both prophets of Yahweh, is but one such instance (Jeremiah 27–
29).[20] A second source of undermined confidence in the prophets
is the apparently undeserved fate, according to prophetic belief
and assumption, of a sincere reformer like King Josiah, a major
figure in what is now known as the Deuteronomic Reform. It is
clear that in the last years of the seventh century B.C., roughly
around 610 B.C., the Judahites undertook a thoroughgoing religious reform. Yet when Josiah went out to battle the Egyptians,
he was killed and ignominiously returned to Jerusalem with his
body sprawled across a donkey. Within twenty years, Jerusalem
was devastated, the Temple destroyed, the people in exile in Babylon, and the Davidic monarchy soon was extinguished. Reform
had not staved the wrath of Yahweh.[21] Thirdly, when after two or
three generations, those Jews who chose to do so returned to
what was left of Judah, what they found was painfully unlike the
promised glorious restoration spoken of by Second Isaiah (40–
55). By the time of Deutero–Zechariah (9–14), probably the last of
the fifteen canonical Hebrew prophets, prophecy was itself being
ridiculed in a prophetic text (13:2–6). The notion of a morally
conditioned future lost cogency. Neither reform nor sincerity had
altered God's designs. What was left? The emerging assurance of
apocalypse.

And here, Pope's *Dunciad* uncannily and coincidentally captures most salient characteristics of how the emerging religious
form of apocalypse supplants prophecy. In a note to *Dialogue II*,
the last poem, apart from *The Dunciad*, he completed, Pope an-

nounced he was giving up satire because it had proved hopeless: "Ridicule was become as unsafe as it was ineffectual." The poem, at best, is a protest "against that insuperable corruption and depravity of manners, which he had been so unhappy as to live to see."[22] If, as I have argued elsewhere, prophecy and satire share a most important common subject matter—judgment or criticism[23]—Pope, I assume unconsciously, was announcing the abandonment of his career as a prophet just a few years before consummating his most substantial venture into apocalypse. Living in a time of great trial for the artistically and morally elect, Pope claimed to have abandoned satire because no human agency could rectify wrong. His assumption reflects the central conviction of apocalypse that only God can provide deliverance.

Apocalypse, consequently, as a third characteristic, speaks to those in need of encouragement, to those confronted, like Pope, with "insuperable corruption and depravity of manners." In the history of Israel this was the fate of the Jews, from the fall of Jerusalem and the Babylonian Captivity in the sixth century B.C. through centuries of foreign domination, from the Persians and the Greeks, to the Romans, and for centuries after. It was, after all, only in A.D. 1948 that Israel again emerged as a sovereign, independent state, after two millennia of captivity and domination. In the irony of *The Dunciad*, of course, Cibber and the dunces are the ones who need reassurance.

How does apocalypse offer encouragement? This "lifting of the veil," which is what the term literally means in Greek, claims to know the inner or hidden meaning of history as God himself understands it. This meaning will be revealed to all through an imminent, irresistible divine intervention into human history. The future, unlike that in prophecy, is no longer conditional upon human action. The future has been determined. God himself will intervene; God himself will deliver—and that moment is at hand. The cosmic *deus ex machina* is waiting in the wings (or in the clouds).[24] However dreadful and violent the present moment, however discouraging and relentless for believers, their deliverance is at hand. They need only persevere.

The apocalyptist is, of course, privy to these divine designs. So he writes to encourage the faithful, as Cibber is himself encouraged in *Dunciad*, Book 1, despite initial despair, to remain true to the Dulness he had always served. Dulness herself, quasi-erotically, looks forward to the divine consummation, to this cosmic union of Sable Dulness with her Chosen Son:

O! when shall rise a Monarch all our own,
And I, a Nursing-mother, rock the throne,
'Twixt Prince and People close the Curtain draw,[25]
Shade him from Light, and cover him from Law;
Fatten the Courtier, starve the learned band,
And suckle Armies, and dry-nurse the land:
'Till Senates nod to Lullabies divine,
And all be sleep, as at an Ode of thine. (1.311–18)

Dulness's enemies, the enchained Arts and Sciences around her throne (4.21–44), are the goats, the reprobates in this upside-down apocalypse.

Here, as elsewhere in *The Dunciad*, Pope provides his own types and antitypes within the poem itself. The reference to the soporific effect of Cibber's odes foreshadows the universally soporific consequence of the Reading Contest in Book 2, which, in turn, foreshadows the silence that ends the poem. Illustrations that accompany William Warburton's edition of Pope's *Works* provide hilariously graphic images of this contest. In "Plate XXI" all are asleep, one dunce has his head propped up comfortably, using Blackmore's *Job* as a pillow, and Dulness herself, with her head thrown back and her mouth open, is obviously in what my students would call a "deep zonk."[26]

In "A Mock-Biblical Controversy: Sir Richard Blackmore and *The Dunciad*," I argue that the Reading Contest in Book 2, which ends with all the contestants and audience asleep, prefigures the apocalyptic silence that concludes the poem. Given the prominence of Sir Richard Blackmore's *Job* as the poetic ordeal in this early Olympic competition, I argue as well that Blackmore, well known as an enemy of Wit and the Wits, might be the intended but unsuccessful winner of this trial and thus in line to become "Judge of all present, past, and future wit" (2.376). But in Pope's joke, Blackmore, overcome by his own poetry, fails to achieve this distinction as a Daniel-like Judge, because everyone, himself included, falls fast asleep. The apocalypse is put on hold, until Book 4, where Dulness, who "was Pertness once" (1.112), herself assumes the responsibility. As a central incident in all versions of *The Dunciad*, this apocalyptic foreshadowing of the Judgment finally accomplished in 1742 and 1743 provides major evidence of Pope's creative flirtation with a mock-apocalypse in *The Dunciad* from its very first version in 1728.[27]

Fourthly, an air of mystery surrounds apocalypse. Alluding to Milton's invocation to Light in *Paradise Lost*, Pope prays, "Of

Plate XXI.

Vol. V. facing p. 121.

F. Hayman inv. et del.

C. Grignion sculp.

And now to this Side, now to that, they nod,
As Verse or Prose infuse the drowsy God.

Dunciad. Book II.

The end of the Reading Contest.

darkness visible so much be lent, / As half to shew, half veil the
deep Intent" (4.3–4). Apocalypse is mysterious because it is intended for the select few, the elect who can understand God's unfolding purposes. The pseudonymity characteristic of apocalypse
is not a feature of Pope's inversion, perhaps because of the widespread assumption in Pope's time that biblical writings were actually authored by those to whom they are attributed. But offered
is a revelation that fulfills promises of long ago. Alchemizing the
precious metals of the Book of Revelation, *The Dunciad* celebrates the hatching of a "new Saturnian age of lead" (1.28) to
replace and improve the old one.

Daniel affords a fine example of this apocalyptic convention of
opportune discovery. The apocalypse was written in the 160s B.C.,
but was set back in the time of the Babylonian captivity, that is,
into sixth-century-B.C. history, about which the Book of Daniel
makes innumerable errors. In the fiction of apocalypse, however,
Daniel is given this revelation centuries before the present distress,
so his lifting of the veil of history can be revealed at a most opportune time for the distressed, that is, in the middle of the second
century B.C.. This same fiction of an earlier composition revealed
now at an opportune moment for the distressed faithful appears
in Revelation, in the apocalyptic sections of Mark, and, to some
extent, in *The Dunciad*. Cibber, after all, is the one foretold of
ancient times. If he was foretold, and is now, then apocalyptic deliverance is at hand. Apocalypse thus pretends to be a much earlier prediction, very specific in its forecast, that anticipates
exactly what is going on today. In this specificity and accuracy of
prediction (accurate because it is after the fact), apocalypse dif-
fers radically from prophecy, in which prediction plays no significant role. In his use of typology, Pope seems to accept the
common eighteenth-century assumption among Christians—not
widely held even among contemporary Catholic biblical scholars—that the Hebrew scriptures do foretell events to be accomplished in the life of Christ.

Apocalypse, furthermore, deals in dualities: good versus bad,
anti-Christ versus Christ, Dulness versus Light. No middle
ground is available. Courage is the order of the day. A grand new
time of redemption, vindication, and triumph is at hand. The veil
will be fully lifted, and everyone and everything will be seen finally for what they are. In a poem that celebrates the undoing of
God's creative act, which, in Genesis, is the spoken Word, how
appropriate it is that the dunces, on their way to the Paradise
that awaits them, are given the prelapsarian gift and forecast of

"Want of Shame." Whatever they do, whatever coarseness in which they vie, whatever foolishness they proclaim, "they are stupid, and they feel no shame": Adam and Eve in a Garden of Fools.

How do the dunces, for example, respond to the presence of Dulness? Spontaneously. An inward impulse enables them to recognize themselves for what they are and to respond unhesitatingly to any summons from Dulness: to the games in Book 2 or to her throne in Book 4. This spontaneity and excitement, a very apocalypse-like response to the imminence of final vindication, pervades *The Dunciad*. Throughout Book 1 Cibber never once questions that he is a dunce. The Argument to Book 4 reinforces this pervasive sense of never-doubted dunce-like self-identity: *"All her Children, by a wonderful attraction, are drawn about her; and bear along with them divers others, who promote her Empire. . . . All these crowd round her"* (547; original italics). After "Fame's posterior Trumpet" summons "all the Nations . . . to the Throne":

> The young, the old, who feel her inward sway,
> One instinct seizes, and transports away.
> None need a guide, by sure Attraction led,
> And strong impulsive gravity of Head:
> None want a place, for all their Centre found,
> Hung to the Goddess, and coher'd around.
> Not closer, orb in orb, are seen
> The buzzing Bees about their dusky Queen.
> The gath'ring number, as it moves along,
> Involves a vast involuntary throng,
> Who gently drawn, and struggling less and less,
> Roll in her Vortex, and her pow'r confess. (4.71–84)

As Jesus says in Matthew, "And he shall send his angels with a trumpet and a great voice and they shall gather together his elect from the four winds, from the farthest parts of the heavens to the utmost bounds of them. . . . So you also, when you shall see these things, know ye that it is nigh, even at the doors" (24: 31, 33, Rheims NT). In the Argument to Book 2, we read: "Hither flock the Poets and Critics . . ." (495). No one sits out the General Judgment. The dunces come to romp and play in the fecal fields: "The shudder in [their] loins engenders there," not "Agamemnon dead" but the final, triumphant progeny of Dulness.

This impulsive, inward, knowing, yet involuntary, response provides a recognizable, recurring quality to the dunces' activi-

ties in the poem. Innocent in their shameless prelapsarian spontaneity, they are eager: winner in the Phantom Poet Contest,
Curll "stretch'd his eager hand" (2.109). As the mobs continue to
surge near her throne: "Now crowds on crowds around the Goddess press, / Each eager to present the first Address" (4.135–136).
In seeking her divine sentence, the Flower Collector and the But-
terfly Collector appeal to her throne "with earnest zeal, / And aspect ardent" (4.401–402). Earlier, as Dulness finishes her
fashioning of the phantom poet, "All gaze with ardour . . ." (2.51).
In Book 1, Cibber describes himself as "desp'rate in my zeal"
(1.209). Just as the prodigal Cotta in Pope's *Epistle to Bathurst*
uses his patriotism to rationalize ridiculously excessive expenditure—"Zeal for that great House [of Brunswick] which eats him
up" (l. 208)—so throughout *The Dunciad* Swiftian zeal and enthusiasm for Dulness's house eat up the dunces. They come prepared for any event, for their entire lives and careers have
awaited this moment: "With ready quills the Dedicators wait;
/ . . . And, instant, fancy feels th' imputed sense . . ." (2.198, 200).
Freed from restraint, they compete and vie for honors furiously
without any need hypocritically to pay even lip service to civilized
values because the veil has been lifted. The dunces gladly accept
themselves for what they are. Possessed by a god, theirs is the
Dulness-inspired frenzy, the shameless delight of unaware, irrational children.[28]

The games of Book 2 demonstrate the thoroughness with
which Pope captured this particular apocalyptic feature of enthusiastic behavior in his dunces. "Herald Hawkers . . . summon all
her Race: An endless band / Pours forth, and leaves unpeopled
half the land" (2.18–20).[29] Stationers, like authors, "obey'd the
call" (2.31). "Dauntless Curl" accepts the challenge of the Phantom Poet at once (2.88). Then, striving to be a two-letter varsity
athlete, Curll challenges Osborne in "the glorious strife" of the
Urinating Contest (2.167), which "all follow with their eyes"
(2.185).[30] Though a loser, Osborne walks contentedly home ("In
my Father's house there are many mansions" [John 14:2, Rheims
NT]). Leonard Welsted "strives" (2.208) in a competition in
which the "ready quills" and "instant fancy" of the competing
ticklers have already been noted. In the Sewage Diving Contest,
Dulness urges her Olympians: "here at once leap in" (2.275).
Concanen perseveres, but finds himself outshone when "Next
plung'd a feeble, but a desp'rate pack" (2.301, 305). Of "bold Ar-
nall," we read: "Furious he dives, precipitately dull" (2.315, 316).
As the locale of the various contests shifts, the mob continues its

impetuous and impulsive movement through the streets (2.359–62). Finally, of course, the works of the dunces spontaneously, inevitably reduce all to slumber.[31]

The activities of the Goddess and her sons and daughters have an apocalyptic excitement about them. The dunces are about to be eternally vindicated. Dulness will regain her Paradise. Their ardor, zeal, and excitement convey a beatific quality to their expectations and activities. "Raptures . . . overflow" Cibber's head (3.5). His vision brings him joy, the beatific emotion par excellence, especially associated with the sight and possession of the divine: "Joy fills his soul, joy innocent of thought; / What pow'r, he cries, what pow'r these wonders wrought?" (3.249–50). The universality and immediacy of the response to Dulness provide a thoroughgoing apocalyptic quality to the poem, which reaches its climax, of course, in Book 4, where all come, all follow and dispute with interest, all seek their rewards, and all succumb to the yawn of Dulness. Pope has gathered us at the Valley of Jehosophat in a coming together he has planned since the first version of *The Dunciad* in 1728. Indeed, the final *Dunciad* is the mammoth expansion of a theme that intrigued him, he said, as early as his mid-teens.

From Silence to Silence

Alexander Pope "consistently asserted," so the Twickenham editors claim, that his poem "On Silence," written in imitation of Rochester's "Upon Nothing," was composed when the poet was in his mid-teens.

> Silence [Pope begins]! Coeval with Eternity;
> Thou wert, e're Nature's self began to be,
> 'Twas one vast Nothing, All, and All slept fast in thee.
> Thine was the Sway, e'er Heav'n was form'd or Earth,
> E'er fruitful *Thought* conceiv'd Creation's Birth,
> Or Midwife *Word* gave aid, and spoke the Infant forth. (1–6)

Several stanzas later, Pope concludes:

> The Parson's Cant, the Lawyer's Sophistry,
> Lord's Quibble, Critick's Jest; all end in thee,
> All rest in Peace at last, and sleep eternally. (40–42)[32]

With the Genesis-to-Revelation framework of the 1743 *Dunciad* inchoately present, the young Pope also flirts here, and satirically, with three themes and symbols, as I will discuss later, so central to the substance of *The Dunciad*: Silence, Creation, and Word. How delightful it would be to have the assurance that Pope was, indeed, fourteen or fifteen when, in "On Silence," he envisioned the mock-celebration of triumphant apocalyptic silence that closed his career three decades later.

What we do know is that "On Silence" was published by the time Pope was twenty-four, in 1712, the same year in which he published "Messiah." Taken out of context, only four lines of many from "Messiah" can, with no change at all, be appropriately fitted into *The Dunciad*. Simply consider these Isaian–Virgilian messianic and apocalyptic themes through the spectacles of *The Dunciad*:

> The Saviour comes! by ancient Bards foretold!
> Hear him ye deaf, and all ye Blind behold!
> He from thick Films shall purge the visual Ray,
> And on the sightless Eye-ball pour the Day. (37–40)[33]

The millennium, after all, effects the paradoxes central to religious belief and mystery. An apocalyptic section of Isaiah (34–35)—the one William Blake refers to in the opening section of his *Marriage of Heaven and Hell*—provides a characteristic instance of these biblically familiar contraries:

> The land that was desolate and impassable shall be glad, and the wilderness shall rejoice, and shall flourish like the lily. . . . Then shall the eyes of the blind be opened, and the ears of the deaf shall be unstopped. Then shall the lame man leap as a hart, and the tongue of the dumb shall be free: for waters are broken out in the desert, and streams in the wilderness. And that which was dry land, shall become a pool, and the thirsty land springs of water. In the dens where dragons dwelt before, shall rise up the verdure of the reed and the bulrush. . . . No lion shall be there, nor shall any mischievous beast go up by it, nor be found there: but they shall walk there that shall be delivered. And the redeemed of the Lord shall return, and shall come into Sion with praise, and everlasting joy shall be upon their heads: they shall obtain joy and gladness, and sorrow and mourning shall flee away. (Isaias 35:1, 5–7, 9–10, Douai OT)[34]

In *The Dunciad*, Dulness views these Isaiah-like types in the achievements of the Cibberian stage, where

. . . Tragedy and Comedy embrace;
. . . Farce and Epic get a jumbled race;
. . . Time himself stands still at her command,
Realms shift their place, and Ocean turns to land.
Here gay Description Aegypt glads with show'rs,
Or gives to Zembla fruits, to Barca flow'rs;
Glitt'ring with ice here hoary hills are seen,
There painted vallies of eternal green,
In cold December fragrant chaplets blow,
And heavy harvests nod beneath the snow. (1.69–78)

Dunces, like saints, inhabit an eternity of oxymoronically apocalyptic delights.

Korshin describes *The Dunciad* as "a shadowy prefiguration of a glorious antitype which . . . will arrive at some future time."[35] *The Dunciad*, in its ironic celebration of Dulness, is a comedy because it assures the dunces of their final vindication and provides for them the satisfying ending of comedy, which Northrop Frye epitomizes in the reaction: "This should be."[36]

Apocalypse, it is well to recall, was the single most popular form of religious writing in the Holy Land during the three-century intertestamental period that began early in the second century B.C. and that exercised a profound influence on the emerging Christian canon, for example, on the way the Gospel of Mark read the character and mission of Jesus. Its highly symbolic, visionary treatment of what theologians today call the end-time announces an imminent divine intervention that will vindicate the elect if only they remain steadfast through the catastrophes and persecutions that are tangible signs of just how soon the divine will rectify the earthly. Remain steadfast, apocalypse urges; deliverance is at hand. This ineluctable divine triumph, wholly impervious to human will or action, reveals for once and all the meaning of history, the divine plan that has guided all human activity, all human history all along. Apocalypse, true to its name, thus lifts the veil from the hitherto shrouded understanding of divine intention. And the agent of this revelation, the instrument of interpretation, is the apocalyptic writer himself. As the sole instance of apocalypse in the Christian canon, Revelation provides the finally delightful resolution to the comedy, which, Northrop Frye reminds us, is the Christian Bible as a whole.[37] The distresses of the elect end, the threatening monsters are conquered, marriage—a conventional ending in comedy—announces a new beginning, and a universe of loyal guests follows the Lamb and the

New Jerusalem into just-beginning and never-ending felicity. Apocalypse closes, but also opens; it ends, but it also begins.[38]

But in *The Great Code*, the first of his two books on the Bible and literature, Frye also reminds us that Revelation is a deliberately allusive work using many, many echoes of the Hebrew scriptures in particular to underscore its central conviction that Jesus' coming as Judge ends human history, provides history its real meaning, and ushers in a phase of unimaginable bliss for the elect. The interrupted promise of Genesis thus lies at the root of an alchemy that finally transforms the Garden of Eden into the mineral-rich New Jerusalem. "A mosaic of allusions to the Old Testament," Frye calls Revelation, in "a vision of . . . primarily the true meaning of the Scriptures."[39] In his 1968 study of the Gospel of Matthew's use of the Hebrew scriptures, Krister Stendahl cites Revelation as one of these biblical texts "abounding in allusions." Indeed, he continues: "Without a single true quotation, [Revelation] is nevertheless interwoven with O[ld] T[estament] material to a greater extent than any other writing in the N[ew] T[estament]."[40]

This allusive, rather than directly quoted, technique characteristic of biblical writing generally holds true for Pope's *Dunciad*, which, in this regard as in many others, captures—at least coincidentally—a number of the external and internal features of apocalypse.[41] With its added last book, *The Dunciad* becomes, indeed, a mini-Bible, with an extensive and in a way breathtaking panorama of a salvation history the Christian Bible also claims to be. Biblical typology, furthermore, creates a situation in which any single allusion, incident, reference, or the like necessarily calls others to mind at the same time, a wealth of simultaneous reference.

The Salvation History of the Dunces

Of great significance, however, is how the Apocalypse of John the Apostle provides Pope with the apocalyptic structure that all versions of *The Dunciad*, most, of course, its final form, display. In a framework that moves from the upside-down Creation hints at the beginning of the poem to the triumph of apocalyptic darkness at the end, Pope's mock-apocalypse captures the basic premise of belief that underscores the Apocalypse of John the Apostle, as the Book of Revelation is called in the Rheims New Testament and in later Roman-Catholic English versions well into the mid-

dle of the twentieth century. The Apocalypse embodies the deliberately stylized attempt of the apocalyptic writer or writers of
Revelation to reinforce the central conviction of this admittedly
weird and even violent conclusion to the scriptures as a whole:
viz., that Jesus fulfills salvation history. His Second Coming in
triumph realizes all the promises of scripture and takes the elect
into the New Jerusalem. This city of incalculable riches and enjoyment replaces the riches and enjoyment of the Garden lost to
humankind in the man and the woman who embodied the human
race as a whole at Creation. In this religiously colonial appropriation and assimilation of the earlier Hebrew scriptures as well as
their later Christian equivalents, the apocalyptist does not follow
the roughly chronological order of the two scriptures—from Creation, through Exodus, into the Kingdom of Israel and its later
captivity in Babylon, to the redeeming life of Jesus, and, at last,
the promised restoration of bliss at the end of history. Rather, the
Apocalypse of John introduces this intra-Genesis-to-Revelation
material, as it might be termed, in whatever manner and at whatever point suits the apocalyptic text at hand. The religious and
theological anatomy of salvation history, as Northrop Frye might
call it, provides thus considerable flexibility for the apocalyptic
writer.

Alexander Pope's mock-inversion of this framework and anatomy provides him with a comparable flexibility in *The Dunciad*.
The poem's pervasive use of biblical material makes no attempt
to follow the roughly chronological pattern of its biblical source
within the mock Genesis-to-Revelation pattern. For example, although the apocalyptic visions of the Book of Daniel provide a
conclusion of sorts to salvation history for the Jews, Christian
scripture transfers that finish to the apocalyptic discourses of
Jesus in the Gospels as a foreshadowing of the historical completion to come, symbolically described and achieved in the Book of
Revelation. So too, the apocalyptic conclusion that remains unful-
filled at the ends of Books 2 and 3 in any version of *The Dunciad*
is achieved only at the conclusion of Book 4 in 1743.[42]

So in Pope's *Dunciad* we are with the Creator at the very beginning and likewise with the Word (1:1–16). We witness the Last
Judgment (Book 4). The Urinating Contest that splashes the by-
standers harmlessly recalls the rainbow of Genesis and the bap-
tism of Jesus with a different Jordan (2.157–90). No one, by the
way, seems to have suggested that a "Jordan" (2.190), certainly
a chamberpot, can also be a biblical river, here a yellow one. For
an entire book (3), we descend into Shadwell's Bosom, not Abra-

ham's, where the dearly departed dull await the harrowing of the messianic Cibber: "He descended into hell." An Exodus-like pillar of cloud announces divine presence in the desert of Cibber's despair (1.257–72), and later Dulness anoints him king in a rite simultaneously Hebrew–Davidic and Christian–Messianic (1.287–310). King Cibber enters London–Jerusalem to the triumphant echoes of Psalm 44, a key feature of the Palm Sunday liturgy (1.301–10). Cibber's near-one-hundred-line prayer to Dulness, "Great Tamer of All Human Art," captures the hymnology of the Psalter (1.163–242)[43] and alludes later, in that same prayer, to one of the most famous items among the Psalms, David's so-called *"Miserere,"* Psalm 51: "O born in sin, and forth in folly brought! / Works damn'd, or to be damn'd! (your father's fault)" (1.225–26)[44]—Cibber as repentant David. The unmartyred faithful among the dull are "confessors," that Catholic liturgical term for saints whose witness to Christ is a lifetime of service rather than a shedding of blood (2.146). We witness the Moses-like vision from Pisgah, which is also Book 3 and which explicitly draws attention to Adam's vision of salvation history in Books 11 and 12 of *Paradise Lost.*[45] Cibber and Dulness, as Williams points out,[46] obscenely parody Madonna and Child (3.1–6): Cibber is in the lap of Dulness for Books 3 and 4. Behind this, I assume, is Milton's obscene, incestuous parody of Satan, Sin, and Death in Book 1 of *Paradise Lost*, here suggesting an incestuous relationship between Cibber and Dulness. If so, Pope has provided us with a ludicrously fulfilled kinky coition that resolves the *coitus interruptus* imaginatively hinted at in the Genesis story of the Fall of the first man and the first woman (1.265–72).[47] Immediately prominent in *The Dunciad* is the Temple (1.265–73), an edifice whose building, rebuilding, and destruction is central to both scriptures. Throughout Book 3, Dulness recalls earlier triumphs of her chosen dull, now on their way to imminent, never-ending success. The prophetic tradition and its typological assimilation into the Christian scriptures pervade *The Dunciad*. In a Eucharist-like ritual, a cup of oblivion is passed around, where, as in the sacrament, a new identity is achieved (4.517–28). The illustration preceding Book 4 of *The Dunciad* in Warburton's edition shows the priest clearly garbed in a Roman-Catholic–like chasuble and standing before a chalice.[48] A priest-chef presides over the transubstantiation of hallucinogenic cuisine (4.549–64). Given the imminence of Dulness's triumph, this is her Last Supper. Dulness pronounces her universal missionary command to make dunces of all nations (4.579–604). Then, in a stunning

F. Hayman inv. et del.   *C. Grignion Sculp.*

Then blessing all, Go Children of my Care!
To Practice now from Theory repair. —
All my Commands are easy, short and full,
My Sons be proud, be selfish, and be dull.

                                Dunciad, Book IV.

A Priest in Chasuble and with Chalice Watches as Dulness confers her Blessing.

blackout scene like that which pitched Manhattan Island into darkness quite a number of years ago, Creation's first command is reversed as light after light inexorably goes out, the city falls into darkness, and Dulness witnesses the triumph of silence and night at her Second Coming: "Thy hand, great Anarch! lets the curtain fall; / And Universal Darkness buries All" (4.655–56).

This astonishingly extensive biblical panorama appears, as I said earlier, within a Genesis-to-Revelation framework, the Genesis part of which pervades the eighteen lines or three verse paragraphs that open the 1743 *Dunciad* and appear likewise in the opening sixteen lines of the 1728 and 1729 versions of the poem. The first two-and-a-half lines announce the imminent accomplishment of the dark mysteries in Book 4, when the "Smithfield Muses" actually appear at "the ear of Kings," at the Temple/ Court where the action of Book 4 occurs. At its outset, thus, the poem apocalyptically proclaims Daniel's sign of the end-time: "And there shall be in the temple the abomination of desolation" (9:27, Douai OT). As she awaits this universal anti-birth, Dulness pours out her anti-creative, anti-Pentecostal spirit and bids "Britannia sleep" (1.7). Her unholy Ghost dispenses with the need for tongues: there will be no Word. Indeed, the very next line—"In eldest time, e'er mortals writ or read" (9)—takes us back to a time before literacy. In the beginning, or, if you prefer, before the beginning, there was no Word.

"Light Dies Before Thy Uncreating Word"

In the background of these lines are the first Creation account of Genesis (1:1–2:4a) and the very abstract statement of Creation and divine relationship that begins the Gospel of John (1:1–18). Dulness, Pope claims, initially reigned before Words, in Chaos and Night, the antitheses of Creation's Order and Light. Her reign ended with God's creative Word: "Let there be Light." Pope subtly reminds us that God's creative activity was solely and uniquely to speak, and to speak a supremely efficacious Word: "And God said," and it was so—the "midwife *Word*," Pope called it in "On Silence," that "spoke the Infant [Creation] forth." Word in its manifold richness is thus Pope's central theme, concern, image, and symbol, the expression of all that brings into being the unbounded richness, variety, and dynamism of creation threatened by all those who abuse the Word. The hints of Genesis and John in this three-paragraph introduction draw on Hebraic and Hellenic traditions of the Word.

For the Hebrews, Words are powerful, dynamic, and efficacious. The prophet's Word, as scripture scholar Johannes Lindblom points out, "is charged with energy and power, . . . effective and creative, . . . [a] spoken Word [that] was also a deed."[49] At the very beginning, with his life-infusing, hen-like spirit brooding over the dark waters,[50] God's Word irrevocably shatters the formless, dark, silent reign of Chaos and Night—or almost irrevocably, as Pope soon reminds us. Characteristically, the Words of the dunces are sluggish, torpid, abrasive, miscarrying in their effects. Noise, din, and bellowing replace harmony, energy, and power: Kurt Vonnegut's "busy, busy, busy," frenetic, time-consuming, but finally purposeless, activity.

For John, in the Hellenized prologue to his gospel, the Word is a supremely intellectual artifact, at its best the perfect expression of an idea that itself conforms to the real. And this triangle of correspondence becomes the divine nature expressed in: "In the beginning was the Word, and the Word was with God, and the Word was God" (1:1). What is expressed corresponds perfectly with what is thought. And so the Jesus who tells his disciples, fittingly, also in John's Gospel, "He that seeth me seeth the Father also" (14:9, Rheims NT), finds his perfect symbolic expression as personified Word. The Genesis Creation account reinforces this sense of Word by reminding us that Words distinguish, identify, separate, signify: what is light is not darkness; earth, not sea; animal, not human; good, not bad.

When the dunces speak, however, they blur: the magus of Book 4 offers loss of human identity in his potion (4.517–28); in the Cave of Poverty and Poetry, "nameless Somethings in their causes sleep" (1.56); masses are called forth: "hints, like spawn, scarce quick in embryo lie" (1.59); "Maggots half-form'd in rhyme exactly meet, / And learn to crawl upon poetic feet" (1.61–62). The Cave is a snug, miscarrying womb of "motley Images" (1.64), of the "jumbled race" of Farce and Epic (1.69)—a haven of dramatic and literary monstrosities that defies the power of Words to name. The distinction, discrimination, and identification that was God's Creation is inexorably overturned in a poem that returns us, if you like, to Genesis-minus-one. To abuse the Word is finally to undo Creation.

This three-paragraph introduction closes with a succinct, terrifying reminder: "Still her old Empire to restore she tries, / For, born a Goddess, Dulness never dies" (1.17–18). Here is Pope's re-

minder of the cultural death-wish, the warning reinforced elsewhere in the poem, that civilization is not a given. If Aquinas,
among others, testifies to an instinct for self-preservation and
Freud to one of self-extinction, these polarities, Pope insists, op-
erate collectively as well. To tamper with the Word is to threaten
civilization, frivolously to play a Dr. Strangelove-like game of
"Let's try it and see what happens." The Genesis and Johannine
hints of Pope's opening eighteen lines in the 1743 *Dunciad* are an
integral part of the Word-versus-Anti-Word dialectic that governs
the movement of the history within the poem as the dunces
march insouciantly forward to their millennium of dark, silent,
and formless delights: "Eye hath not seen, nor ear heard, neither
hath it entered into the heart of man what things [Dulness] hath
prepared for them that love [her]" (1 Cor. 2:9). Amen.

"Writing Nonsense": Pope, Rabelais, and the Fair

CLAUDIA N. THOMAS

I

IN *THE POLITICS AND POETICS OF TRANSGRESSION*, PETER STALLY-brass and the late Allon White sketch a broad view of the relationships among the literary profession, the carnival, and the refinement of middle-class manners in the eighteenth century.[1] In this essay, I build on their necessarily brief discussion of Alexander Pope's *Dunciad*, further considering the poem's Rabelaisian qualities. By "Rabelaisian," I mean the imagery and purpose of the Renaissance satirist as Pope understood them. I propose that Pope's poem is more "Rabelaisian" than either Stallybrass and White's analysis suggests or than Mikhail Bakhtin's theory of the carnivalesque accommodates. I attempt to distinguish in my argument between the historical evolution of popular amusements and their use as metaphor, a distinction that Bakhtin as well as Stallybrass and White somewhat elide. My essay concludes by contrasting Pope's carnival imagery in *The Dunciad* with his positive image of marketplace activities in the *Epistle to Lord Bathurst*, a wistful metaphor for the cultural hierarchy he desired, but feared would never be established.

Pope's poem, despite his prophetic pretension, did not accurately predict the historical process by which popular amusements became middle-class amusements. Pope and his conservative allies warned against the dangers to middle and upper ranks of mingling with the lower sort in their pastimes. *The Dunciad* imagines this trend spreading from amusements into all aspects of civic life, making "one mighty Dunciad of the land!" In pastimes, professions, and politics, Pope foresaw a "motley mixture" of high and low. In some ways, his vision seems startlingly apt, when one views, for example, a modern political campaign. Conversely, many plebeian pastimes have metamor-

189

phosed into middle- or upper-class events. Today, middle-class people do not merely "slum it" by occasional visits to local fairs and carnivals: they are the chief participants in modern versions of these activities. The poor can ill afford to frequent the giant amusement parks, urban "festival marketplaces," and ballparks that are the current incarnations of plebeian holiday sites. No longer sponsored by the church or benevolent landowners, these attractions are run by governments or corporations for profit as well as mass diversion. But when the tour buses and BMWs roll away from, for example, a municipal stadium, the nearby poor retain variants of other immemorial amusements. Empty lots have replaced the village greens; block parties or church suppers, the holiday feasts. On the sinister side, drug dealers and armed gangs have replaced alehouses and cudgel-wielding mobs. Despite the pronouncements of Robert Malcolmson and others, plebeian amusements have not disappeared.

And, contrary to analyses such as Stallybrass and White's and Terry Eagleton's,[2] the middle class has never learned to forego the pleasures of an outdoor crowd. Pope's masterpiece did little to disturb these ongoing pastimes, let alone halt literature's eventual integration into an "entertainment industry." Pope's achievement lies not in any literal outcome, of course, much as he may have hoped to wreck his enemies' careers and dissuade readers from attending operas or fairs. Rather, he created a Rabelaisian fantasy so astutely realized that his enemies were almost helpless to respond. Whether assuming with Pope a degenerate culture or denying his allegations, they were forced to cope with Pope's fiction. Engaging Pope's fictional carnival proved for many to be like entering a funhouse with no exit: despite their protests, they were returned again and again to the poem and its proliferating footnotes. Although Bakhtin would have found Pope's assumptions about Rabelais contrary to his own in their monologia and physical phobia,[3] Pope's *Dunciad* fulfilled the mythic potential of carnival latent in seventeenth- and early eighteenth-century writings. Building on more than a century of negative associations, Pope immersed himself, his victims, and his readers in pungent carnival metaphors.

Stallybrass and White distinguish their project from the overly idealistic theory of carnival proposed by Mikhail Bakhtin (19). Recognizing that carnival was probably never the pure expression of popular vitality that Bakhtin describes, they examine instead the politics of carnival, its manipulation as both specific ritual and as metaphor. Bakhtin discerns in Rabelais the creator of a genuinely carnivalized literary text, a feat not duplicated until the novels of Dostoevsky. These two writers exemplified for Bakhtin his theory of carnival's liberating function. Early eighteenth-century writers, however, had diverse conceptions of Rabelais compatible with their views of cultural and literary history. To Jonathan Swift, Rabelais appeared a precursor, exposing hypocrisy and castigating human pride. Rabelais's influence is manifest not only in Swift's "excremental" imagery but in the fantastic, scandalous, and mixed-generic nature of his texts.[4] To Pope, Rabelais's imprecision reduced his value as a satiric predecessor. Disappointed by Rabelais's obscurity, Pope sought in *Gargantua and Pantagruel* the same kind of sustained analogy that made keys or Scriblerian notes indispensable to much contemporary satire. "Everybody allows that there are several things without any manner of [design or] meaning in his *Pantagruel*," Pope observed to Joseph Spence in 1738. "Dr. Swift likes it much, and thinks there are more good things in it than I do" (Spence, 1:218).[5] Probably encouraged to elaborate by Spence, Pope illustrated his complaint: Rabelais's "concealed characters are touched only in parts, and by fits—as, for example, though the King's mistress be meant in such a particular related of Gargantua's mare, the very next thing perhaps that is said of the mare will not at all agree with the mistress" (1:218). Where Bakhtin discovered exuberance and plenitude, or Swift multiple strategies for revealing human folly, Pope vainly sought a coherent satiric purpose.

Pope's remark, however, reflects eighteenth-century satiric preferences. Four years before Pope's conversation with Spence, Voltaire had remarked in his *Philosophical Letters* that Rabelais "was a drunken philosopher who only wrote when he was drunk." Voltaire also accused Rabelais of writing "volumes of rubbish" for every two good pages, before praising Swift as "a sensible Rabelais living in civilized society."[6] Kinder than Voltaire although equally bound by contemporary assumptions, Pope believed that Rabelais had at least intended consistency in his writings although incapable of sustaining his satiric allegory. Swift, whose taste was formed during the Restoration—when harsh and even obscene satire emanated from courtly circles— was much more capable of appreciating Rabelais's methods. Just as Bakhtin found in Rabelais a vehicle for subtly anti-Stalinist argument, Swift found a model for Christian satire of *vanitas*. Pope, born a generation after Swift, found merely a crude forebear in need of refinement. Similar to his estimates of Homer,

Chaucer, Shakespeare, and Donne, Pope viewed in Rabelais another writer from a less fastidious era, whose genius was obscured by lapses into vulgarity and incoherence. Pope chose to rescue the four previous writers by translating, editing, or paraphrasing until each appeared more worthy of fastidious modern readers. He removed the worst grossness or, at least, clarified the author's purpose. In *The Dunciad*, Pope followed a different strategy. He adopted what he considered the crude satirical manner of Rabelais, but incorporated it into a recognizable allegory regarding the literary, now metamorphosed into the carnival, marketplace. Pope's project is thus roughly analogous to Bakhtin's. Each regarded himself as comprehending Rabelais's "true" intentions while failing to recognize many salient cultural differences.

I deduce Pope's intention to revise Rabelais from his dedication of *The Dunciad* to Swift, in the dean's guise of a modern Cervantes or Rabelais.[7] The dedication has been read usually as an acknowledgment of Swift's career rather than as descriptive of Pope's poem; in relation to Swift, *The Dunciad* is usually described as Scriblerian.[8] But *The Dunciad* is both a quixotic attempt to hold back the curtain of universal darkness, as Pope viewed his cultural predicament, and a Rabelaisian exposure of his rivals' grotesque pretensions. Pope believed that Rabelais, a priest and physician, had been driven to stylistic and thematic extremes by neglect of his more conventional writings. "Rabelais had writ some sensible pieces . . . which the world did not regard at all," he informed Spence in 1738. " 'I will write something,' says he, 'that they shall take notice of,' and so sat down to writing nonsense" (Spence, 1:217–18). While this conversation occurred ten years after the initial *Dunciad*'s publication, it reveals Pope's opinion that prolonged neglect goaded Rabelais into adopting a style so obscure as to appear deliberate "nonsense." In defense of *The Dunciad*'s brutality, Pope had offered an analogous explanation that years of provocation had driven him to take distasteful but expedient measures (Pope, 5:49–50). And while Pope's remedy was far from nonsensical in his sense of Rabelais's inconsistency, it did include, by the second edition, Scriblerus's deliberately inane commentary. Moreover, for Pope's generation, the physical spectacle of popular festivity was rapidly becoming nonsensical to the extent that writers were now discouraging participation as worthless or foolish for middling and genteel people. While Stallybrass and White see Pope and his contemporaries obsessively depicting the carnivalesque because they loathed and feared contamination by the low, I believe Pope deliberately chose to wallow in Rabelaisian nonsense because he wanted to "write something that they shall take notice of." Schooled in Horace's maxim that writing should both instruct and delight, but aware that his readers often chose to divert themselves with scandal, Pope designed a poem that would—in a deliberately perverse departure from Horace's dictum—both instruct and *shock*.

When Pope undertook to write a Swiftian or Rabelaisian satire, he was developing a model that Bakhtin traced to its classical origin, the mennippea (Bakhtin, 112–22). Whether Swift and Pope had familiarized themselves with the characteristics of this ancient genre, as they had the Horatian, Juvenalian, or Persian satires, is debatable. They were certainly familiar with the genre through Rabelais and his humanist precursors.[9] Continental contemporaries were well aware of the genre; Voltaire, in his *Philosophical Letters*, mentioned French mennippea among the ancestors of Samuel Butler's *Hudibras* (107). Swift would have found, in what Pope thought a fragmented style ("the very next thing said of the mare does not agree with the mistress"), the perfect vehicle for covert, potentially dangerous political satire. By emulating Rabelais, Swift arrived at the intermittent satiric episodes in *Gulliver's Travels*, in which analogies to the Hanoverian court alternate with self-mockery, fantasy, and other modes and objects of satire. While Pope found this method incoherent, Swift chose it precisely because of its apparent lack of design.

Swift's and Pope's "Rabelaisian" techniques had additional benefits for both writers. Rabelaisian literalized metaphors yielded fantastic yet seemingly "realistic" narratives, making it difficult for their enemies to respond. One tactic was simply to pretend that the satire was "nonsense," too unrealistic to convey any meaning. This left opponents open to accusations of obtuseness, as befell the Whig prelate who remarked of *Gulliver's Travels* that he didn't believe above half of it. The fate of most of Pope's respondents as well has been the assumption that they lacked a sense of irony. Another defensive recourse was to invent a counterfantasy similar to the original but reversing its objects. *Swiftiana* and *Popeiana* are full of such attempts, in which the Scriblerians replace the brothers of *A Tale of a Tub* or emerge as the "true" dunces. Although some of these efforts participate in the crude vigor of their models, none surmount Swift's or Pope's insinuations. Instead, the "paper wars" surrounding their publications took on lives of their own, and, in Pope's case, the replies became part of *The Dunciad*'s evolving fantasia.

As Stallybrass and White observe, Pope's use of the Smithfield metaphor was far from original, explosively controversial, and ultimately futile. This is partly because, as they explain, writers contaminated themselves each time they described the dangers of popular culture (Stallybrass and White, 104–6, 108, 116–18). But it is also true that the classical satiric structure to which Pope assimilated his Rabelaisian material further prevented any resolution. Pope's satiric structure invariably implies the normative role of the speaker who exposes vice and folly. In Rabelais's novels, the author's presence in his own narrative excludes nobody from the panorama of bodily excess. In Swift's writings, the narrator is usually implicated in the foolish phenomena he describes. Pope's choice of a Juvenalian observer, painfully aware of but uninvolved in the dunces' activities, guaranteed the outraged replies of his victims, who viewed Pope as sharing their professional dilemma.[10] In Stallybrass and White's analysis, this stalemate reflects the fact that all professional writers were distancing themselves from plebeian associations.

At Pope's historical moment, however, an even more particular distinction was being made. A firmly established middle class was subdividing itself into upper, middle, and lower categories.[11] As I have argued elsewhere, the urgency of both *The Dunciad* and of Pope's anguished exchanges with his victims arose from his attempt to define an upper-middling professional strata of authorship aligned with the elite—comparable to barristers and physicians—and a lower, occupational level of "hacks" resembling attorneys and apothecaries or, worse, artisans.[12] *The Dunciad*'s gross imagery rankled so much not because, as some scholars have argued, it was such an appropriate metaphor for Pope's enemies' literary activities, but because it so vividly illustrated his conservative, exclusive vision of their profession.[13] I turn now to the "high, heroic games" of *Dunciad* 2, which illustrate both Pope's "Rabelaisian" method and the two patterns of his victims' replies.

II

The Politics and Poetics of Transgression links Pope with Ben Jonson and William Wordsworth in their mutual representations of Bartholomew Fair. Like Jonson, Pope associated the fair with political enemies.[14] Like Wordsworth, he believed himself one of the few "stragglers" left to perceive its distastefulness.[15] But

Wordsworth's concern with the fair's danger to the "slaves unres-
pited of low pursuits" (700) indicated not only his implied opinion
of all who toiled in the city for gain, but his particular concern for
the urban working poor, contrasted with the country folk who
held their fair beneath Helvellyn. Although disgusted like Wordsworth with the adverse effects of indiscriminate amusements,
Pope did not record an actual experience of the fair but a scene as
visionary as Dulness's prophecy in Book 3. Far from commiserat-
ing with those for whom fair-going is their sole respite from toil,
Pope's literalized metaphor assailed literary competitors and
their sponsors by claiming their affinity with such amusements.
In *Dunciad* 2, members of the book trade herd together to participate in a travesty of the heroic games featured in ancient epics.
Drawn to the contests,

> . . . An endless band
> Pours forth, and leaves unpeopled half the land.
> A motley mixture! in long wigs, in bags,
> In silks, in crapes, in Garters, and in rags,
> From drawing rooms, from colleges, from garrets,
> On horse, on foot, in hacks, and gilded chariots.[16]

The "true Dunces" next engage in Pope's symbolic, degrading
contests, while "all who knew those Dunces to reward" amuse
themselves with the spectacle (25–26). The scene as well as the
numbers involved are grotesque, reminiscent of Pope's Rabelaisian model.

Pope's indecorous portrait of gentry as the chief audience of his
scabrous contests particularly vexed his critics. An anonymous
writer complained,

> Here we see Gentlemen, Beaus, Divines, and Knights of the Garter,
> all *Hail Fellows well met* with the *Grub-street Rags*.
>   He tells you before, that they flock'd in so fast that they *unpeopl'd
> half the Land*: by which he gives us to understand, I suppose, that
> most part of *England* are blockheads, without any Exception to Qual-
> ity or Character. . . . In the first place the Author calls Men of Letters
> all *Dunces*, and then he falls foul upon our great Patrons of Learning,
> and gives them the same scandalous usage.[17]

Such usage led this writer to conclude that the poem "was never
the Employment of a Gentleman, and much less of Mr. Pope" (7).
According to the statement's logic, Pope should either expect a
challenge for insulting other gentlemen, or admit he betrayed his

lack of gentility by suggesting such preposterously assorted spectators. Although this critic construed Pope's fiction as a metaphor ("he gives us to understand, I suppose"), he claimed to be affronted by its "unrealistic" numbers and assortment. By quarreling with the metaphor rather than with Pope's intention—an assault on the Whig grandees who patronize paid writing—the critic attempted to discredit Pope's authority.

Deliberately obtuse, the complaint that Pope's scenario defies decorum ignores its fantastic exaggeration. Even if Pope had meant this scene literally, his critic seemingly forgot that gentry customarily sponsored plebeian activities. John Dennis also tried to invalidate the same passage by questioning its probability. "Is it not monstrous," he asked, "to imagine any Thing like that in the Master Street of a populous City; a Street eternally crowded with Carriages, Carts, Coaches, Chairs, and men passing in the greatest Hurry about Private and Publick Affairs?"[18] Dennis's query, besides pointing out the daily indiscriminate mingling of carriages and carts, and thus of gentry and laborers, in the city's streets, ignored the fact that many sizeable towns, if not cities, closed their principal streets during holidays to accommodate football matches and other sports. Dennis's declaration that such a scene was unthinkable reflected his membership in a mercantile society increasingly intolerant of periodic interference with "Private and Publick Affairs."

Dennis's disgust indicated his participation in literary efforts to wean the middle class from lower-class amusements, the phenomenon documented by Stallybrass and White. By declaring such activities "monstrous," Dennis maintained his own distance from what were in fact familiar events. A review of these amusements reveals the cleverness of Pope's extended metaphor. Much as Rabelais presented an exaggerated version of Renaissance carnival, in his "high, heroic games," Pope invented the bizarre counterparts of contemporary festive activities. If, as I have suggested, Pope sought in Rabelais a satiric "allegory," he refined Rabelais's technique through consistent use of literalized metaphors suggested by traditional carnival pastimes. Robert Malcolmson describes the plebeian feasts and pleasure fairs firmly woven into the pattern of English life.[19] The often week-long holidays, of which London's St. Bartholomew's Fair was among the most notorious, generally commemorated local patron saints or agricultural hiatuses, and involved entire communities. The laborers caroused usually at the expense of the gentry, with genteel onlookers or even participants. The gentry particularly supported sports such as football, cock-fighting, and boxing, on which they could bet.

The most popular and deeply rooted sports, such as football and bull-baiting, often involved closing down and boarding up a whole village so that crowds could surge through its streets, sometimes for several days. As might be expected, such reversals of normal order and restraint led to "behavior which was not merely more relaxed but which actually countered the dominant mores of people's working lives" (Malcolmson, 77), particularly those relating to drunkenness, sexual indulgence, and expressions of hostility toward outsiders and social superiors. In a society that rarely acknowledged them, the poorer people could win recognition and self-esteem through participation in these activities, whether for athletic or sexual prowess, or taste in dress (85).

Malcolmson's book traces the decline of the feasts and fairs, and the popular recreations that accompanied them, through their demise after the mid-nineteenth century. But as Stallybrass and White observe, plebeian recreations were first assailed in the seventeenth century when writers articulated the necessity for a genteel mode of behavior distinct from that of common people. The gentry's traditionally benign attitude toward plebeian sports was criticized by writers preoccupied with refinement. Men and women newly awakened to their need for cultivated manners, restrained behavior, reasonable minds, and exquisite morals were supposed less likely to flock to the village green and wager on a cock-fight (Malcolmson, 163). The paternal landlord envisioned by Addison and Pope did not extend his care for villagers' well-being to abetting their holiday frolics. Throughout their periodical essays, Addison and Steele disparaged even such aristocratic blood-sports as hunting, and encouraged their aspiring middle-class readers to distance themselves from vulgar pastimes. "You see in Elections for Members to sit in parliament, how far saluting Rows of Old Women, drinking with Clowns, and being upon a level with the lowest part of Mankind in that wherein they themselves are lowest, their Diversions, will carry a Candidate," observed Steele with disgust in *Spectator* 394 (2 June 1712).[20]

Addison and Steele, with their condescension toward Sir Roger de Coverley, insinuated the Whig preference for urbane manners embodied in Sir Andrew Freeport. Neither Pope nor his Tory associates willingly ceded the guardianship of middle-class and genteel manners to the Whigs. Pope's Homeric commentary, for example, dispensed refinement to an audience of both sexes. Among the Scriblerians, John Gay especially enjoyed ridiculing plebeian recreations. *The Shepherd's Week* (1714) abounds in references to wakes and feasts, exposing the naivete and ignorance of his rustic louts. In "Saturday; Or, the Flights," the drunken Bowzybeus entertains the swains with ballads celebrating the attractions of country fairs.[21] One of the most threatening passages in *Trivia* (1716) describes the pensive narrator's attempt to visit St. Paul's, Covent Garden: "Here oft my course I bend, when lo! from far / I spy the furies of the football war."[22] Gay contrasts a gentleman pedestrian with a mob of laborers intent on their rude sport. In the first half of the eighteenth century, Covent Garden was known as a locale where people of every class mingled, some lounging, some engaging in trade.[23] But Gay's speaker disassociates himself from the pursuit of pleasure, whether in theater, auction room, or bagnio—not to mention the exhilaration of mingling with London's demimonde—that usually drew the middle class and gentry to Covent Garden. He claims a monument of religion and architecture as his destination. Unlike his peers, he presumably seeks a respite from the hawkers and prostitutes associated with the Garden district.[24]

Pope's *Dunciad* 2 develops the aversion to lower-class pastimes expressed earlier by Steele and Gay. Like Gay's footballers, the dunces romp through the Covent Garden locale. Their games resemble village rowdiness more than the heroic contests he ostensibly parodies. The dunces gather on the former site of the maypole, that phallic landmark associated with sensual village revelry. The locale recalls the peasant recreations gentlemen should be learning to despise, while the dunces' aristocratic spectators resemble those squires who tolerate, reward, and even join in such games. When the hack authors vie for patronage, a cry is heard: "Room for my Lord! three jockeys in his train, / Six huntsmen with a shout precede his chair" (2.192–93). A youth willing to prostitute his sister in return for a secretaryship wins the ensuing competition. The scene expresses Pope's disdain for the humiliating scramble for rewards imposed on paid writers, but it also suggests Steele's earlier disgust with the symbiotic, mutually degrading relationship between the political candidate and his dependents.

The patron's characterization as a huntsman exploits contemporary stereotypes of the ignorant country squire, ill qualified to exercise the cultural influence entrusted to his class. His entrance surrounded by professional riders and pack-managers suggests familiarity with social inferiors whose employment in sports distracts the gentleman from intellectual pursuits. The dunces tickling contest represents the degrading efforts required to win attention when no intellectual appeal is possible. But the patron-huntsman and his entourage also diminish the dunces into village laborers, their contests judged by the local squire, whose verdict might depend on permission to exercise his *droit du seigneur*. In a more sinister reading, the hack writers dwindle to a version of prey, and the winning youth's sister to a hare run to ground by the huntsmen's hounds.

Many of the games in *Dunciad* 2 suggest aspects of Malcolmson's observations about rural sports. As arenas for the display of physical prowess, for example, football, running, and wrestling "were among the few kinds of opportunities which laboring men had to perform publicly for the esteem of their peers" (Malcolmson, 85). From this perspective, what Emrys Jones has described as the childlike shamelessness of the dunces as they vie gleefully in the games resembles also the sheer pride in physical ability of competing laborers, another reminder of Pope's distinction between literature as trade and as profession.[25] When Curll challenges Lintot in the race for the phantom poet ("The race by vigour, not by vaunts, is won" [2.59]), and when "Osborn and Curll accept the glorious strife" of the pissing contest ("One on his manly confidence relies, / One on his vigour and superior size" [2.169–70]), Pope implied that the prestige of all their accomplishments equals that of the winner of a cudgelling match. And while the prizes Dulness distributes allude facetiously to the vases, slave women, and rich cloaks distributed by Aeneas at Anchises' funeral games, they also resemble the sexual conquests and humbler prizes for which laborers vied at local festivals. One such feast, in 1736, featured "running round the Hill for a Petticoat" (Malcolmson, 66)—a race comparable to Curll's and Lintot's race for the "shaggy Tap'stry" bedspread (2.143).

Besides helping create *The Dunciad*'s aura of carnival, the heroic games enabled Pope to define his competitors as a mob without having to acknowledge their threat. The mob, as Pat Rogers observes, was a frightening contemporary image (*Hacks and Dunces*, 99). The Fleet-ditch diving contest, in which hacks strip and dive enthusiastically into a filthy sewer, resembles less an imminent riot than a dare among ignorant boys. When the contest is won by a clergyman, Smedley, on behalf of all clerics who engage in party-writing for hire, the corrupt divines appear in a ludicrous light that invites jeering laughter (2.356–58). This is perhaps a healthier response to "the black troop" in question than Warburton's indignant note, denouncing such priests, who tho' educated under an entire ignorance of the world, aspire to interfere in the government of it, and, consequently, to disturb and disorder it; in which they fall short only of their Predecessors . . . in supporting arbitrary power, or in exciting rebellion (2:314, n.355).

Warburton's note recalls the anti-Stuart clerical factions who promoted the Civil War, Restoration unrest, and the Glorious Revolution. Pope, too, undoubtedly wished his readers to believe the cultural danger posed by the multiplication of paid writers, but he placed those writers in situations the refined reader could laugh at and dismiss, and thus disarm. As "William Cleland" remarks of Pope's method of answering his critics, "He has laugh'd and written *The Dunciad*" (12). Pope probably also intended to counter accusations that his own writings promoted Jacobite unrest, with a suggested link between his Whig competitors and a mob.[26]

As the day of heroic games ends, Dulness proposes a final contest. Whoever can stay awake through a reading of Henley's and Blackmore's writings will assume "full, and eternal privilege of tongue" as critical arbiter (2.346). Various professional writers, including Susanna Centlivre, compete for the privilege, but Pope's image suggests the crowd of spectators at a boxing match. A pair of "gentle readers" bring the books, then takes their seats while "the vulgar form a ring" (2.352). This configuration irresistibly suggests local gentry, sponsors of a plebeian contest, looking on while villagers circle the contestants. As at most feasts or fairs, "the clam'rous crowd is hush'd with mugs of Mum" (2.353), more evidence of patriarchal largesse. The Brunswick origin of the brew suggests the national scale of this unhealthy relation between governing and governed. Pope's joke becomes clear when his contest materializes not as a physical combat but as a reading duel between three undergraduates and three barristers. Its emphasis on simple endurance of the mind-deadening powers of poor writing recalls the purely physical nature of plebeian contests that inspired Steele's, Gay's, and later, Oliver Goldsmith's, condescension.[27] Pope did not fear potential violence but the imaginative and intellectual lowering that presumably accompanies both participation in popular amusements and reading his enemies' writings.

Later in the century, football matches were often pretenses for trampling enclosures, a situation that accelerated the gentry's disassociation from such sports. In Pope's day, however, the major complaint of the refined regarding these boisterous exhibitions concerned their thoughtlessness, and their lack of any intellectual or moral value. Like the glazier in Gay's *Trivia* who kicks a football through a window (2.355–56), Pope suggested, his enemies' broadsides, gazettes, and miscellanies damaged rather than promoted literature. As they tumble pell-mell through the city's purlieus, the dunces resemble a pack of rowdy footballers, making a spectacle of themselves and rudely destroying property, except that the property they damage is the work and reputations of other writers. Pope thus associated his literary competitors with the very kinds of activities, familiar and even cherished in the countryside, that aspiring urban middle-class readers were being taught to avoid. The braying contest (2.246–67), which skewers both Blackmore's epics and contemporary dissenting preachers, fantastically resembles country-fair contests for the funniest grin. Most professional writing, insinuated Pope, was no more appropriate entertainment for the gentry or middle class than was such a competition. When Pope's enemies accused him of resorting to the same tactics he deplored, they were correct: *Dunciad* 2 resembles an elaborate skimmington. In creating his vivid carnival of literary sports, Pope intended a systematic satire such as he presumed Rabelais had failed to achieve by "writing nonsense."

One more aspect of plebeian recreation relevant to Pope's games was its tendency to create solidarity among participants. Communal feasts "served to articulate a vision of the social harmony for which its members wished; festivities celebrated those ideals which transcended self, they reinforced the individual's sense of his social identity" (Malcolmson, 85). *Dunciad* 2 suggests this effect by collecting a "motley mixture" of poets, journalists, dramatists, booksellers, divines, noblemen, and paupers, uniting them under Queen Dulness. The games of Book 2, like all the poem's activities, represent various "ideals" of Dulness, such as the substitution of manipulative noise for psychological insight or technical virtuosity:

> To move, to raise, to ravish ev'ry heart,
> With Shakespear's nature, or with Johnson's art,
> Let others aim: 'Tis yours to shake the soul
> With Thunder rumbling from the mustard bowl. (2.223–26)

Pope's insulting characterization ignores distinctions among his enemies. Daniel Defoe, Pope's best-known victim, is valued today especially for his imaginative insight into the minds of his characters.[28] Several of Susanna Centlivre's plays, contrary to Dulness's assumption here, remained part of theatrical repertory for generations because of her ability to craft comic plots and roles.[29] But by amalgamating all of his literary enemies, regardless of gender, class, or ability, Pope created the illusion of a mob similar to those found at the newly despised wakes and fairs.

The Dunciad succeeded in creating temporary solidarity among Pope's victims. Several "Dunces" responded with poems such as James Ralph's "Sawney," dedicated "to the Gentlemen Scandaliz'd in *The Dunciad*,"[30] or Edward Ward's "Durgen," "amicably Inscrib'd . . . to those Worthy and Ingenious Gentlemen misrepresented in a late invective Poem, call'd *The Dunciad*."[31] In the latter poem, designed "to return [Pope] a scratch for his bite" ("The Author to the Reader"), Ward rebuked Pope in mock-heroic verse for his "Heroick Scandal" (3). He invented numerous, ingenious lowering similes in an attempt to degrade Pope to the level of his dunces. Scandal-mongering Pope metamorphoses into a boy playing with a ball:

> For Scandal, tho' it titillates the Town,
> Like a Ball tost against a Wall of Stone,
> Reverb'rates on the Wretch by whom the Dirt is thrown. (7)

In his 1744 *Occasional Letter,* Colley Cibber also attempted to turn the tables on Pope and associate him with imagery borrowed from plebeian entertainment:

> Trust me, Alexander, if thou goest on at this wild rate, thou will soon make the Throne of thy Laureat Vacant; and who knows, then, but the second Thought of thy Readers may humourously mount thee into it; as the merry Mob, at a Cock-match hoist up a Cheat into the basket, for having lost a Bet he was not able to pay.[32]

Cibber's image cleverly deflates Pope's pretension. He grants Pope's lofty perspective, but claims his vantage-point will soon be that of the cheat, exposed in a basket tied to the ceiling for failing to pay his gambling debts. Cibber paradoxically lowers Pope by imagining the poet hoisted up in shameful display. Cibber's metaphor also characterizes Pope's readers as a mob, and the literary marketplace as a cock-fight. Among the most ubiquitous of the blood sports, cock-fighting traditionally drew as many genteel as plebeian spectators. By the late seventeenth century, cock-fighting attracted criticism by gentlemen disgusted with its brutality, association with betting, and unseemly mingling of classes (Malcolmson, 49). While belittling Pope, Cibber implicated himself and the reading public in the very milieu that *The Dunciad* envisioned and deplored. In fact, none of those Pope described as dunces were able to conjure up an alternative to his images of popular amusements. He may have inspired in his enemies a sense of solidarity, but he could claim it resembled the brotherhood of village louts cavorting about a maypole.

Bartholomew Fair and its associated amusements inspired comparisons with contemporary social and intellectual pursuits for many more years. In a recent study, Derek Jarrett finds in Hogarth's "Southwark Fair" (1733) a recollection of the Bartholomew Fair spectacles of the artist's youth.[33] While satirizing the foolish, even dangerous shows that competed for the fairgoers' attention, Hogarth nevertheless suggests that the fair's escapist entertainment is relatively benign compared with the genteel pastimes he depicts in *The Rake's Progress* (158). Averse to gambling and cock-fighting, Hogarth nevertheless appreciated the healthy outlet afforded by a battle royal or a game of hopscotch (151). Hogarth's attitude is probably more representative of mid-century genteel opinion of popular sports than is Pope's. Much as Bakhtin, under the Stalinist regime, championed a writer whom he believed exalted freedom, Pope discovered in Rabelais a satiric ally against "leveling" in all aspects of culture. Many English, in contrast, seem to have cherished their feasts, fairs, and contests as among the last vestiges of a traditional, rural way of life.

In this context, Pope's attitude toward Bartholomew Fair and its kindred sports appears anachronistic. From the perspective of Leah S. Marcus's recent study of seventeenth-century poets who defended royal encouragement of holiday sports, Pope's disdain apparently contradicted his nostalgic attitude toward Stuart rule.[34] But Pope's generation was preoccupied not with absolutist control but with post-Revolution opportunities for mobility and participation. Critics caricatured Pope, for example, as the upstart son of a bankrupt hatter. In turn, Pope insisted that genius and virtue, even more than training and successful publication, made him the professional equivalent of a barrister or physician. Pope's version of the fair, nearly void of nostalgia, constituted a kind of middle-class warfare. By demoting his competitors to the level of artisans and day-laborers at a fair, he insisted on distinguishing among kinds of paid writing as among occupations. Steele's and Gay's competing efforts to promote refinement inspired Pope's metaphor for an emerging literary hierarchy. By associating his enemies with the laboring class in relation to an undiscriminating class of patrons, he intended to associate them with marginal or lower-middling status. Pope, disavowing patronage, claimed professional, upper-middling status for himself. The fact that critics continue to refer to Pope's subjects en masse as "the Dunces," ignoring the variety of their circumstances and abilities, testifies not to the accuracy of Pope's cultural assessment, but to his skillful association of competitors with a crowd of laborers, enjoying carnivalesque sports.[35] While Bakhtin, in a far different cultural context, envisioned Rabelais as an ancestral proponent of liberation, Pope—sharing the preoccupations of his own time and place—resurrected their mutual predecessor's texts as a flawed model for his satire of the literary marketplace. It simply would not have occurred to Pope, nor to Addison, Steele, or Gay, to construe a marketplace overflowing with bodily fluids as an image of healthy self-acceptance.

III

Pope feared the apparent metamorphosis of literary production (an endeavor he had formerly compared, in "The Temple of Fame," to a sacred enclosure) into a chaotic festival marketplace. But this glum assessment of his vocation does not indicate that Pope was averse to all potential manifestations of the emerging market economy. A clever businessman, Pope was equally capable of imagining a marketplace directed by conservative principles and thus less vulnerable to the kinds of abuse he ascribed to Whig influence. In stark contrast with *The Dunciad*'s metaphoric image of a carnivalized literary "marketplace" abandoned to degrading activities, Pope did create one positive image of a literal, although not literary, marketplace. In his *Epistle to Allen Lord Bathurst* (1732), he devoted several eulogistic paragraphs to a man who combined paternal regulation of the marketplace with progressive economic policies. Colin Nicholson, in his recent study of *Writing and the Rise of Finance* (1994), describes Pope's transformation of "the historical John Kyrle, the Man of Ross . . . into an ideal portrait of independent squirearchy."[36] Nicholson observes the awkwardness of Pope's effort to promote as his ideal a "Christ-like, compassionate figure [hovering] in the background of a market-place signifying a traditionally moral rather than an innovatively monetarised economy" (153), but he attributes the apparent strain of the image to a different cause than I do. Nicholson asserts that Pope's devotion to an outmoded economic order led him to idealize a landlord "who belonged more rather than less to the preceding century" (153). Pope's blindness to the changing nature of British society led to such unconvincing devices as his evocation of "Age and Want . . . smiling" as they await Kyrle's ration of bread (152–53). While I concur with Nicholson in the awkwardness of Pope's portrait of Kyrle, I credit the poet with greater awareness that his nation's economy and hence society were changing, and not entirely for the worse. I attribute the strain in the Ross passage to Pope's effort to incorporate some of the features of a whiggish, professionalized relation between landlord and laborer into his Tory patriarch's activities. The outcome of our interpretations is similar, in that Pope's solution was impracticable whether he in fact failed to see changes in his society or was attempting to adapt the old order to utterly changed circumstances. But rather than attributing certain features of the Man of Ross to gaps in Pope's vision, I believe that the squire in the marketplace represented his promotion of the Tory squire as a better "manager" of rural labor than the occasionally resident Whig grandee.

The Man of Ross imitated great landowners by hiring local laborers to carry out landscaping projects, including a picturesque prospect of the surrounding valley (251–61). Unlike the creators of pleasure grounds whose enclosures deprived local inhabitants of conveniences, however, Kyrle's reservoir augmented the town's water supply. He contributed to engineering projects such as a causeway and a church steeple, which employed laborers while enhancing Ross. Unlike Joseph Addison's caricature of a Tory squire, Sir Roger de Coverley, who donated an occasional flitch of bacon to poor households, Kyrle created meaningful employment. He apprenticed young men and dowered young women, discouraging poverty by promoting early establishments in both occupations and marriages rather than by erecting a workhouse. Pope's invitation to "Behold the Market-place with poor o'erspread" (263) places the reader in Kyrle's vantage-point, observing the scene from a window of his home. But Ross harbored no rowdy dunces attracting patronage by vying in absurd spectacles. Under the benevolent gaze of Kyrle, the poor "[sat] smiling" (266) as they awaited their benefactor's assistance. He not only fed but provided medicines for the inhabitants of the almshouse, the older and kinder alternative to the workhouse for the "deserving" poor, usually aged and children. And Kyrle regulated the behavior of not only the poor: farmers and gentry who frequented the Ross marketplace were also fed, and dissuaded from scandalous legal wrangles. Acting as the traditional justice of the peace, Kyrle resolved disputes before legal underlings could prolong them. Nicholson is certainly correct in stating that Pope's Ross is a fantasy, but the fantasy takes place in a present where the poor have been relegated to disease and starvation in Whig-sponsored workhouses, and where prosperity seemed threatened by proliferating legal disputes and vain expenditures in search of medical panaceas.[37]

Most suggestive is Kyrle's banishment of "Despairing Quacks" and "vile Attornies" (272–73), the upstart medical and legal occupations analogous to the hacks whom Pope, as a professional writer, despised. Kyrle, with no more income than Pope, had effectively driven such pretenders to authority, as well as all riot and disorder among the poor, from his marketplace. He achieved literally what Pope dreamed of securing metaphorically through his *Dunciad*: a marketplace void of contention, where all deferred to the gentleman distinguished by his vision, generosity, and disinterestedness. That Pope idealized Kyrle, a man of similar class status who surpassed many grandees in social achievement, is hardly surprising. But that, as Ronald Paulson suggests, he identified himself with Kyrle,[38] is unlikely except as a poignant fantasy. It is most suggestive that when Pope wrote his *Epistle,* Kyrle was dead and, the poet feared, fading into oblivion, while *The Dunciad* takes place in the recent past but concludes with a prophetic vision. For the gentleman who pulls aside his curtain and beholds from his window the marketplace crowd, docile and smiling as they await food and medicine or troop off to the trades in which he has placed them, is the comic obverse of *The Dunciad*'s narrator. In *The Dunciad*, Pope's speaker beholds an unruly, motley crowd of booksellers and mercenary writers who should have chosen other occupations. Far from appreciating his satiric "medicine," they persist in publishing what he regards as trash. Any pretense of his disinterestedness soon evaporates, as edition after edition of *The Dunciad* compiles the attacks and counterattacks of Pope and his competitors. By the final *Dunciad in Four Books* (1743), Pope's kinship with the practical, masterful Kyrle is even less apparent. A helpless observer of what he construes as chaos, Pope's narrator ceases as Dulness "lets the curtain fall" (4.655).

Pope's vision of a Rabelaisian marketplace overflowing with dunces effectively conveyed his phobias. By indulging in carnivalesque imagery, he degraded his competitors and initiated several long-running feuds. By adopting the Juvenalian stance of outraged, unsullied, beleaguered opponent, he guaranteed his poem's controversy and, ultimately, its futility. The distinctions he sought to make between himself and other professional writers too often were based on personal dislike or political allegiance rather than on the "objective" criteria, such as originality and decorum, he claimed. Scholars who conflate Pope's actual rivals with his duncical creations miss the source of the poem's deliberate provocation. By "writing nonsense"—that is, what he conceived as Rabelaisian satire—Pope achieved his Swiftian goal of vexing the age. His grotesque characterizations were fantastic enough to be assailable; his normative presence in the poem, debatable. Unlike the village patriarch in an ideal marketplace, the literary arbiter could neither regulate behavior nor control access to his profession. He could not produce a satire that effectively halted what he considered creeping vulgarity. He could neither prevent nor resolve disputes. He could only convey his distress through the most distasteful metaphors available to his culture, then "let the curtain fall."

Notes

Notes to "Introduction: 'More Solid Learning': Pope, *The Dunciad*, and the Academy"

1. Richard Savage, *A Collection of Pieces in Verse and Prose . . . By Mr. Savage* (London: L. Gilliver, 1732), vi.

2. James Ralph, *Sawney: An Heroic Poem. Occasion'd by the Dunciad*, 1728; reprinted in *Popeiana: The Dunciad I, 1728* (New York: Garland, 1975), 42–43.

3. Alexander Pope, *The Dunciad in Four Books*, 1743; reprinted in *The Twickenham Edition of the Poems of Alexander Pope*, John Butt et al., eds., 11 vols. (London: Methuen, 1953), n.1, 5:339. All quotations of Pope's poems are taken from this edition and cited within the text throughout the introduction, unless otherwise specified. (*Twickenham Edition* is hereafter referred to as *TE*.)

4. Pat Rogers, *Grub Street: Studies in a Subculture* (London: Methuen, 1972), 211.

5. See Pope's letters of 13 January 1742/3 and of 9 February 1742/3, in *The Correspondence of Alexander Pope*, 5 vols., George Sherburn, ed. (Oxford: Clarendon Press, 1956). All further citations of Pope's correspondence are cited by volume and page number within the text.

6. TE 5:xxxii.

7. Samuel Richardson, *Selected Letters of Samuel Richardson*, John Carroll, ed. (Oxford: Clarendon Press, 1964), 100.

8. George Sherburn, *The Early Career of Alexander Pope* (Oxford: Clarendon Press, 1934); William Wimsatt, *The Portraits of Alexander Pope* (New Haven: Yale University Press, 1965); Maynard Mack, *Essential Articles for the Study of Alexander Pope* (Hamden, CT: Archon Books, 1964), *The Garden and the City: Retirement and Politics in the Later Poetry of Pope, 1731–1743* (Toronto: University of Toronto Press, 1969); Reuben Brower, *Alexander Pope: The Poetry of Allusion* (Oxford: Clarendon, 1959); Nicolson and Rousseau, *"This Long Disease, My Life": Alexander Pope and the Sciences* (Princeton: Princeton University Press, 1968); Emrys Jones, "Pope and Dulness," in *Publications of the British Academy* (1969): 232–63; Elias Mengel, *"The Dunciad* Illustrations," *Eighteenth-Century Studies* 7 (1973/74): 161–78; John Sitter, *The Poetry of Pope's Dunciad* (Minneapolis: University of Minnesota Press, 1971). One might also put Aubrey Williams, *Pope's Dunciad; A Study of Its Meaning* (London: Methuen, 1955) in this category.

9. G. Douglas Atkins, *Quests of Difference: Reading Pope's Poems* (Lexington: University Press of Kentucky, 1986).

10. Erskine-Hill does mention Book 4 of *The Dunciad* (pp. 276–78) in the context of his discussion of Pope's representation of eighteenth-century Britain and the decline of empire. *The Social Milieu of Alexander Pope: Lives, Example, and the Poetic Response* (New Haven: Yale University Press, 1975). Isaac Kram-

nick's *Bolingbroke and His Circle: The Politics of Nostalgia in the Age of Walpole* (Cambridge: Harvard University Press, 1968; reprinted Ithaca: Cornell University Press, 1992) falls into the same category. Indeed, the timeliness of Kramnick's book is suggested by its 1992 reprint. Colin Nicholson's more theoretically informed book explores some similar issues: *Writing and the Rise of Finance: Capital Satires of the Early Eighteenth Century* (Cambridge: Cambridge University Press, 1994).

11. *Pamphlet Attacks on Alexander Pope, 1711–1744: A Descriptive Bibliography* (New York: New York University Press, 1969).

12. *Alexander Pope: A Bibliography, Volume II* (Austin: University of Texas, 1927), xlvii.

13. *Alexander Pope: A Life* (New York: W. W. Norton, 1985); *The Politics and Poetics of Transgression* (London: Methuen, 1986).

14. G. S. Rousseau, "Perils of Articulation: A Review Essay of Maynard Mack's *Alexander Pope*," *South Atlantic Quarterly* 86:3 (1987); republished in Wallace Jackson and R. Paul Yoder, eds., *Critical Essays on Alexander Pope*, (New York: G. K. Hall, 1993), 37.

15. And, as Brean Hammond observes, "by sprinkling his style with unacknowledged quotations from the great authors in the Western cultural tradition, Mack implicitly presented himself as standing alongside Pope in the doomed struggle against the new barbarism." See *Pope*, edited and introduced by Brean Hammond (London: Longman, 1996), 6.

16. James Winn, *A Window in the Bosom: The Letters of Alexander Pope* (Hamden, CT: Archon Books, 1977); Dustin H. Griffin, *Alexander Pope: The Poet in the Poems* (Princeton: Princeton University Press, 1978); James Grantham Turner, "Pope's Libertine Self-Fashioning," *The Eighteenth Century: Theory and Interpretation* 29 (1988): 123–44.

17. Laura Brown, *Alexander Pope* (Oxford: Basil Blackwell, 1985), 130.

18. Felicity Nussbaum and Laura Brown, eds., *The New Eighteenth Century: Theory, Politics, English Literature* (New York: Routledge, 1987).

19. "Journalism, Carnival and *Jubilate Agno*," *ELH* 59 (1992): 358.

20. Felicity Nussbaum, *The Brink of All We Hate: English Satires on Women, 1660–1750* (Lexington: University Press of Kentucky, 1984); Ellen Pollak, *The Poetics of Sexual Myth: Gender and Ideology in the Verse of Swift and Pope* (Chicago: University of Chicago Press, 1985); Valerie Rumbold, *Women's Place in Pope's World* (Cambridge: Cambridge University Press, 1989). More recently, Marilyn Francus, "The Monstrous Mother: Reproductive Anxiety in Swift and Pope," *ELH* 61.4 (1994): 829–51, continues the project of feminist interpretations of Pope. Claudia Thomas's *Alexander Pope and His Eighteenth-Century Women Readers* (Carbondale: Southern Illinois University Press, 1994) examines Pope's relationships with his female readers from a feminist perspective.

21. Catherine Ingrassia, "Women Writing/Writing Women: Pope, Dulness, and 'Feminization' in *The Dunciad*," *Eighteenth-Century Life* 14 (1990): 40–58, offers a feminist reading of *The Dunciad* that looks specifically at the figure of Dulness.

22. Carolyn Williams, *Pope, Homer, and Manliness: Some Aspects of Eighteenth-Century Classical Learning* (New York: Routledge, 1993); Kristina Straub, *Sexual Suspects* (Princeton: Princeton University Press, 1992).

23. Dennis Todd, *Imagining Monsters: Miscreations of the Self in Eighteenth-Century England* (Chicago: University of Chicago Press, 1995); Mark Rose, *Authors and Owners: The Invention of Copyright* (Cambridge: Harvard University

Press, 1993); Marlon B. Ross, "Authority and Authenticity: Scribbling Authors and the Genius of Print in Eighteenth-Century England," in Martha Woodmansee and Peter Jaszi, eds., *The Construction of Authorship: Textual Appropriation in Law and Literature* (Durham, NC: Duke University Press, 1994), 231–57. Another relevant discussion about the construction of authorship can be found in David Saunders and Ian Hunter, "Lessons from the 'Literatory': How to Historicize Authorship," *Critical Inquiry* 17 (1991): 479–509.

24. *Alexander Pope, The Genius of Sense* (Cambridge: Harvard University Press, 1984).

25. *Pope and the Early Eighteenth-Century Book Trade,* revised and edited by James McLaverty (Oxford: Clarendon Press, 1991). Such fine articles as Shef Rogers, "Pope, Publishing and Popular Interpretations of the *Dunciad Variorum*," *Philological Quarterly* 74.3 (1995): 279–95, owe a great deal to Foxon's study.

26. *TE* 5:xliv.

27. Helen Deutsch, *Resemblance & Disgrace: Alexander Pope and the Deformation of Culture* (Cambridge: Harvard University Press, 1996), 184.

Notes to " '*et in Arcadia homo*': Opera, Gender, and Sexual Politics in *The Dunciad*"

1. For the semantic difficulties, see G. S. Rousseau, "The Pursuit of Homosexuality in the Eighteenth Century: 'Utterly Confused Category' and/or Rich Repository?," in Robert Purks Maccubbin, *'Tis Nature's Fault: Unauthorized Sexuality During the Enlightenment* (Cambridge: Cambridge University Press, 1987), 132–69.

2. G. S. Rousseau, "Perils of Articulation: A Review Essay of Maynard Mack's *Alexander Pope* and *The Prose Works of Alexander Pope, Volume II,* Rosemary Cowler (ed.)," *South Atlantic Quarterly* 86.3 (1987): 327–39.

3. M. Mack, *Alexander Pope: A Life* (London: Yale University Press, 1985), 104, 187, 372.

4. This announcement is made after an exhaustive search of the sources and in wide consultation with theater and opera historians on both sides of the Atlantic. Pope undoubtedly saw at least one Handelian opera; the issue here is Italian opera, home of the castrati. Sutherland alone addresses the matter in his notes to *The Dunciad,* noting that Pope had read Rolli's libretto of the Italian opera *Polifemo.* See *The Poems of Alexander Pope,* gen. ed. John Butt, 11 vols. (London: Methuen, 1967), 5:334–35. (All further quotations of Pope's poems are taken from this edition and cited within the text.) Brownell and Winn are silent in their various studies of the arts of Restoration and Georgian England. Mack cautiously speculates in the biography while discussing Gay's other opera that "it would not be unfair to guess . . . that the vehement prejudice of many at that time (including Pope) against Italian opera—the opera of which Gay's own Opera makes continuous fun and in the face of which its songs flaunt native English sentiments expressed in honest kersey English words set to traditional English tunes—carried in suspension antipathies to other forms of foreign infiltration . . ." (455). Prejudice of a fierce sort it may have been, but was it sufficient to deter Pope? The reasons are inexplicable, but Pope was of the type to blast his trumpet if he had witnessed an Italian opera. Besides, he did

not circulate with the groups who frequented them in London, and therefore had little opportunity. The letter showing that Pope solicited subscriptions for the engraved musical scores of Buononocini proves little. See *The Correspondence of Alexander Pope*, George Sherburn, ed., 5 vols. (Oxford: Clarendon, 1956), 2: 99–100. The more complex question, surely, is how Pope could feel himself qualified to launch such a vehement attack against a new form of spectacle he himself had never seen, and why his curiosity wasn't greater than it was. It is possible that he did attend one, but unlikely in view of his own diligence to record anything curious he ever saw; and Italian opera, of all the new metropolitan public forms of entertainment, is surely just the sort of event he himself would have written about, or which Spence would have recorded. Therefore the conclusion must be that, whereas Pope had heard debate pro and con, he himself never saw the new entertainment his great didactic poem showed him to be so strongly opposed to, and it is not to his credit that he appears never to have attempted to see one. Italian opera would signify to him, of course, its entirety: its music, libretto, spectacle and machinery, setting, costume, boy singers, castrati, and especially its foreign origins in the Mediterranean. See also J. M. Knapp's chapter in S. S. Kenny's *British Theatre and the Other Arts, 1660–1800* (Washington, DC: Folger Shakespeare Library, 1984), and Winton Dean, *Handel's Operas, 1704–1726* (Oxford: Clarendon Press, 1987). R. Ness (n.25, below) does not ask whether Pope ever saw an Italian opera.

5. The phrase comes from Linda and Michael Hutcheon, *Opera: Desire, Disease, Death* (Lincoln: University of Nebraska Press, 1996).

6. New York: Poseidon Press, 1993. See also Wayne Koestenbaum's "Listening to Schwarzkopf: The Reich and the Soprano," *New Yorker* (2 September 1966): 162. The role of the libretto in opera is, of course, a complex matter, especially as dramatic purveyor of the tragic story, and not one I wish to ponder here.

7. See R. Trumbach, "The Birth of the Queen: Sodomy and the Emergence of Gender Equality in Modern Culture, 1600–1750," in Martha Vicinus, George Chauncey, and Martin Duberman, Jr., eds., *Hidden from History: Reclaiming the Gay and Lesbian Past* (New York: New American Library, 1989), 129–40.

8. See the line of studies extending from M. H. Nicolson and G. S. Rousseau through H. Deutsch.

9. I borrow the phrase from Carol Flynn in her perceptive article entitled " 'A Softer Man': Pope's, Swift's, and Farquhar's Feminine Ideal," *South Atlantic Quarterly* 84 (1985): 51, but also see James Turner, "Pope's Libertine Self-Fashioning," *The Eighteenth Century: Theory and Interpretation* 29:2 (1988): 123–44, and James Winn, "Pope Plays the Rake," in H. Erskine-Hill and A. Smith, eds., *The Art of Alexander Pope* (London: Vision, 1979). See also Oscar Reutersvard, *The Neo-Classic Temple of Virility and the Buildings with a Phallic Shaped Ground-Plan* (Lund: Gleerup, 1971).

10. 1 December 1742, *Corr.*, 4:428, Pope to Allen.

11. 8 December 1742, *Corr.*, 4:431, Pope to Allen.

12. The passage sheds light on his mindset. "One of my amusements has been writing a Poem, part of which is to abuse Travelling. . . . I little thought 3 months ago to have drawn the whole polite world upon me, as I formerly did the Dunces of a lower Species, as I certainly shall whenever I publish this poem. An Army of Virtuosi, Medalists, Ciceronis, Royal Society-men, Schools, Universities, even Florists, Free thinkers, & Free masons, will incompass me with fury: It will be once more, Concurrere Bellum atque Virum" (*Corr.*, 4:377, dated winter 1742–1743 while Pope was hard at work revising all four books).

13. Clark Lawlor, "The Classical and the Grotesque in the Work of Alexander Pope and Jonathan Swift" (unpublished Ph.D. thesis, University of Warwick 1994), 132–33; the pages within Lawlor's citation are from the important study by Faulkner and Blair, "The Classical and Mythographic Sources of Pope's Dulness," *Huntington Library Quarterly* 43 (1979–80): 213–46.

14. John Ray, *Three physico-theological discourses, concerning I. The primitive chaos, and creation of the world. II. The general deluge, its causes and effects. III. The dissolution of the world, and future conflagration* (London, 1713), 2–3, which Pope may have read.

15. Ibid., 4.

16. N. Katherine Hayles, *Chaos Bound: Orderly Disorder in Contemporary Literature and Science* (Ithaca: Cornell University Press, 1990), 19. See also E. Panofsky, "Et in Arcadia Ego," in E. T. Lincoln, ed., *Pastoral and Romance: Modern Essays in Criticism* (Englewood Cliffs, NJ: Prentice-Hall, 1969), 25–46, who considers Eros and Anteros as crucial for the birth of the world. In all the myths of the creation of the world, love as Eros and Anteros—the rational check upon the blind Eros or Cupid—had played a part (40–41). In *Studies in Iconology: Humanistic Themes in the Art of the Renaissance* (New York: Harper and Row, 1962), Panofsky commented on their antiphony and rivalry: "the rivalry between Eros and Anteros which in the Renaissance was often misrepresented as a struggle between Sensual Love and Virtue. The function of the classical Anteros . . . had been to reassure reciprocity in amorous relations" (126).

17. See Jack Lindsay, *The Origins of Alchemy in Graeco-Roman Egypt* (London: Frederick Muller, 1970), 2.

18. Lawlor, n.13, makes much of *The Dunciad*'s grotesquerie.

19. Panofsky, *Studies in Iconology*, 126.

20. The subject is further developed in C. Gallant, *Blake and the Assimilation of Chaos* (Princeton: Princeton University Press, 1978), 82.

21. Susan Gubar developed ideas about genderized monstrosity in "The Female Monster in Augustan Satire," *Signs* 3 (1977): 380–94. It was also embedded in the age for males; see Thomas Artus, *Description de l'Isle des hermaphrodites* (Cologne, 1726) and below.

22. A. Williams, *Pope's Dunciad; A Study of Its Meaning* (London: Methuen, 1955), 73.

23. Ibid., 238.

24. Pope's xenophobia must not be underestimated, as in his fierce denunciation of "Italian song" in the prologue to *Cato*. Steele was equally virulent in his xenophobia and homophobia, despite his own relationship to male homoerotic culture, as were others at the time.

25. There is no sustained study of English responses to Italian opera before 1760; see F. Petty, *Italian Opera in London, 1760–1800* (Ann Arbor: University of Michigan Press, 1980). Immensely useful is R. Ness, "*The Dunciad* and Italian Opera in England," *Eighteenth-Century Studies* 20 (1986–1987): 172–94, on which I have drawn throughout this exploration. Also useful now is R. L. Woof, "Italian Opera and English Oratorio as Cultural Discourses Within Eighteenth-Century English Literature, with Particular Reference to the Novels of Samuel Richardson and Fanny Burney" (unpublished Ph.D. thesis, Oxford University, 1996).

26. Sutherland, V, xxx.

27. Very little is known about the audiences of Italian opera in England of the eighteenth century, if compared with the kind of analysis that Paris has re-

ceived in the nineteenth; see James H. Johnson, *Listening in Paris: A Cultural History* (Berkeley: University of California Press, 1995).

28. For their masculinities, see R. F. Gleckner, *Gray Agonistes: Thomas Gray and Masculine Friendship* (Baltimore: Johns Hopkins University Press, 1997).

29. H. Erskine-Hill, *The Social Milieu of Alexander Pope: Lives, Example, and the Poetic Response* (London: Yale University Press, 1975), 277–78.

30. Ibid., 278.

31. T. Laqueur, *Making Sex: Body and Gender from the Greeks to Freud* (Cambridge: Harvard University Press, 1990), 135–41.

32. See Anonymous, *Les Alienes Voyageurs* (Paris, 1887) and Ian Hacking, "Les alienes voyageurs: How Fugue Became a Medical Entity," *History of Psychiatry* 7 (September 1996): 425–49.

33. No English translation has been found after an extensive search.

34. A. Heriot, *The Castrati in Opera* (London: Calder and Boyars, 1956; 2nd ed., 1975), 37; for Burney, 42–43. Martin Schurig, a German physician practicing in the 1720s, asked whether the sperm of castrati was identical to that of other men; see his *Spermatologia Historico-Medica, . . . de hermaphroditis & sexum mutantibus . . .* (Frankfurt, n.p.: 1720).

35. A. Evans, *The Apparition. A Poem* (London: The Booksellers, 1710), 13–14.

36. Pietro Francesco Tosi, *Observations on the Florid Song* (London: J. Wilcox, 1742).

37. Heriot, *Castrati*, 30, 34, 37.

38. This was Filippo Balatri's *Frutti del Mondo, esperimentati da Filippo Balatri nativo dell'Alfea in Toscana*, published in 1728, which I have not seen. Balatri was programmed to sing for Queen Anne in the summer of 1714, but she died; see Heriot, *Castrati*, 20–23.

39. Most of this information derives from Heriot, *Castrati*, but also see P. Brett et al. (eds.), *Queering the Pitch: The New Gay and Lesbian Musicology* (London: Routledge, 1994).

40. Heriot, *Castrati*, 54; the Casanova passages are from his *Diary* for 1745. There was also a popular quasi-religious literature; Samuel Smith (1584–1662), for example, produced popular tracts called *The Ethiopian Eunuch's Conversion* (1632), for which he was later ejected from his Worcester living.

41. *Hell upon Earth* (1729), 53, whose xenophobic author continues to compare England's effeminacy in Pope's era to that in Greece and Rome; see also *Satan's Harvest Home* (1749), and the edition of both works by Randolph Trumbach (New York: Garland, 1985).

42. These words—"sick" and "unnatural"—were explicitly invoked; see the first issue of *Gentleman's Magazine* (1731): 56; hereafter cited as *GM*.

43. Heriot, *Castrati*, 25.

44. Walpole's correspondence abounds with references demonstrating the degree to which the castrati (Farinelli, Balatri, etc.) were perceived as individual international stars by the 1730s and known as household names in England (see the Yale *Walpole*, W. S. Lewis et al., eds., 17: 248, 274); among the drollest is the playful "gift of eunuchs" made in the young Walpole's famous "Persian Letter" to the equally post-pubescent and "most potent" Lord Lincoln, "whose vigour is nine times beyond that of our prophet" (30: 35–36). For the eunuchs and orientalism, see G. S. Rousseau, "The Sorrows of Priapus: Anticlericalism, Homosocial Desire, and Richard Payne Knight," in G. S. Rousseau and Roy Porter (eds.), *Sexual Underworlds of the Enlightenment* (Chapel Hill: University of North Carolina Press, 1988), 101–53.

45. Heriot, *Castrati*, 26. Marjorie Garber has a more sophisticated explanation in *Vested Interests: Cross-Dressing & Cultural Anxiety* (New York: Routledge, 1992).

46. Heriot, *Castrati*, 32–33.

47. Naples, 1664. Heriot, *Castrati*, 53–54.

48. *GM* (1734): 693, complained that the castrati were bleeding the English by stealing their jobs and keeping their male musicians out of work.

49. For a specimen of this anti-opera sentiment, see *GM* (1738–1739) *passim* and Heriot, 99. *Fog's Journal* for 26 April 1735, No. 338, printed an attack on opera and its castrati, asking whether "Farinelli" and the castrati "have inspired any of our Mercenary" audiences toward nobler morality; this was reprinted in other newspapers including *London Magazine* (1735): 204–205. The newspapers of the 1730s are permeated with negative attacks on Italian opera.

50. The *DNB* is uncertain of the date of death but Heriot provides it as 1736.

51. John Evelyn wrote in his *Diary* that he had "never heard a more excellent voice; one would have sworn it had been a woman's it was so high."

52. Heriot, *Castrati*, 34.

53. Heriot, *Castrati*, 12–13.

54. Heriot, *Castrati*, 13; emphases mine.

55. Quoted in Ness, 186.

56. Lawlor citing Pat Rogers, *Literature and Popular Culture in Eighteenth Century England* (Sussex, UK: Harvester, 1985), 106–107, 138.

57. Rogers, *Literature and Popular Culture*, 106–107.

58. Ness, 186.

59. Ibid., 187.

60. Catherine Ingrassia, "Women Writing/Writing Women; Pope, Dulness, and 'Feminization' in *The Dunciad*," *Eighteenth-Century Life* 14 (1990): 49.

61. Ness, 187.

62. Ibid., 186–87.

63. Ingrassia, 49.

64. W. Koestenbaum, *The Queen's Throat: Opera, Homosexuality, and the Mystery of Desire* (New York: Poseidon Press, 1993). Had Koestenbaum glanced at the eighteenth century when writing *Double Talk: The Erotics of Male Literary Collaboration* (New York: Routledge, 1989), he would have been elated by the Pope–Warburton collaboration, erotic, homoerotic, or otherwise.

65. Critics of his life and works have documented this point especially from the biographical angle: Nicolson and Rousseau in their study of Pope's body and his health, Mack in the biography, and more recently Helen Deutsch in *Resemblance & Disgrace: Alexander Pope and the Deformation of Culture* (Cambridge: Harvard University Press, 1996).

66. D. B. Morris, *Alexander Pope, The Genius of Sense* (Cambridge: Harvard University Press, 1984), 275.

67. See Lawlor, 148; see below for the symbology of this castration and the castrato's body.

68. Originally titled *The Fatal Contract* (1653), it was a political intrigue couched in libertinism that circulated privately during the Restoration; Etherege thought it dead wood.

69. K. Silverman, *Male Subjectivity at the Margins* (London: Routledge, 1992), 447.

70. Further contexts are found in M. Bronski, "Opera: Male Queens and Other Divas," in *Culture Clash: The Making of Gay Sensibility* (Boston: South

End Press, 1984) 134–43; T. Bauman and Marita Petzoldt McClymonds, eds., *Opera and the Enlightenment* (Cambridge: Cambridge University Press, 1995).

71. See G. C. Thomas, "Was George Frideric Handel Gay?," in Philip Brett et al. (eds.), *Queering the Pitch: The New Gay and Lesbian Musicology* (London: Routledge, 1994), 155–203, and the debates it has initiated. For Handel and the castrati, see R. Strohm, *Essays on Handel and Italian Opera* (Cambridge: Cambridge University Press, 1985), 213–17.

72. Ingrassia, 40.

73. Ibid., 40.

74. Ness, 187.

75. Ilya Prigogine and Isabelle Stengers, *Order out of Chaos: Man's New Dialogue with Nature* (London: Heinemann, 1984), especially Toffler's introduction, xv.

76. See W. K. Wimsatt, *The Portraits of Alexander Pope* (New Haven: Yale University Press, 1965).

77. Readers who wonder what this mindset can amount to historically should consult Laurence Goldstein, ed., *The Male Body: Features, Destinies, Exposures* (Ann Arbor: University of Michigan Press, 1994).

78. 8 December 1742, *Corr.*, 4:431.

79. J. Saslow, *Ganymede in the Renaissance: Homosexuality in Art and Society* (New Haven: Yale University Press, 1986).

80. Thomas, *Queering the Pitch*, 177.

81. Cited by Thomas, *Queering the Pitch*, 178.

82. In G. S. Rousseau and Pat Rogers, eds., *The Enduring Legacy: Alexander Pope Tercentenary Essays* (Cambridge: Cambridge University Press, 1988), I argued for a tradition and a discourse of rage from Pope to Byron that continues to go unnoticed.

83. Jonathan Goldberg, *Sodometries: Renaissance Texts, Modern Sexualities* (Stanford: Stanford University Press, 1992).

84. D. H. Lawrence, *Lady Chatterley's Lover* (Harmondsworth, UK: Penguin, 1961), 77. See the interesting discussion of this passage in Jungian psychiatrist Rosemary Gordon, *Bridges: Metaphor for Psychic Processes* (London: Karnac, 1993), 81.

Notes to "Ideology and Opportunism: The Role of Handel in Pope's *The Dunciad in Four Books*"

I would like to thank Rosamond McGuinness and Ruth Smith for their patience in answering my questions and helping me locate sources for this paper.

1. 4.45–70. All references are to *The Dunciad in Four Books* (London, 1743).

2. *Opera seria*, the kind of opera fashionable in London at this period, was a staged and costumed musical drama in Italian, performed entirely by a small number of soloists, with dialogue between arias set as recitative, the plot usually hinging on heroic love in the tradition of historical romance. Oratorio, as developed by Handel, had a comparable dramatic structure, but differed in being in English and featuring a chorus separate from the soloists. In addition, it was characteristically performed without stage action or costume, and usually dealt with a sacred topic. It has been widely recognized—contrary to the interpretations of Pat Rogers (*Literature and Popular Culture in Eighteenth Century En-*

gland [Brighton, UK: Harvester Press, 1985], 112) and Carolyn Williams (*Pope, Homer, and Manliness: Some Aspects of Eighteenth-Century Classical Learning* [London: Routledge, 1993], 179)—that the praise of Handel at 4.63–70 alludes not to Handel's operas but to his English oratorios, and in particular to *Saul* (Sutherland in *TE* V, 4.64, n.; Morris R. Brownell, "Ears of an Untoward Make: Pope and Handel," *Musical Quarterly* 62: [1978], 554–70; Deborah J. Knuth, "Pope, Handel, and the *Dunciad*," *Modern Language Studies* 10 [1980], 22–28). For the long neglect of Handel's operas, the distortion of the oratorio performance tradition, and the relatively retarded condition of textual scholarship relative to Handel, see Winton Dean, "Scholarship and the Handel Revival," in Stanley Sadie and Anthony Hicks, eds., *Handel Tercentenary Collection* (London: Macmillan, 1987), 165–81. In his pioneering vindication of Handel's oratorios, *Handel's Dramatic Oratorios and Masques* (London: Oxford University Press, 1959), Dean disassociated Handelian oratorio from the embarrassingly pietistic and anachronistic implications of its popular performing tradition by focusing on its dramatic representation of character and conflict (which enabled him to pass over what was at that time the most embarrassing exhibit in the case against Handel, namely *Messiah*). Ruth Smith has more recently argued for an interpretation conditioned less by twentieth-century aesthetic criteria and more by contemporary religious, moral, and artistic ideals (Ruth Smith, *Handel's Oratorios and Eighteenth-Century Thought* [Cambridge: Cambridge University Press, 1995], 5–8).

3. Only since the 1970s, for the first time since Handel's lifetime, has it been possible to see stage productions of some of his operas in which original editions are consulted, correct tessituras restored, cuts avoided, and contemporary performing conventions respected. A body of recent scholarship analyzes the operas as complex musical and dramatic works, rendered the more impressive by the variety between the different operas, by Handel's pragmatic ability to work within prevailing artistic and marketing conventions, and by the sheer scale of his productivity (see particularly Winton Dean and John Merrill Knapp, *Handel's Operas, 1704–1726* [Oxford: Clarendon Press, 1987], especially chap. 1; Reinhard Strohm, *Essays on Handel and Italian Opera* [Cambridge: Cambridge University Press, 1985]; Donald Burrows, *Handel*, in *Master Musicians* series [Oxford: Oxford University Press, 1994], especially 134–56; and Steven C. LaRue, *Handel and his Singers: The Creation of the Royal Academy Operas, 1720–1728* [Oxford: Clarendon Press, 1995]).

4. It is hard to be sure how far to take this as a declaration of Pope's distaste for the entertainment as such, and how far as a recognition of the strain that crowds, confinement, and late nights placed on his delicate health (*The Correspondence of Jonathan Swift*, Harold Williams, ed., 5 vols. [Oxford: Clarendon Press, 1965], 3, 243–44; Rogers, *Literature and Popular Culture*, 127–28).

5. For the draft, now known only from a later transcription, see Maynard Mack, ed. and transcr., *The Last and Greatest Art: Some Unpublished Poetical Manuscripts of Alexander Pope* (Newark: University of Delaware Press; London: Associated University Presses, 1984), 97–100, 127. David L. Vander Meulen argues that the original manuscript dated from before first publication in 1728, but James McLaverty suggests that it need not have all been completed at this time, and links the section that anticipates the procession to the throne in Book 4 with developments of the early 1730s (David L. Vander Meulen, ed., *Pope's Dunciad of 1728: A History and Facsimile* [Charlottesville: University Press of Virginia, 1991], 48–59; James McLaverty, "Facsimiles and the Bibliographer: Pope's *Dunciad*," a review of the foregoing, *Review* 15 (1993), 1–15; 11–14).

6. Smith, 70–80.

7. Joseph Spence, *Observations, Anecdotes, and Characters of Books and Men, Collected from Conversation*, James M. Osborn, ed., 2 vols. (Oxford: Clarendon Press, 1966), 1, no.398.

8. See Simon Alderson, "Iconic Forms in English Poetry of the Time of Dryden and Pope," Ph.D. dissertation (University of Cambridge, 1993), particularly chap. 2, 5, and 6; and his "Alexander Pope and the Nature of Language," *Review of English Studies*, 47 (1996), 23–34.

9. *TE* 5, 608; Spence, I, no.396.

10. *Essay on Criticism*, 337–83.

11. The basic unit of *opera seria*, the *da capo* aria, has an ABA' structure completed by an ornamented repetition of the first section of the music to the same words, a recurrence to a previous verbal formulation that would hardly ever be called for by solely dramatic criteria. Though conservative commentators like Pope, along with audiences who admired Handel principally for his setting of English sacred texts, persisted in treating music as trivial except when subservient to text, the future lay in extended instrumental forms, notably the sonata and symphony, in which the unfolding of internal compositional logic would make possible a self-sustaining development independent of text or quasi-linguistic referentiality. See James A. Winn, *Unsuspected Eloquence: A History of the Relations Between Poetry and Music* (New Haven and London: Yale University Press, 1981), 199.

12. Winn, 200–201, 241–49.

13. For the unity of music, dance, and poetry in early culture, see Winn, chap. 1, "The Poet as Singer: The Ancient World." For the separation and its conseqences, see page 30. For the gradual decline in the prestige of analogies between musical harmony and the creativity of God and of poets, see John Hollander, *The Untuning of the Sky: Ideas of Music in English Poetry, 1500–1700* (Princeton: Princeton University Press, 1961), particularly p. 13 and chap. 6.

14. The epigraph quotes Ovid's account of how Phoebus Apollo, god of music and poetry, prevented a serpent from devouring the murdered Orpheus: "Tandem *Phoebus* adest, morsusque inferre parentem / Congelat, et patulos, ut erant, indurat hiatus" ("'At last Phoebus appears, and freezes him as he is about to bite, and turns to stone, just as they were, his gaping jaws'": for original context, see Latin text in *Ovid: Metamorphoses*, ed. and trans. Frank Justus Miller, rev. G. P. Goold, 2 vols. [London: Heinemann, 1977], XI.58, 60). The implication is that, through Pope's text, the power of poetry will similarly turn his enemies into ludicrously petrified images of their futile malice.

15. For the passions as objects of musical imitation, see Winn, 197, 232–37; for motion as an imitative principle in word-setting, see Manfred Bukofzer, "Allegory in Baroque Music," *Journal of the Warburg and Courtauld Institutes* 3 (1939–1940): 1–21; Winn, 217–18.

16. Spence, 1, no.34.

17. Norman Ault and Rosemary Cowler, eds., *The Prose Works of Alexander Pope*, 2 vols. (Oxford: Blackwell, 1936–1986), 2, 15–16. The supposed excesses of stage spectacle frame the apocalyptic climax of Book 3 (from line 228).

18. For an assessment of the contribution of librettists to Handel's operas, see Dean and Knapp, 15–19 and *passim*. Strohm points out that in Italy, where in comparison to London there was little spoken drama, opera was seen as "primarily the music-dramatic recitation of poetry" (96–97).

19. Frequently cited as an index of the pressure from English audiences to keep recitative to a minimum is the advice given to a would-be librettist by the commercially minded Giuseppe Riva (George E. Dorris, "Paolo Rolli and the Italian Circle in London 1715–1744," *Studies in Italian Literature* 2 [The Hague and Paris: Mouton, 1967], 42–43).

20. Charles Burney, *A General History of Music, from the Earliest Ages to the Present Period (1789)*, Frank Mercer, ed., 2 vols. (London: G. T. Foulis, 1935), 2, 497–506. Of the twelve chapters of Book 4 (devoted to the eighteenth century), seven deal explicitly with music-drama; and the chapter on Italian opera in London (chap. 6) accounts for approximately half the length of the whole. Burney also confronts the early eighteenth-century literary onslaught on opera by mobilizing technical and historical detail to undermine Pope's credibility, and by mounting a respectful but firm critique of Addison and Steele's operatic satires (2, 640–41, 675–78).

21. Otto Erich Deutsch, *Handel, A Documentary Biography* (London: Adam and Charles Black, 1955), 303–304; Judith Milhous and Robert Hume, "The Charter for the Royal Academy of Music," *Music and Letters* 67 (1986): 50–58.

22. Smith concludes that "In relation to his oratorios (and for that matter his operas) political implications seem to have come a long way down Handel's list of priorities" (200).

23. Carole Taylor, "Handel and Frederick, Prince of Wales," *Musical Times* 125 (1984): 89–92; Robert D. Hume, "Handel and Opera Management in London in the 1730s," *Music and Letters* 67 (1986): 347–62 (359); Christine Gerrard, *The Patriot Opposition to Walpole: Politics, Poetry, and National Myth, 1725–1742* (Oxford: Clarendon Press, 1994), 61; Elizabeth Gibson, *The Royal Academy of Music (1719–1728): The Institution and Its Directors*, Outstanding Dissertations in Music from British Universities, John Caldwell, ed. (New York: Garland, 1989), 68–69; Burrows, 198. It is not clear either that the king and queen systematically snubbed the Opera of the Nobility: according to Burney, the entire royal family, not just the prince of Wales, attended the opening night of Porpora's *Polifemo* in 1735 (Burney, 2, 791–92).

24. Smith, 76.

25. Compare James Miller, who considered Handel a corrupter of national taste up to 1735, but later that year exempted him from blame, presumably also on account of oratorio: see Smith, 76.

26. For the process and probable motives of Handel's cessation of operatic enterprises, see Carole Taylor, "Handel's Disengagement from the Italian Opera," in Sadie and Hicks, 165–81.

27. Graydon Beeks, " 'A Club of Composers': Handel, Pepusch and Arbuthnot at Cannons," in Sadie and Hicks, 209–21; 212. For the first private performance of *Acis and Galatea*, see Georg Friedrich Händel, *Acis and Galatea (1. Fassung) HWV 49ª*, Wolfram Windszus, ed., Hallische Händel-Ausgabe 9.1 (Kassel: Bärenreiter, 1991), xiv–xvii; Pat Rogers, "Gay and the World of Opera," in Peter Lewis and Nigel Wood, eds., *John Gay and the Scriblerians*, (London: Vision Press, 1988), 147–62 (153); and John Fuller in his edition of *John Gay, Dramatic Works*, 2 vols. (Oxford: Clarendon Press, 1983), 1, 32. Although David Nokes, in his *John Gay, A Profession of Friendship* (Oxford: Oxford University Press, 1995), dismisses allegations that Pope shared authorship of the libretto (e.g., *TE*, 6, 215–17) as "a further instance of the scholarly habit of attributing, wherever possible, Gay's works to one of his more celebrated colleagues," their currency among musicologists has been renewed on the basis of a letter in which

Sir David Dalrymple reports from Cannons that "the words are to be furnished by Mrs Pope & Gay" (276, n.31; Beeks, 212). Brian Trowell, proceeding from the supposition of joint authorship established by the Twickenham edition and supported by Dalrymple's letter, considers the relation of the libretto to pastoral and metrical theory very much from the standpoint of Pope's published views, but concludes that because Pope was so fully occupied at this time in translating Homer, he "is unlikely to have contributed more than a few lines of verse"; and he argues that even the portion of the libretto he regards as its original core (in contrast to portions he attributes to later revision by John Hugues) has several numbers marked by the metrical hiatus that Pope considered a serious fault, from which Trowell concludes that these numbers are unlikely to have been written or revised by Pope (Brian Trowell, "Acis, Galatea and Polyphemus: A 'Serenata a tre voci'?," in Nigel Fortune, ed., *Music and Theatre: Essays in Honour of Winton Dean* [Cambridge: Cambridge University Press, 1987], 31–93; 83, 87–88). The unfortunate misattribution to Pope of large portions of the libretto by Windszus rests on a misreading of Trowell (Windszus, xvi).

28. For the most recent assessment of Pope's probable contribution to the original *Esther*, see Smith, 277–81. See also Brownell, 566–70, and, for a reconstruction of the text, *TE* 6, 423–25. The work is now included in the Halle edition: Georg Friedrich Händel, *Esther: Oratorio in Six Scenes (1. Fassung) HWV 50ª*, Howard Serwer, ed., Hallische Händel-Ausgabe I.8 (Kassel: Bärenreiter, 1995).

29. See Deutsch, 602; Smith, 37–38. For the expressive genius of the English language as analyzed in popular grammars, see Alderson, "Alexander Pope and the Nature of Language." For Handel's recovery from this setback, see Burrows, 281–84.

30. *The Dunciad* revision of 1735 recorded the presentation on 12 March 1729 in the note to the first line of the poem, the revision of 1743 in the note to the title that precedes the note to line 1. The king's response was recorded (or, it may be, to an extent invented) in a jocular account of recent Scriblerian triumphs sent by Arbuthnot to Swift in the same month (*The Correspondence of Jonathan Swift*, 3, 236). The presentation was made public by Richard Savage in the dedication to *A Collection of Pieces . . . publish'd on Occasion of the Dunciad* (London: L. Gilliver, 1732), vi.

31. Smith, 169.

32. Ibid., 327–33.

33. Georg Friedrich Händel, *Saul*, Percy M. Young, ed., Hallische Händel-Ausgabe I.13 (1962), 109–11. For the wordbook and evidence that this number was omitted in performance, see the companion volume of critical notes, 19–20, 34. It is included in the 1989 recording by John Eliot Gardiner (Philips CD 426–265–2).

34. See Hollander, chap. 6.

35 For discussion of contemporary political readings of *Israel in Egypt*, see Smith, 213–15, 288–92.

36. As constructed in *The Dunciad in Four Books*, oratorio apparently provides a satisfactory contrast with the frivolously theatrical devotional music of which Pope disapproved (for remarks typical of the conventional insistence on a distinct and more solemn church style, see the "Light quirks of Musick, broken and uneven" that "Make the soul dance upon a Jig to Heaven" [*Epistle to Burlington*, lines 143–44], and, in the present passage, the "One Trill" that is to "Wake the dull Church, and lull the ranting Stage"). For some elements in

Handel's audience, however, the theatrical venue and associations of oratorio remained problematic: see Smith, 43–49.

37. Since the Hallische Händel-Ausgabe edition of *Israel in Egypt* has not yet appeared, I cite the unsatisfactory but generally available *Israel in Egypt. An Oratorio by Georg Frederic Handel*, Friedrich Chrysander, ed., German Handel Society (Leipzig: Breitkopf and Härtel, 1863). I have also consulted the notes accompanying the 1978 recording by John Eliot Gardiner (Erato CD 2292–43399–2). Miriam's part is anticipated by alto and tenor on p. 254 of Chrysander's text, and she emerges briefly from the chorus at 258–60.

38. Chrysander, 109–110.

39. Ibid., 3–16, 17–22. For the emotive power of Handel's setting of Biblical words for contemporaries, see Smith, 125–36.

40. Chrysander, 23–26 (frogs), 27–40 (flies), 41–54 (hailstones).

41. Ibid., 195–96, 210–11, 173–84, 185–94, 153–62.

42. Ibid., 41–42, 55, 58.

43. Ibid., 27–40.

44. Smith, 77.

45. George Sherburn, "The *Dunciad*, Book IV," *Texas Studies in Literature and Language* 24 (1944): 174–90, n.4. Sherburn also adds that Handel "so appreciated Pope's praise that in his next opera [*sic*] (*Semele*, 1743) he inserted in Congreve's libretto the famous aria, 'Where'er you walk'," a statement I have been unable to verify (for various uses of Pope material in Handel's oratorios, see index under "Pope, Alexander" in Dean, *Handel's Dramatic Oratorios*). For periodic but unfounded rumors of Handel's bankruptcy, see Deutsch's index under "Handel, bankruptcy (alleged)"; for a vigorous refutation of the traditional account of Handel's alleged sufferings, see Hume, 356–62.

46. For a generally positive interpretation of Handel's management of his various projects in the years 1741–1745, see Burrows, 259–84.

47. Deutsch, 515–17; for Handel's scorn for the operas mounted without him, 520, 530–31.

48. For the progress of the printing during 1742, see *The Correspondence of Alexander Pope*, George Sherburn, ed., 5 vols. (Oxford: Clarendon, 1956), 5, 393, 425–26, 427–28, 429–30.

49. Burrows, 280–84, 300–301.

50. The claim is made in the preface to the three-book *Dunciad*s, reprinted as Appendix I in *The Dunciad in Four Books*.

51. Richard Luckett, *Handel's Messiah: A Celebration* (New York: Harcourt Brace, 1992), 25.

52. Deutsch, 424, 472.

53. Ibid., 310.

54. The note cited is cued as "VER. 614, 618" but I quote only the lines relevant to opera (lines 616–18). The cue to line 614 may be an error.

55. *Poems on Affairs of State . . . Vol. III* (n.p., 1704), 407. The poem has been attributed to Halifax: see Charles Montagu, Earl of Halifax, *The Poetical Works of Charles Montague Earl of Halifax . . .* (Edinburgh: Mundell and Son, 1793), 770.

56. *Poems on Affairs of State*, "Tofts and Margarita," 455.

57. Beeks, 213–24.

58. Stanley Sadie, ed., *The New Grove Dictionary of Music and Musicians*, 20 vols. (London: Macmillan, 1980), "Margherita L'Epine."

Notes to " 'Trials of Manhood': Cibber, *The Dunciad*, and the Masculine Self"

I wish to thank Helen Deutsch and the editors of this volume for their insights and suggestions.

1. "Women Writing/Writing Women: Pope, Dulness, and 'Feminization' in *The Dunciad*," *Eighteenth-Century Life* 14 (November 1990): 40–58. See also Margaret Doody, who argues that Augustan society placed limits on the kind of poetry acceptable for women to write (*The Daring Muse: Augustan Poetry Reconsidered* [Cambridge: Cambridge University Press, 1985], 130).

2. Lance Bertelsen provides a recent significant exception in his "Journalism, Carnival, and *Jubilate Agno*," *ELH* 59 (Summer, 1992): 357–84. While not taking up this particular question, Kristina Straub's *Sexual Suspects: Eighteenth-Century Players and Sexual Ideology* (Princeton: Princeton University Press, 1992) analyzes Pope and Cibber with equal seriousness; similarly, J. Paul Hunter calls much-needed attention to the kind of writers whom Pope attacks in *Before Novels: The Cultural Contexts of Eighteenth-Century English Fiction* (New York: W. W. Norton, 1990). See also Philip Pinkus, *Grub St. Stripped Bare . . .* (Hamden, CT: Archon Books, 1968) and Pat Rogers's fine study, *Grub Street: Studies in a Subculture* (London: Methuen, 1972). Rogers, however, remains firmly in Pope's corner.

3. See "Journalism, Carnival, and *Jubilate Agno*," cited earlier, 357.

4. Bertelsen, 358.

5. *Women's Place in Pope's World* (Cambridge: Cambridge University Press, 1989), 166–67. See also Penelope Wilson, "Feminism and the Augustans: Some Readings and Problems," *Critical Quarterly* 28.1 (Spring, Summer 1986): 80–92; Ellen Pollak, *The Poetics of Sexual Myth: Gender and Ideology in the Verse of Swift and Pope* (Chicago: University of Chicago Press, 1985). In his discussion of *The Dunciad*, David B. Morris points out that "the formula 'man of sense' conveys an implicit suggestion that sense is specifically a masculine virtue." See his *Alexander Pope, The Genius of Sense* (Cambridge: Harvard University Press, 1984).

6. "The Monstrous Mother: Reproductive Anxiety in Swift and Pope," *ELH* 61 (1994): 832. For Francus, "the accelerated demonization of the fertile mother in Swift and Pope is primarily a result of their extended punning on reproduction, in which literary production is fused with its theological and biological counterparts" (834).

7. *The Dunciad* (B) in *The Twickenham Edition of the Poems of Alexander Pope*, 11 vols., John Butt, gen. ed., James Sutherland, vol. ed. (New York: Routledge, 1993), 5: 277, 107–108. References from this edition are cited in the text; references to *The Dunciad Variorum* are cited in the text as A.

8. *Sawney: An Heroical Poem: Occasion'd by the Dunciad* (London: J. Roberts, 1728), 7.

9. "The 'Blunted Arms' of Dulness: The Problem of Power in *The Dunciad*," *Studies in Philology* 79 (Spring 1982): 177–204; 178.

10. For a fine discussion of *The Dunciad* as an attack on the feminization of culture, see Ingrassia, "Women Writing/Writing Women."

11. On feminine monstrosity in *The Dunciad*, see Francus; for Augustan misogyny in general that often takes the form of monstrosity, see Felicity Nussbaum, *The Brink of All We Hate: English Satires on Women, 1660–1750* (Lexington: University of Kentucky Press, 1984).

12. Straub, 67–77.

13. Ibid., 24–46.

14. Ibid., 74–75; 79–82.

15. Ibid., 78.

16. On this point, see Susan Staves, "A Few Kind Words for the Fop, " *SEL* 22 (Summer 1982): 413–28. While taking up with question in very different terms, Staves similarly understands foppishness as an alternative and not necessarily negative construction of masculinity.

17. *The Bonds of Love: Psychoanalysis, Feminism, and the Problem of Domination* (New York: Pantheon Books, 1988), 46–47. Future references cited in the text.

18. Carol Barash, "Violence and the Maternal: Swift, Psychoanalysis, and the 1720s," in Jonathan Swift, *Gulliver's Travels,* Christopher Fox, ed. *Case Studies in Contemporary Criticism* (New York: Bedford Books, 1995), 443.

19. Christopher Fox, *Locke and the Scriblerians: Identity and Consciousness in Early Eighteenth-Century Britain* (Berkeley: University of California Press, 1988).

20. Terry Eagleton, *The Ideology of the Aesthetic* (Oxford: Basil Blackwell, 1990), 16. For more about Pope and the ideology of the aesthetic, see Susan Staves, "Pope's Refinement," *The Eighteenth Century: Theory and Interpretation* 29 (Spring 1988): 145–63.

21. Eagleton, 16, 23.

22. Francus makes a similar point when she observes that "[t]he crux of the problem for Swift and Pope is the menace of multiplicity, which dilutes integrity (in its etymological and common senses), so that individuality, and consequently autonomy, are forfeit" (834). Cibber *is,* however, feminized in particular images I discuss later.

23. For eighteenth-century associations of effeminacy and aristocracy, see Michael McKeon, "Historicizing Patriarchy: The Emergence of Gender Difference in England, 1660–1760," *Eighteenth-Century Studies* 28 (Spring 1995): 295–322.

24. I discuss the problem of Cibber's plagiarism at greater length in *Playwrights and Plagiarists in Early Modern England: Gender, Authorship, Literary Property* (Ithaca: Cornell University Press, 1996).

25. *A Letter from Mr. Cibber, to Mr. Pope, Inquiring into the MOTIVES that might induce him in his SATYRICAL WORKS, to be so frequently fond of Mr. CIBBER'S Name* (1742), facsimile reprint (New York: Garland, 1975), 18. Future references cited in the text.

26. *The Player's Passion: Studies in the Science of Acting* (Newark: University of Delaware Press, 1985).

27. David B. Morris, *Alexander Pope, The Genius of Sense* (Cambridge: Harvard University Press, 1984), 283. Morris also makes the following point about Cibber: "Exhibition and self-exposure are the consistent signs of insanity in the eighteenth century, epitomized by the odd spectacles at Bedlam. In an age that considered social decorum an expression of communal wisdom, Cibber's zest for confession and self-exposure far exceeded the range of amiable eccentricity. In fact, as actor, theater manager, and author, Cibber could be said to have earned his living by exhibiting folly" (284).

28. See also Ingrassia, 44–45.

29. For another view, see Howard D. Weinbrot, "*The Dunciad,* Nursing Mothers, and Isaiah," *Philological Quarterly* 17 (Fall 1992): 479–94. Richard

Nash also comments on the birth imagery in Pope; see his "Translation, Editing, and Poetic Invention in Pope's *Dunciad*," *Studies in Philology* 89 (Fall 1992): 470–84.

30. See Richard Nash, "Translation, Editing, and Poetic Invention in Pope's *Dunciad*." The Toft case has recently been discussed by Dennis Todd in *Imagining Monsters: Miscreations of the Self in Eighteenth-Century England* (Chicago: University of Chicago Press, 1995). See also Alan Shepard, "The Literature of a Medical Hoax: The Case of Mary Toft, 'The Pretended Rabbet-Breeder,' " *Eighteenth-Century Life* 19 (May 1995): 59–77; Glennda Leslie, "Cheat and Impostor: Debate Following the Case of the Rabbit Breeder," *The Eighteenth Century: Theory and Interpretation* 27 (1986): 269–86; Lisa Cody, " 'The Doctor's in Labour; or a New Whim Wham from Guilford,' " *Gender & History* 4 (1992): 175–96.

31. Eagleton, 25.

32. Valerie Rumbold, in fact, points out that Pope had quite a close relationship with his own mother.

33. Richard Nash, "Translation, Editing, and Poetic Invention in Pope's *Dunciad*," 470.

34. Straub, *Sexual Suspects*, chap. 1. See also chaps. 2–4 on Colley Cibber, to which my reading is indebted.

35. For chronologies of the dispute between Pope and Cibber, see Norman Ault, *New Light on Pope* (London: Methuen, 1949), chap. 20; Richard Hindry Barker, *Mr Cibber of Drury Lane* (New York: Columbia University Press, 1939), chap. 12; Leonard R. N. Ashley, *Colley Cibber* (Boston: Twayne, 1989), chap. 9.

36. Kristina Straub points out that "Colley Cibber's 1740 *Apology for the Life of Mr. Colley Cibber* shows the rhetorical control over his 'feminine,' abject status that professionalism afforded the actor" (39). In the *Apology*, "Cibber presents himself as both the object of public gaze and the keen self-observer" (40).

37. "The World as Stage and Closet," in *British Theater and Other Arts, 1660–1800,* Shirley Strum Kenney, ed. (Washington, DC: Folger Shakespeare Library, 1984), 277.

38. "The Insistent I," *Novel: A Forum on Fiction* 13 (Fall 1979): 19–36. See also Christopher Fox, *Locke and the Scriblerians*.

39. See Straub, 39–40.

40. *An Apology for the Life of Colley Cibber*, B. R. S. Fone, ed. (Ann Arbor: University of Michigan Press, 1968), 6.

41. *Colley Cibber*, 100.

42. See *Memoirs of Laetitia Pilkington*, A. C. Elias, Jr., ed., 2 vols. (Athens: University of Georgia Press, 1977).

43. *Apology*, 43.

44. Ibid., 167.

45. Ibid., 103.

46. Ibid., 27–28.

47. Colley Cibber, *The Egotist; Or, Colley upon Cibber* (London, 1743), 58.

48. For the connection between aristocratic masculinity and effeminacy in the eighteenth century, see Michael McKeon, "Historicizing Patriarchy."

49. Cibber, *The Egotist*, 30.

50. Ibid., 47.

51. *Apology*, 279, 280, 281.

52. Ibid., 3.

53. *A Letter from Mr. Cibber, to Mr. Pope*, 8. Future references cited in the text.

54. Straub offers a different reading of Cibber's boxing metaphor: "Cibber associates his professed lack of literary skill with a nonaggressive, asexual masculinity that looks healthy in relation to the fevered and pathetic heterosexual drive to conquest he associates with Pope's satiric virtuosity" (*Sexual Suspects*, 44).

55. See also Helen Deutsch, " 'The Truest Copies' and the 'Mean Original': Pope, Deformity, and the Poetics of Self Exposure," *Eighteenth-Century Studies* 27 (Fall 1993): 1–26. Deutsch shows the ways in which Pope, on the other hand, uses his body as a source of authority.

56. Straub, 44.

57. Ibid., 45.

58. *Between Men: English Literature and Male Homosocial Desire* (New York: Columbia University Press, 1985).

59. *Another Occasional Letter from Mr. Cibber to Mr. Pope. Wherein The New Hero's Preferment to his Throne, in the* Dunciad, *seems not to be Accepted. And the Author of his Poem His more rightful Claim to it, is Asserted* (1744), facsimile reprint (New York: Garland, 1975), 7. Future references cited in the text.

60. *Nobody's Story: The Vanishing Acts of Women Writers in the Marketplace, 1670–1820* (Berkeley: University of California Press, 1994), 150. See also Robert Folkenflik, "Patronage and the Poet-Hero," *Huntington Library Quarterly* 48 (1985): 363–79.

Notes to "Pope's 'Girl of the Game': The Prostitution of the Author and the Business of Culture"

1. For example, see Jacqueline Pearson, *The Prostituted Muse: Images of Women & Women Dramatists, 1642–1737* (New York: St. Martin's, 1988); Janet Todd, *The Sign of Angellica: Women, Writing, and Fiction, 1660–1800* (New York: Columbia University Press, 1989); and Catherine Gallagher, *Nobody's Story: The Vanishing Acts of Women Writers in the Marketplace, 1670–1820* (Berkeley: University of California Press, 1994).

2. Shannon Bell, *Reading, Writing and Rewriting the Prostitute Body* (Bloomington: Indiana University Press, 1994), 2.

3. Marilyn Francus, "The Monstrous Mother: Reproductive Anxiety in Swift and Pope," *ELH* 61 (1994): 829.

4. This did not just apply in England. For example, the association of prostitution, writing, information-gathering, and police surveillance in France in the second half of the eighteenth century is explored in Pamela Cheek, "Prostitutes of 'Political Institution,' " *Eighteenth-Century Studies* 28 (Winter 1994–5): 193–219.

5. Quoted in Howard William Troyer, *Ned Ward of Grubstreet: A Study of Sub-Literary London in the Eighteenth Century* (Cambridge: Harvard University Press, 1946), 3.

6. Jonathan Swift, *The Writings of Jonathan Swift*, Robert A. Greenberg and William B. Piper, eds. (New York: W. W. Norton, 1973), 274.

7. Daniel Defoe, *A Vindication of the Press*, Augustan Reprint Society no. 29 (Los Angeles: Clark Library, 1951), 21.

8. Alexander Pope, *The Twickenham Edition of the Poems of Alexander Pope*, John Butt, gen. ed., 11 vols. (London, Methuen, 1939–1969), 6: 326. Henceforth referred to as *TE* in notes; subsequent line references are made parenthetically.

9. Colley Cibber, *A Letter from Mr. Cibber to Mr. Pope, Inquiring into the Motives That Might Induce Him in His Satyrical Works, To Be So Frequently Fond of Mr. Cibber's Name* (London: Lewis, 1742), 47–48. All subsequent references are made parenthetically.

10. For the assaults against Pope that Cibber's story motivated, see Joseph V. Guerinot, *Pamphlet Attacks on Alexander Pope, 1711–1744* (London: Methuen, 1969), 288–311. For a list of materials generally relating to the "Pope–Cibber Controversy" from 1717 to 1744, see also C. D. Peavy, "The Pope–Cibber Controversy: A Bibliography," *Restoration and Eighteenth-Century Theatre Research* 3 (1964): 51–55.

11. *The Universal Spectator* (14 August 1742).

12. Ibid., (21 August 1742).

13. Norman Ault, *New Light on Pope* (London: Methuen, 1949), 306. Besides Ault, who enumerates the most interesting materials this episode generated and tries to evaluate the story's biographical veracity, a number of other scholars touch upon Cibber's tale. In *Sexual Suspects: Eighteenth-Century Players and Sexual Ideology* (Princeton: Princeton University Press, 1992), Kristina Straub analyzes some of the tropes that Cibber employs in both his *Letter from Mr. Cibber* and other self-representations, but does not give close attention to the figure of the whore. In "Colley Cibber's Good Nature and His Reaction to Pope's Satire," *Papers on Language and Literature* 2 (1966), 361–71, Thomas B. Gilmore compares Cibber's response to Pope's satires to other "dunce" attacks on the poet and finds "distinct and numerous similarities" (371). In the various Pope and Cibber biographies, the episode gets duly narrated or at least mentioned: for example, on Pope, see Maynard Mack, *Alexander Pope: A Life* (New York: W. W. Norton, 1985), 292–93 and 779–81; George Sherburn, *The Early Career of Alexander Pope* (Oxford: Clarendon, 1934), 156–59; and Bonamy Dobrée, *Alexander Pope* (New York: Greenwood, 1969), 113–14; on Cibber, Helene Koon, *Colley Cibber: A Biography* (Lexington: University Press of Kentucky, 1986), 81–82 and 157–65; Richard Hindry Barker, *Mr Cibber of Drury Lane* (New York: AMS, 1966), 210–20; and Leonard R. N. Ashley, *Colley Cibber*, in *Twayne's English Authors* series (New York: Twayne, 1965), 140–50. In some of the earlier biographies, the story of the whore gets very brief and euphemistic mention: in *Alexander Pope*, in *English Men of Letters* series (London: Macmillan, 1914), Leslie Stephen simply calls the tale an "irritating anecdote" that describes "Pope as introduced by Cibber and Lord Warwick to very bad company" (135); in *The Life of Alexander Pope*, in *The Works of Alexander Pope*, 10 vols. (London: Murray, 1889), William John Courthope says no more than that it is "a ridiculous story calculated to show that Pope was not the person to reflect upon his [Cibber's] morals" (5: 334); in *The Life and Times of Colley Cibber* (London: Constable, 1928), F. Dorothy Senior discusses Cibber's "Quarrel with Pope" (126–43) but demurely fails to refer to the story at all.

14. Isaac Disraeli, *Quarrels of Authors* (London: Murray, 1814), 222–23.

15. Straub, 87.

16. We must remember that, if it were not for the story of Pope with the "Girl of the Game," Cibber's pamphlet would mostly be forgotten. It is this story (essentially divorced from the rest of the pamphlet) that gets retold, discussed, and

repeatedly illustrated. With its wonderful visual contrasts—the diminutive hunchback poet or the "little hasty . . . *Tom Tit*," whose deformed figure was already well established in both satirical prints and literature, and the huge-by-comparison prostitute, the "Mount of Love"—logically inspired several engravings. Besides the two reproduced here, there were also "The POETICAL TOM-TITT perch'd upon the Mount of Love: *Being the Representation of a Merry Description in Mr.* Cibber's *Letter to Mr. Pope*" and "*An* Essay *on* Woman, *by the* Author *of the* Essay *on* Man: Being HOMER PRESERV'D, OR, THE TWICKENHAM SQUIRE CAUGHT BY THE HEELS." Ault observes that the last print "must have been extremely popular, for there seems to have been at least three issues of it with different titles" (303). William Kurtz Wimsatt characterizes all these prints as "Nominal Portraits" in *The Portraits of Alexander Pope* (New Haven: Yale University Press, 1965), 364. The fact that "Pope was probably the most frequently portrayed English person of his generation, perhaps of the whole eighteenth century" and that he worked obsessively to have "an adequate image of himself made public" (Wimsatt, xv), especially as a high-culture defender and producer, makes the narrative and graphic representation of the poet in the lap of the whore behind a closed door, which Cibber flings open ultimately to expose Pope to all, particularly relevant and poignant as an image subverting the poet's representational efforts. See Eric V. Chandler, "The Publishing Imagination: The Cultural Warfare of Alexander Pope and Edmund Curll," Ph.D. thesis, University of California at Berkeley, 1998, esp. chaps. 3–5, for a discussion of other satirical images of Pope.

17. See J. G. A. Pocock, "Between Machiavelli and Hume: Gibbon as Civic Humanist and Philosophical Historian," *Daedalus* 105 (Summer 1976): 153–56, and *The Machiavellian Moment: Florentine Political Thought and the Atlantic Republican Tradition* (Princeton: Princeton University Press, 1975) 423–505; also John Barrell, *The Political Theory of Painting from Reynolds to Hazlitt: "The Body of the Public"* (New Haven: Yale University Press, 1986), 3–10.

18. As Mary Douglas explains in *Purity and Danger: An Analysis of Concepts of Pollution and Taboo* (New York: Praeger, 1966), "The body is a model which can stand for any bounded system. Its boundaries can represent any boundaries which are threatened or precarious. . . . The functions of [the body's] different parts and their relation afford a source of symbols for other complex structures" (115). Recourse to corporeal metaphor—defecation, urination, flatulence, sex of all sorts, reproduction, and disease—is everywhere in the eighteenth-century satire about "degenerate" cultural production. Among these metaphors, the metaphor of prostitution seems particularly apt in representing commercial/cultural abjection, since the prostitute body (on which the identity of the prostitute as such depends) works in a system of exchange—sexual access for money. Her commercial self-abjection makes the prostitute particularly monstrous. After quoting the 1725 pamphlet *A Conference about Whoring*, in which the author describes the prostitute as "Monster and Dunghill" and as "quite another Creature" from normative womanhood, Felicity A. Nussbaum in *Torrid Zones: Maternity, Sexuality, and Empire in Eighteenth-Century English Narratives* (Baltimore: Johns Hopkins University Press, 1995) argues that prostitutes "are conceptualized in eighteenth-century England as a species set apart from woman" (100); the prostitute is associated with fluidity, exchange, ambiguity, disease, and both barrenness (sex grotesquely without the burden of reproduction) and unwanted or uncontrolled fertility (sex with the burden of unwanted, bastard offspring). In " 'Monstrous Generation': The Birth of Capital in Defoe's

Moll Flanders and *Roxana*," *Publications of the Modern Language Association of America* 110 (1995), Ann Louise Kibbie shows that the eighteenth-century use of the prostitute as a metaphor in "the evolving discourse of capitalism" (1023) was partially prefigured in sixteenth- and seventeenth-century condemnations of usury, in which the more general "figure of the woman represents a more natural, self-limiting, 'moral' economy at some moments, at others it symbolizes the destructive energies of capitalism" (1025). In "Sentimental Properties: *Pamela* and *Memoirs of a Woman of Pleasure*," *ELH* 58 (1991), Kibbie elaborates on Steven Marcus's understanding in *The Other Victorians: A Study of Sexuality and Pornography in Mid-Nineteenth-Century England* (New York: W. W. Norton, 1985) that "the principle imagery in which sexuality was represented in consciousness was largely drawn from the sphere of socioeconomic activity and had to do with concerns and anxieties about the problems of accumulation, production, and excessive expenditure" (xiii). Kibbie shows that "the inverse of [Marcus's] model is equally true: the principal imagery in which the economic was represented in consciousness was largely drawn from the sphere of sexual activity"; after showing how economic and sexual discourses draw on each other, Kibbie argues that the pornographic/sentimental *Memoirs of a Woman of Pleasure* presents "an erotic fluid economy" that "dissolves distinctions between the sexual and commercial" (569). This association of the whore and her story with problematical or provocative conflation provides Aphra Behn, in *Nobody's Story*, with a compelling strategy for dealing with the charge of prostitution that perniciously confuses the circulating prostitute body with the circulating text of the female author. Rather than try to deflect the charge, as Gallagher shows, Behn as author immerses herself in or embraces prostitute ambiguity and playfully compounds confusion (see chap. 1).

19. In *Authors and Owners: The Invention of Copyright* (Cambridge: Harvard University Press, 1993), Mark Rose states, "Pope was not the first English author to go to court. . . . But Pope was the first author to make regular and repeated use of the [copyright] statute" (59).

20. Carolyn D. Williams, *Pope, Homer, and Manliness: Some Aspects of Eighteenth-Century Classical Learning* (New York: Routledge, 1993), 1.

21. Colley Cibber, *An Apology for the Life of Mr. Colley Cibber* (Ann Arbor: University of Michigan Press, 1968), 279. All subsequent references are made parenthetically.

22. *Another Occasional Letter from Mr. Cibber to Mr. Pope* (London: Lewis, 1744), 19.

23. About this advertisement, Pope wrote to Warburton on 27 November 1742, "I have scratched out a sort of *avis au lecteur*, . . . which if you disapprove not, you will make your own." This statement seems to confirm Pope's authorship of the section. See *The Correspondence of Alexander Pope*, George Sherburn, ed., 5 vols. (Oxford: Clarendon, 1956), 4: 428. See also James Sutherland's note (Pope, *TE* 5: 251 n. 4).

24. In a letter to Warburton dated 28 December 1742, Pope refers to this section as "your Discourse in the Name of Aristarchus" (*Corr.* 4: 434) and thus seems to confirm Warburton's authorship.

25. Warburton's phrase "in that Society," emphatically set off by commas, functions as a kind of wink to the reader: does "that Society" refer to the theater or to the whorehouse? It does not matter, because the whole point is to conflate the two in an exploitation of the contemporary perception that female theater performers, like female authors, are necessarily prostitutes and that the

theater is one place where whores could conveniently peddle themselves. Warburton implies that Cibber's view of mankind as normally consorting with whores is the grotesque result of a life spent in the theater.

26. See Guerinot for the precedents in attributing the authorship of this pamphlet and *The Difference between Verbal and Practical Virtue* to Hervey (296, 299–300).

27. *A Letter to Mr. C—b—r, On his Letter to Mr. P—* (London: Roberts, 1742), 16–17.

28. *The Difference between Verbal and Practical Virtue* (London: Roberts, 1742), 1; 5. Ibid., 5.

29. For the rise of commercialism in the eighteenth century, see Neil McKendrick, John Brewer, and J. H. Plumb, *The Birth of a Consumer Society: The Commercialization of Eighteenth-Century England* (London: Europa, 1982), esp. 265–285. For considerations of Pope's problematical relationship to literary commercialism, see Catherine Ingrassia, "Women Writing/Writing Women: Pope, Dulness, and 'Feminization' in the *Dunciad*," *Eighteenth-Century Life* 14 (November 1990): 40–58; Brean S. Hammond, " 'Guard the sure barrier': Pope and the Partitioning of Culture," *Pope: New Contexts*, David Fairer, ed. (New York: Harvester Wheatsheaf, 1990), 225–40; Peter Heaney, Introduction, in *An Anthology of Eighteenth-Century Satire* (Lewiston, NY: Edwin Mellen, 1995), esp. 15–16 and 24–25; Laura Brown, *Alexander Pope*, in *Rereading Literature* series (New York: Blackwell, 1985), 128–58; Nicholson, 1–26; Anne Hall Bailey, "How Much for Just the Muse?: Alexander Pope's *Dunciad*, Book IV and the Literary Market," *The Eighteenth Century* 36 (1995): 24–37; Eric Chandler, "Pope's Emetic: Bodies, Books, and Filth," *Genre* 28 (Winter 1994): 351–76; Claudia Thomas, "Pope and His *Dunciad* Adversaries: Skirmishes on the Border of Gentility," in James Gill, ed., in *Cutting Edges: Postmodern Critical Essays on Eighteenth-Century Satire*, (Knoxville: University of Tennessee Press, 1995), 275–300.

30. *Sawney and Colley, A Poetical Dialogue: Occasioned by a Late Letter from the Laureate of St. James's, to the Homer of Twickenham* (London, [1742]), 5–6. According to *The Compact Edition of the Oxford English Dictionary*, 3 vols. (Oxford: Oxford University Press, 1971–1987), a "Pother" is a "Disturbance, commotion, turmoil, bustle; a tumult, uproar; a noise, din" (2: 2257).

31. Eric Partridge, *MacMillan Dictionary of Historical Slang* (New York: Macmillan, 1973), 974.

32. While it sometimes is a solecism for "teat," "tit" at this time is not yet slang for the female breast. Partridge indicates that this usage is a late-nineteenth-century and twentieth-century Australian colloquialism (974). *The Compact OED* identifies it as twentieth-century American slang (3: 1270).

33. "Mr. C—b—r to Mr. P," in *The Difference between Verbal and Practical Virtue*, [by John Hervey] (London: Roberts, 1742), [i–ii].

34. bell hooks, *Teaching to Transgress: Education as the Practice of Freedom* (New York: Routledge, 1994), 137.

35. Nicholson, 181.

36. Introduction, *Two Poems Against Pope*, The Augustan Reprint Society no. 114 (Los Angeles: Clark Library, 1965), i.

37. Pat Rogers, *Grub Street: Studies in a Subculture* (London: Methuen, 1972), 404.

38. Jerome J. McGann, *The Romantic Ideology: A Critical Investigation* (Chicago: University of Chicago Press, 1983).

39. Kathy MacDermott, "Literature and the Grub Street Myth," *Literature and History* 8 (Autumn 1982): 159–68.

Notes on "Not 'The Only Trifler in the Nation': Pope and the Man of Leisure in *The Dunciad*"

1. Mary Wollstonecraft, *A Vindication of the Rights of Woman* (New York: A. Knopf, 1992), 60.

2. Vicesimus Knox, *Essays Moral and Literary*, 2 vols. (London: Charles Dilly, 1782), 2:186.

3. Richard Savage, "Article I," in *A Collection of Pieces in Verse and Prose, which have been publish'd on Occasion of the Dunciad* (London: L. Gilliver, 1732), 4.

4. Anonymous, *The Poet finish'd in Prose. Being a Dialogue Concerning Mr. Pope and his Writings* (London: E. Curll, 1735), 17–18.

5. Claudia N. Thomas, *Alexander Pope and His Eighteenth-Century Women Readers* (Carbondale:Southern Illinois University Press, 1994), 13. Steve Clark traces remarks made over the past two centuries about Pope's feminine characteristics in " 'Let Blood and Body bear the fault': Pope and Misogyny," in David Fairer, ed., *Pope: New Contexts* (London: Harvester, 1990), 81–101, and Carolyn D. Williams's *Pope, Homer, and Manliness: Some Aspects of Eighteenth-Century Classical Learning* (London: Routledge, 1993) examines charges that Pope's effeminacy perverted his translation of Homer.

6. Colley Cibber, *A Letter from Mr. Cibber, to Mr. Pope* (London: Roberts, 1742), 49.

7. Studies detailing various prejudices against castrati include John Rosselli's *Singers of Italian Opera: This History of a Profession* (Cambridge: Cambridge University Press, 1992); James P. Carson's "Commodification and the Figure of the Castrato in Smollett's *Humphrey Clinker*," *The Eighteenth Century: Theory and Interpretation* 33 (1992): 24–46; and Todd Gilman's "The Italian (Castrato) in London," in Richard Dellamora and Daniel Fischlin, eds., *The Work of Opera: Genre, Nationhood, and Sexual Difference* (New York: Columbia University Press, 1997), 49–70.

8. Anonymous, *A Compleat Collection Of all the Verses, Essays, Letters and Advertisements, which Have been occasioned by the Publication of Three Volumes of Miscellanies, by Pope and Company* (London: A. Moore, 1728), 27.

9. Giles Jacob, *The Mirrour: or, Letters Satyrical, Panegyrical, Serious and Humorous, On The Present Times* (London: J. Roberts, 1733), 7.

10. Walter Harte, *An Epistle to Mr. Pope, On Reading his Translations of the Iliad and Odyssy [sic] of Homer* (London: J. Wilford, 1731), 11; Bezaleel Morrice, *Three Satires. Most Humbly Inscribed and Recommended to that Little Gentleman, of Great Vanity, who has just published, A Fourth volume of Homer* (London: J. Roberts, 1719), 8. Lord Hervey draws a similar analogy between the styles that poets adopt and female adornment: "Nor will the finest Versification, the most flowing Numbers, the best chosen and best sorted Words, without any other Merit, make a fine Poem, any more than the best chosen and best made Apparel will make a fine Woman," *A Letter to Mr. C—b—r* (1742), 12.

11. Joseph Warton, *An Essay on the Genius and Writings of Pope*, 2 vols. (London: W. J. and J. Richardson, 1782), 2:481.

12. William Cowper, *Table Talk, The Complete Poetical Works of William Cowper*, H. S. Milford, ed. (London: Henry Frowde, 1905), 11.654–55.

13. As David B. Morris points out, "many of the difficulties and dangers [Pope] recognized in poetry depend upon the central role which Pope grants to pleasure. . . . The means for pleasing readers, like the readers to be pleased, belong to a continuum ranging from the worthiest to the most contemptible" ("Pope and the Arts of Pleasure," in G. S. Rousseau and Pat Rogers, eds., *The Enduring Legacy: Alexander Pope Tercentenary Essays* [Cambridge: Cambridge University Press, 1988], 104–5.) Yet the "characteristic doubleness" with which Pope responds to pleasure—affirming its power while rejecting it as temporary—may be less a manifestation of Pope's personality than a response to complex political and cultural circumstances.

14. Alexander Pope, *Preface to the Works of Alexander Pope, The Poems of Alexander Pope*, John Butt, ed. (New Haven: Yale University Press, 1963), xxv. All further references to Pope's poems are to the Yale edition.

15. Alexander Pope, *The Correspondence of Alexander Pope*, George Sherburn, ed., 5 vols. (Oxford: Clarendon, 1965), 1:109–10.

16. Robert Halsband offers an account of the escalating tensions between Pope and Hervey in *Lord Hervey: Eighteenth-Century Courtier* (Oxford: Oxford University Press, 1974), 141–44.

17. John, Lord Hervey, *An Epistle from a Nobleman to a Doctor of Divinity: In answer to a Latin letter in verse. Written from H—N-C—T, Aug. 28, 1733.* (1733), 7. References to this poem are cited by page number.

18. John, Lord Hervey, "To Stephen Fox" (1731), as quoted in Earl of Ilchester, ed., *Lord Hervey and His Friends, 1726–38* (London: John Murray, 1950), 83–84.

19. Hervey himself drew criticism for his poetry. The early eighteenth-century elite remained suspicious of the compatibility between ruling-class masculine behavior and the composition of verse; for instance, Hervey's father, Lord Bristol, "feared that his [son's] constant rhyming would stand in the way of his advancement in the world," and Hervey's patron, George II, concurred: "You ought not to write verses; 'tis beneath your rank: leave such work to little Mr. Pope." See Halsband, 37, 144.

20. Alexander Pope, *Letter to a Noble Lord, On occasion of some Libels written and propagated at Court* (1733), in Rosemary Cowler, ed., *The Prose Works of Alexander Pope*, 2 vols. (Hamden, CT: Archon Books, 1986), 2:443.

21. Jean Baudrillard, *For a Critique of the Political Economy of the Sign*, Charles Levin, trans. (St. Louis: Telos Press, 1981), 32.

22. Baudrillard, 32. Baudrillard examines the shift in values that occurs as capitalist production and a consumer market gain complete dominance over residual systems of creating wealth (like estate ownership): "One must wonder whether social salvation by consumption, whether prodigality and sumptuous expenditure (formerly the appendage of chiefs and notables) is not today *conceded* to the lower and middle classes. For this selective criterion has long ago given way as the foundation of power to the criteria of productive responsibility, and economic and political decision" (*Critique*, 61–62).

23. Adam Smith, *The Theory of Moral Sentiments*, D. D. Raphael and A. L. Macfie, eds. (Oxford: Clarendon, 1976), 54. For an account of Smith's conflicting attitudes toward commerce and masculinity, see Stewart Justman's *The Autonomous Male of Adam Smith* (Norman: University of Oklahoma Press, 1993).

24. Helen Deutsch analyzes Pope's rhetorical transformation of his disability

into cultural power in *Resemblance & Disgrace: Alexander Pope and the Defor-mation of Culture* (Cambridge: Harvard University Press, 1996).

25. Most readings of *The Dunciad* have focused on the dunces', rather than the aristocrats', threats to culture; Dennis Todd's "The 'Blunted Arms' of Dul-ness: The Problem of Power in *The Dunciad*," (*Studies in Philology* 79 [1982]: 177–204) reviews previous scholarship concerning the seriousness of this threat and concludes that Pope, in the last version of the poem, portrays the dunces as powerful because of their impotence, triviality, and childishness: "[Dulness] destroys culture because she is unable to articulate its values, patterns, and meanings, thus permitting an unmoved audience to gape forever at their own images" (204). Brean Hammond argues that the *"Dunciad's* values enshrine the interests of a highly-educated aristocratic elite," to the detriment of bour-geois professional writers (*Pope*, Harvester New Readings [Brighton: Harvester, 1986], 130). Yet the poem's repeated attacks on the authority of that elite im-plies Pope's critical distance from the ideology of the upper classes.

26. Catherine Ingrassia provides an account of opera as a feminized genre in "Women Writing/Writing Women: Pope, Dulness, and 'Feminization' in the *Dunciad*," *Eighteenth-Century Life* 14 (1990): 49–50. Cameron McFarlane notes that opera's associations with luxury, effeminancy, and ultimately sod-omy arise from anxieties about the preservation of English national purity: "Italian opera is coded as sodomitical because it is a conspicuous site at which foreign culture is seen to penetrate the social body of England" (*The Sodomite in Fiction & Satire 1660–1750* [New York: Columbia University Press, 1997], 32–33).

27. Carolyn D. Williams notes that, although Pope believed that a classical education, including Homer and Virgil, was "the most effective way to teach manliness," he was aware that patterns of effeminate behavior lay within the "fabric of the epic itself" ("Breaking Decorums: Belinda, Bays and Epic Effemi-nacy," in *Pope: New Contexts*, 60). Aristocratic youths, then, may learn effemi-nate conduct from the very institutions that supposedly guard against it.

28. Kristina Straub observes that "Pope's focus on the schoolboy as the ab-ject product of a perverse political and sexual hierarchy foregrounds the failure of masculine sexuality and authority . . . [while he] places that failure 'outside' the poet as the product of a corrupt political and social order" (*Sexual Suspects: Eighteenth-Century Players and Sexual Ideology* [Princeton: Princeton Univer-sity Press, 1992], 80). As a bourgeois outsider to aristocratic institutions, Pope represented himself as untainted by their perversions.

29. Bruce R. Smith argues that throughout the Renaissance and late seven-teenth century, Englishmen "eroticized the power distinctions that set one male above another in their society," in part by designating social inferiors as possible sexual objects (*Homosexual Desire in Shakespeare's England: A Cultural Poetics* [Chicago: University of Chicago Press, 1991], 194). Michael McKeon views a change occurring in the eighteenth century, when the "crite-rion of difference superintends sexual identity as such," rather than the criteria of birth and rank. See "Historicizing Patriarchy:The Emergence of Gender Dif-ference in England, 1660–1760," *Eighteenth-Century Studies* 28 (1995): 309.

30. Owen Ruffhead, *Life of Alexander Pope*, 2 vols. (Dublin: S. Powell, 1769), 2:132.

31. Samuel Johnson, *The Lives of the English Poets*, 3 vols. (1905; reprint New York: Octagon, 1967), 3:199.

Notes to "Dissecting the Authorial Body: Pope, Curll, and the Portrait of a 'Hack Writer' "

1. David L. Vander Meulen, *Pope's Dunciad of 1728: A History and Facsimile* (Charlottesville: University of Virginia Press, 1991), 23.
2. Ronald Paulson, *Popular and Polite Art in the Age of Hogarth and Fielding* (Notre Dame: University of Notre Dame Press, 1979).
3. Pat Rogers, *Grub Street: Studies in a Subculture* (1972; reprint, London: Methuen, 1984).
4. Mikhail Bakhtin, *Rabelais and His World*, Helene Iswolsky, trans. (Bloomington: Indiana University Press, 1984).
5. Peter Stallybrass and Allon White, *The Politics and Poetics of Transgression* (London: Methuen, 1986), 3.
6. Rogers, 280.
7. Montagu to Lady Bute, 23 July 1754, in *The Complete Letters of Lady Mary Wortley Montagu*, vol. 3, Robert Halsband, ed. (Oxford: Clarendon, 1967), 68–69.
8. *Imitations of Horace*, Epistle II,ii. (*TE* 4:169.68–69). All quotations are from *The Twickenham Edition of the Poems of Alexander Pope*, John Butt et. al., eds., 11 Volumes (London: Methuen, 1953). Further references are made by volume, page, and line number in this edition. *The Dunciad* is identified with an "A" and "B" designating the 1929 *Dunciad Variorum* and the 1743 *Dunciad in Four Books*, respectively.
9. The observation occurs in Rose's discussion of Pope's 1741 lawsuit against Curll over the 1735 publication of his letters (*Authors and Owners: The Invention of Copyright* [Cambridge: Harvard University Press, 1993], 62).
10. The quotation continues: "Had it not been for that, the Dunces might have railed against him till they were weary, without his troubling himself about them. He delighted to vex them, no doubt; but he had more delight in seeing how well he would vex them." Boswell, *Life of Johnson*, J. W. Croker, ed. (London, 1887) 11:334 as quoted in Hill 3:241.
11. Shef Rogers, "Pope, Publishing, and Popular Interpretations of the *Dunciad Variorum*," *Philological Quarterly* 74 (1995): 279–95.
12. In *Lives of the English Poets*, Samuel Johnson describes how Pope "was not able to dress or undress himself, and neither went to bed nor rose without help" (Samuel Johnson, *The Lives of the English Poets* in Three Volumes, George Birkbeck Hill, ed. [Oxford: Clarendon Press, 1945] 3:197). While some critics, like Maynard Mack, argue that Pope's own marginality as well as his close associations with women like the Blount sisters increased his sensitivity to the limited opportunities for eighteenth-century women, the simplicity and essentialism of this approach ultimately limits its usefulness in reading Pope.
13. Eve Kosofsky Sedgwick, *Between Men: English Literature and Male Homosocial Desire* (New York: Columbia University Press, 1985), 21. For further discussion of traffic in women, see also Luce Irigarary, *This Sex Which Is Not One*, trans. Catherine Porter (Ithaca: Cornell University Press, 1977), especially chap. 8; Gayle Rubin, "The Traffic in Women: Notes Toward a Political Economy of Sex," in Rayna Reiter, ed., *Toward an Anthropology of Women* (New York: Monthly Review Press, 1976), 157–210. For a discussion of how this paradigm figures in Pope's later exchange with Colley Cibber (in very different

ways), see Kristina Straub, *Sexual Suspects: Eighteenth-Century Players and Sexual Identity* (Princeton: Princeton University Press, 1992).

14. Indeed, as Vander Meulen notes, many people in London, and certainly in the provinces, were confused by the initials and dashes Pope used in his poem and asked the poet for a key to the work (20).

15. Bakhtin, 19.

16. Stallybrass and White, 9.

17. However, as Helen Deustch elegantly details in *Resemblance & Disgrace: Alexander Pope and the Deformation of Culture* (Cambridge: Harvard University Press, 1996), Pope used that hybridity (as manifested by his deformity) in his poetry and representations of self and other: "Throughout the continuous revision that distinguished his poetic career, Pope marked culturally current material with his deformity's singular contradictions" (2).

18. *The Compleat Key to the Dunciad* (London, 1728).

19. *Codrus: Or the Dunciad Dissected Being the Finishing Stroke* (London, 1728).

20. *The Compleat Key to the Dunciad*, 18.

21. *The Female Dunciad* (London, 1728), 44.

22. Terry Eagleton, *The Rape of Clarissa: Writing, Sexuality and Class Struggle in Samuel Richardson* (Minneapolis: University of Minnesota Press, 1982), 20–21.

23. Maynard Mack, *Collected in Himself: Essays Critical, Biographical, and Bibliographical on Pope and Some of His Contemporaries* (Newark: University of Delaware Press, 1982), Appendix A, 395–461.

24. Samuel Johnson, *The Lives of the English Poets*, 3:188.

25. As Maynard Mack observes, "like every writer dependent on a public, Pope had to give as much consideration to what he was perceived to be as to what he was" (*Alexander Pope: A Life*, 655).

26. *The Female Dunciad*, 12.

27. *A Popp upon Pope: or, a True and Faithful Account of a Late Horrid and Barbarous Whipping, Committed on the Body of A. Pope, a Poet* (London, 1728).

28. Mack, *Alexander Pope: A Life*, 490.

29. *The Popiad* (London 1728).

30. Bakhtin, 21.

31. William Kurtz Wimsatt, *The Portraits of Alexander Pope* (New Haven: Yale University Press, 1965), 145.

32. See, for example, David Kunzle, "World Upside Down: The Iconography of a European Broadsheet Type," in Barbara Babcock, ed., *The Reversible World: Symbolic Inversion in Art and Society* (Ithaca: Cornell University Press, 1978), 39–94.

33. Wimsatt, 245.

34. *Mr Pope's Literary Correspondence, Volume the Second* (London 1735).

35. *The Curliad, A Hypercritic upon the Dunciad Variorum* (London 1729).

36. *Mr. Pope's Literary Correspondence, Volume the Second*, xvi.

37. *Mr. Pope's Literary Correspondence, Volume the Fourth* (London, 1736), 148–49.

38. James Ralph, *The Case of Authors by Profession or Trade, stated. With regard to the Booksellers, the Stage, and the Public . . .* (London: R. Griffiths, 1758), 8.

Notes on " '*Consummatum Est*': Alexander Pope's 1743 *Dunciad* and Mock-Apocalypse"

1. Alexander Pope, *The Dunciad*, in Herbert Davis, ed., *Pope: Poetical Works*, intro. Pat Rogers (Oxford: Oxford University Press, 1978), 584. All subsequent references to *The Dunciad* are to this edition and are incorporated into the text. Davis's edition prints the final version of the poem in its entirety. The Twickenham edition uses over 260 cross-references for anything in the 1729 *Dunciad* (or "A" text) repeated verbatim in the 1743 text.

2. Paul J. Korshin, *Typologies in England, 1650–1820* (Princeton: Princeton University Press, 1982), 311, and n.67 (hereafter Korshin). See also Aubrey Williams, *Pope's Dunciad: A Study of Its Meaning* (London: Methuen, 1955) (hereafter Williams).

3. See Williams, 154, and Korshin, 97.

4. For those critics who do admit some mock-apocalyptic quality to *The Dunciad*, especially to its 1743 version, that feature almost exclusively rests in the upside-down General Judgment scene in at least the conclusion of Book 4. For example, Williams speaks of how a passage on the London stage in *The Dunciad Variorum* (3.229–44) "images, in mock-apocalyptic fashion, the final destruction of the real world" (96–97). In her 1980 dissertation "The 'Dunciad' and the Old Testament," Deborah Jane Knuth admits that "discussion of *The Dunciad* in biblical terms is not a new idea" and that "much has been said . . . of the imagery of Book 4 deriving from Revelations." But I am struck by her limiting *The Dunciad* as apocalypse to "the end of the poem." Ironically, in announcing that her study "follows the 'uncreating Word' of Dulness back to Genesis," she inadvertently points to the Genesis-to-Revelation framework that encompasses the poem as a whole and that, I argue, makes the poem as a whole a mock-apocalypse. See Deborah Jane Knuth, "The 'Dunciad' and the Old Testament," unpublished dissertation (New Haven: Yale University, 1980), 6 (hereafter Knuth). All references to *The Dunciad*, unless otherwise indicated, are to the final 1743 version.

Other studies extensively discuss how Pope uses the Bible in *The Dunciad*. One of the most thorough studies of the many biblical sources at work in the poem is Emmett G. Bedford's unpublished dissertation, "Biblical Typology and Related Forms of Christian Symbolism in the Poetry of Alexander Pope" (Carbondale: Southern Illinois University, 1970) (hereafter Bedford). Martin Battestin pursues Pope's satiric use of typology indirectly by focusing on the inversions of Milton's *Paradise Lost*. This analysis appears in the final section of the chapter "Pope: The Idea of Creation" in Martin C. Battestin, ed., *The Providence of Wit: Aspects of Form in Augustan Literature and the Arts* (Charlottesville: University of Virginia Press, 1989; orig. publ. Oxford: Oxford University Press, 1974), 102–18. Finally and more recently, Robert Griffin's essay, "Pope, the Prophets, and *The Dunciad*" (*Studies in English Literature*, [23: 1983], 435–46), provides a number of parallel passages between Pope and Jeremiah but does not account for the specifically apocalyptic form of *The Dunciad* or how the poem as apocalypse might differ from prophecy, a distinction I pursue in the first section of this essay.

5. Because I am convinced of the frequency and even centrality of the ludicrous use in eighteenth-century British satire of religious and biblical material, I am implying by the term mock-biblical a familiar, settled habit of association

on the order of that conveyed by the term mock-epic. Important differences immediately arise, however. Bible, unlike epic, is not a genre. The Hebrew and Christian scriptures, even apart from the artificiality of seeing them as "Books," e.g., the Book of Daniel, offer many literary forms. Secondly, mock-biblical is meant merely to denote such a practice without implying whether religion is itself the object of the satire. In *MacFlecknoe*, mock-biblical has no religiously satiric aims. Its subtitle, "Or a Satire upon a True Blue Protestant Poet, T. S.," not original with John Dryden, has long been recognized as having little connection with Dryden's satiric objectives. Often, mock-biblical can satirize what the writer sees as religious aberrations, as in Jonathan Swift's *Tale of a Tub* or the Puritanism ridiculed in Pope's sketch of Sir Balaam. Thirdly, a more widespread ridicule of religion is possible, as in William Blake's *The Marriage of Heaven and Hell*, where orthodox Christianity of presumably any institutional color is seen as stultifying and finally inimical to genuine religion. Finally, in the likes of David Hume and Edward Gibbon mock-biblical can be so extensive in its religious target as to leave a reader in wonder whether any expression of religion is not, finally, superstition or enthusiasm. The satiric aims of any mock-biblical technique, consequently, will vary from work to work and from writer to writer.

6. The Elijah–Elisha narrative appears in 2 Kings 2:1–18, in the Douai OT 4 Kings 2:1–18. All citations from the Douai–Rheims version are from *The Holy Bible: Translated from the Latin Vulgate* (New York: Douay Bible House, n.d. [1938?]).

7. Although Bernard McGinn admits that "one eminent Old Testament scholar, Gerhard von Rad, has denied that apocalypse as such can be said to constitute a distinctive literary genre," McGinn nonetheless insists that "this view can scarcely be maintained in the light of recent research." See Bernard McGinn, "Early Apocalypticism: The Ongoing Debate," in C. A. Patrides and Joseph Wittreich, eds., *The Apocalypse in English Renaissance Thought and Literature: Patterns, Antecedents, and Repercussions*, (Ithaca: Cornell University Press, 1985), 3 (hereafter McGinn).

8. Korshin, 4.

9. In the Hebrew canon, Daniel is not included among the Prophets. It is one of the Writings. Christian usage in Pope's time and long before considers Daniel the fourth of the major prophets, along with Isaiah, Jeremiah, and Ezekiel.

10. See Daniel 7 and, in the three synoptic gospels, Matthew 24, Mark 13, and Luke 19:41–44 and 21:5–36.

11. Korshin, 65. I prefer, however, to call these texts apocalyptic, rather than prophetic, to reinforce a distinction between a genre that does not predict (prophecy) and one that does (apocalypse).

12. As one example, Jeremiah's bloody predictive vision of the fall of Babylon (Jeremiah 50–51) does not correspond at all with the peaceful surrender of the city to Cyrus some two generations later.

13. As in Daniel, apocalypse often uses the fiction of having been written at a much earlier time to be fortuitously discovered at precisely the moment when the faithful need encouragement. Pope uses something of this ploy in announcing the "discovery" of the lost fourth book of *The Dunciad*, which he publishes separately in 1742 and then as the new concluding book of *The Dunciad* a year later. The separately published Book 4, we are told in "To the Reader" "was found merely by Accident, in taking a survey of the Library of a late eminent

Nobleman; but in so blotted a condition, and in so many detach'd pieces, as plainly shewed it to be not only incorrect, but unfinished." "The Argument" to Book 4 announces that the Poet is "to declare the Completion of the Prophecies mentioned at the end of the former [book]." See Alexander Pope, *The New Dunciad* (London: T. Cooper, 1742), A5, (A7).

14. *The New English Bible* says: "The stories and visions [in Daniel] are set in the Babylonian and Persian periods [6th to 4th centuries B.C.], but they reflect a later time, primarily that of the successors to Alexander the Great. Antiochus IV Epiphanes [175–163 B.C.] and his wars with the Egyptians . . . are especially in view." Of the Revelation of John, the same version observes that it "encourages Christians to keep faith in the face of trial and persecution. . . . [T]he book in its present form probably was written during the reign of Domitian [81–96 A.D.], a period when emperor worship was geographically extensive and coercive." See *The New English Bible, With the Apocrypha*, Oxford Study Edition, gen. ed. Samuel Sandmel, corr. ed. (New York: Oxford University Press, 1976), 945 (in the OT section), 313 (in the NT section) (hereafter NEB).

15. I discuss prophecy and its view of a morally contingent and, hence, not determined future in *Satire and the Hebrew Prophets* (Louisville: Westminster/John Knox Press, 1992), 71–78; 215, n.40 (in Second Isaiah); 216, n.50; 216–17, n.51; and 218, n.55 (in Jonathan Swift) (hereafter *Satire and the Hebrew Prophets*).

16. See McGinn, 4, who quotes this definition from Semeia, vol. 14, in John J. Collins, ed., *Apocalypse: The Morphology of a Genre* (Missoula: Scholars Press, 1979). Collins cites the same definition in *Daniel: With an Introduction to Apocalyptic Literature (Forms of Old Testament Literature, Vol 20)* (Grand Rapids: Eerdmans, 1984), 4. In his essay, McGinn offers the following characteristics of apocalypse as genre: a "deterministic view of history" (10); "the divinely predetermined pattern of crisis-judgment-vindication that marks the End" (10); "the conviction . . . that [this] triple drama has already begun" (11); and often "the dualism of the apocalyptic view of history" (11). These and other apocalyptic qualities emerge in my discussion.

17. See "The Story of Baucis and Philemon," in Rolfe Humphries., trans., *Ovid, Metamorphoses* (Bloomington: Indiana University Press [Midland], 1958), 200–204, and Seneca, *The Apocolocyntosis of the Divine Claudius*, in Petronius, *The Satyricon* and Seneca, *The Apocolocyntosis*, trans., intro., and nn. J. P. Sullivan, rev. ed. (New York: Penguin, 1986), 219–42.

18. See James H. Charlesworth, ed., *The Old Testament Pseudepigrapha: Apocalyptic Literature and Testaments* (Garden City: Doubleday, 1983), Volume 1.

19. See *Satire and the Hebrew Prophets*, esp. 11–12, 15–16.

20. See my discussion of this controversy between the two prophets in *Satire and the Hebrew Prophets*, 131–34.

21. The story of Josiah and the Fall of Jerusalem is told in 2 Kings 22–25, in the Douai OT 4 Kings 22–25.

22. "Dialogue II," in *Imitations of Horace (The Twickenham Edition of the Poems of Alexander Pope: Volume 4)*, 2nd ed., John Butt, corr. ed. (London: Methuen, 1961), 327, n. to l.255.

23. See *Satire and the Hebrew Prophets*, 15, 85–86.

24. The *deus-ex-machina* quality of divine apocalyptic deliverance at the most apparently hopeless time coincidentally reinforces Northrop Frye's reading of the Christian Bible as a comedy and the Book of Revelation as the last act

of that comedy. See Northrop Frye, *The Great Code: The Bible and Literature* (New York: Harcourt Brace Jovanovich, 1983), 169–74 (hereafter *The Great Code*).

25. Is Pope here playing with the notion of the veiled Holy of Holies, in the innermost and most sacred part of the Temple of Jerusalem? Emmett Bedford says yes. See Bedford, 269–73.

26. "Plate XXI," in William Warburton, ed., *The Works of Alexander Pope Esquire. In Nine Volumes Complete. With His Last Corrections, Additions, and Improvements: As They Were Delivered to the Editor A Little Before His Death: Together with the Commentaries and Notes of Mr. Warburton* (London: J. and P. Knapton et al.), 5, facing p. 121. Hereafter Warburton. Many thanks to Laura Fuderer, Rare Books Librarian, and the Department of Special Collections at the University of Notre Dame for permission to reproduce this plate and "Plate XXIII," which appears later.

27. See *Philological Quarterly* 74 (1995): 267–70 (hereafter "A Mock-Biblical Controversy").

28. In *Alexander Pope, The Genius of Sense* (Cambridge: Harvard University Press, 1984), 277, David Morris speaks of this infantile quality of the dunces' behavior in the games of Book 2. This infantile behavior pervades *The Dunciad* as an important feature of the imminent return to a Garden of Prelapsarian Delights that awaits the dunces.

29. The description of those who respond to the summons of Dulness makes clear that even in the early versions of *The Dunciad*, Pope was not limiting himself to literary issues:

> A motley mixture! in long wigs, in bags,
> In silks, in crapes, in Garters, and in rags,
> From drawing rooms, from colleges, from garrets,
> On horse, on foot, in hacks, and gilded chariots:
> All who true Dunces in her cause appear'd,
> And all who knew those Dunces to reward. (2.21–26).

The universality of this response and its expectation of rewarding judgment appears verbatim in *The Dunciad* of 1728 (2.2–8) and in *The Dunciad Variorum* of 1729, another strong indication of the unifying Last Judgment motif apparent from the very first versions of the poem. See Davis, 732 (for the 1728 *Dunciad*) and *The Dunciad* (A), in Alexander Pope, *The Dunciad* (*The Twickenham Edition of the Poems of Alexander Pope: Volume 5*), 3rd ed., James Sutherland, ed. (London: Methuen, 1963), 98.

30. In Mrs. Osborne's reluctance to have her husband participate in the urinating contest, Pope offers a good joke, with bad biology: aware of the deficiencies of her husband's competing instrument in one context, Mrs. Osborne does not wish him to expose it to further ridicule in another. Alas, her fears are vindicated.

31. In Book 3, the Argument makes clear that the visions Cibber will enjoy are caused by the influence of Dulness (525). In Shadwell's Bosom, the "Millions and millions" of dunces (3.31) recognize one another with pride and, dearly departed though they are, recognize Cibber as one of them among the living.

32. Alexander Pope, *Minor Poems* (*The Twickenham Edition of the Poems of Alexander Pope: Volume 6*), John Butt, ed. (London: Methuen, 1964), 17, 19.

33. "Messiah" indisputably demonstrates, at an early point in his career, that Pope knew the typological uses of apocalyptic passages in Isaiah. See "Mes-

siah: A Sacred Eclogue, In Imitation of Virgil's Pollio," in *Pastoral Poetry and An Essay on Criticism (The Twickenham Edition of the Poems of Alexander Pope: Volume 1)*, E. Audra and Aubrey Williams, eds. (London: Methuen, 1961), 109–22. The Introduction is 99–107. These lines appear on 116.

34. *The New English Bible* describes Isaiah 34:1–35:10 as two "exilic or post-exilic" poems, "juxtaposed to contrast the expected devastation of Edom (34:1–7) with the glorious future in store for the exiles (35:1–10)." See NEB, p. 764, n. to Isaiah 34:1–35:10. In his notes to "Messiah," Pope explicitly quotes Isaiah 35:1 and 35:7 (incorrectly identified in Davis as Isaiah 45) and refers to Isaiah 35:2, 35: 5,6; and 35:1,7.

35. Korshin, 311.

36. See Northrop Frye, *Anatomy of Criticism: Four Essays* (New York: Atheneum, 1968), 167.

37. *The Great Code*, 169.

38. Ibid., 137.

39. Ibid., 135.

40. Quoted in David Noel Freedman, ed., *Revelation (Anchor Bible, Vol. 38)*, trans., intro., and comm. J. Massyngberde Ford (Garden City, NJ: Doubleday, 1975), 27.

41. In discussing the doggedly controversial nature of his mock-biblical uses in earlier poetry and in the various versions of *The Dunciad*, I have elsewhere drawn attention to the fact that the Alexander Pope who extensively documents his classical and even Miltonic sources in *The Dunciad* "never once specifically draws attention to [the sources of] the dozens and dozens of biblical and religious images, allusions, incidents and the like that he uses in the poem," a practice far different from what he does earlier in "Messiah." See "A Mock-Biblical Controversy," 265. Knuth points out how Pope, at least once, in his note to the sources of the rainbow that appears in the Urinating Contest, coyly avoids mentioning an obvious source in Genesis, "a mass of almost irrelevant annotation [that] does protect the poet from a charge of blasphemy." See Knuth, 45–47.

42. This argument, consequently, takes issue with the earlier-cited remark of Aubrey Williams that Pope's inverted use of biblical material provides no structural principle for the poem. See Williams, 154. At the other extreme is Knuth's claim that the final *Dunciad* completes an Old Testament (Books 1–3)—New Testament (Book 4) arrangement, an argument I find strained. See Knuth, 149–51. The structural flexibility apparent in the Apocalypse of John does not require such a neat, reasonably chronological pattern for its rich use of earlier biblical material. In addition to which, *The Dunciad* is pervaded by the inescapable sense that the triumph of Dulness is imminent, not a feature I would assign to a work that is supposedly an extensive, roughly chronological adaptation of salvation history as a whole.

43. Pope's long-standing dislike and ridicule of the Sternhold–Hopkins metrical version of the Psalms suggests that parody hymnology is not beyond his capacities. For example, were we to take any four-line combination out of Cibber's psalm-like hymn "Great Tamer of All Human Art" (1.163–242) and eliminate two syllables to transform Pope's iambic pentameter into the tetrameter common to hymns, the words could easily be sung to the *Old Hundredth* tune used in "Praise God from Whom All Blessings Flow," perhaps in a *Dunciad* sing-along students might enjoy. The result would be something like this, beginning at 1.173:

O! ever gracious to . . . mankind,
Still spread a . . . mist before the mind;
And lest we err by Wit's wild . . . light,
Secure us kindly in our . . . night.

In "A Mock-Biblical Controversy," 253–56, I discuss Pope's attempts to defuse the controversy generated by his allegedly blasphemous parody of Psalm 1 as, rather, a spoof of Sternhold–Hopkins.

44. In Psalm 51, David is said to have uttered: "For behold I was conceived in iniquities; and in sins did my mother conceive me" (50:7, Douai OT). In the old Catholic numbering, this was Psalm 50.

45. See Pope's note to *Dunciad* 3.61–62, where he cites *Paradise Lost* 11.411–13, and adds that "there is a general allusion in what follows to that whole Episode."

46. Williams, 149.

47. In the second Creation account in Genesis (2:4b–3:24), the description of a Garden filled with innumerable delights moves provocatively to the familiar statement: "And they were both naked: to wit, Adam and his wife: and were not ashamed" (2:25, Douai OT). Coming as it does immediately after Yahweh's endorsement of the marital state—"Wherefore a man shall leave father and mother, and shall cleave to his wife: and they shall be two in one flesh" (2:24, Douai OT)—the remark leads to the expectation of a paradisiacal intercourse, reinforced but ironically overturned by the verse that follows next: "Now the serpent was more subtle than any of the beasts of the earth which the Lord God had made" (3:1, Douai OT). This common element and symbol of phallic worship in the Near East brings catastrophic rather than erotically satisfying results. The cosmic intercourse of sorts is delayed until the very end of Revelation, when the New Jerusalem descends as a bride for her nuptials with the Lamb. John Mackenzie, S.J., speculates that "the author replaced the original climax, which must have been an epithalamion by the story of the sin, which is in some way, a perversion of the intended union of the sexes." For this stimulating and sensitive response to this narrative, see John Mackenzie, S.J., "The Literary Characteristics of Genesis 2–3," *Theological Studies* 15 (1954): 541–72. The quote appears on 562.

48. See Warburton, "Plate XXIII," 5, facing p. 225

49. See Johannes Lindblom, *Prophecy in Ancient Israel* (Philadelphia: Fortress Press, 1965), 51–52.

50. Creation *ex nihilo*, a medieval view, is not assumed in the Hebrew scriptures. Yahweh works on and informs a formless, dark mass, the *tohu wabohu* of the first Creation account (Genesis 1:2). Pope's Douai–Rheims Bible would have told him that "darkness was upon the face of the deep; and the spirit of God moved over the waters," waters present before God's creative activity begins (1:2, Douai OT).

Notes on " 'Writing Nonsense': Pope, Rabelais, and the Fair"

1. Peter Stallybrass and Allon White, *The Politics and Poetics of Transgression* (Ithaca: Cornell University Press, 1986), chap. 2, 80–124.

2. Terry Eagleton, *The Function of Criticism: From the Spectator to Post-Structuralism* (London: Verso, 1984), proposes that a "bourgeois public sphere"

emerged in the eighteenth century for the purpose of "codifying . . . the norms and regulating . . . the practices whereby the English bourgeoisie [negotiated] an historic alliance with its social superiors" (10).

3. Mikhail Bakhtin, *Problems of Dostoevsky's Poetics*, Caryl Emerson, trans. (Minneapolis: University of Minnesota Press, 1984), asserts that the "consolidation of monologism" took shape during the Enlightenment, "with its cult of a unified and exclusive reason" (82). In a monologic text, even when "voices" other than the author's are present, they are either discredited or serve the author's purpose. Throughout his discussion of carnivalized literature, Bakhtin emphasizes its free and frank attitude toward the body, in contrast to the abstractions of "official" literature (122–37).

4. Bakhtin describes the characteristics of Mennippean satire characteristic of much classical, medieval, and enlightenment satire (114–19). Swift's fondness for Rabelais is documented, for example, in Pope's conversations with Joseph Spence; see Spence, *Observations, Anecdotes, and Characters of Books and Men, Collected from Conversation*, James M. Osborn, ed., 2 vols. (Oxford: Clarendon, 1966), 1:55, 218. For recognition of Swift's mixture of genres, see Frederik N. Smith, ed., *The Genres of Gulliver's Travels* (Newark: University of Delaware Press, 1990).

5. Irvin Ehrenpreis, *Swift: The Man, His Works, and the Age*, 3 vols. (Cambridge: Harvard University Press, 1983), confirms that Swift "never stopped reading" Rabelais (3:328).

6. Voltaire, *Letters on England*, Leonard Tancock, trans. (London: Penguin, 1980), 108.

7. Alexander Pope, *The Dunciad*, James Sutherland, ed., vol. 5 of *The Poems of Alexander Pope*, John Butt et al., eds., 11 vols. (London: Methuen, 1963), 1.19–20. All further quotations of Pope are cited within the text and taken from this edition. I distinguish within the text between *The Dunciad* (meaning *The Dunciad Variorum* of 1729–1742) and *The Dunciad, in Four Books*. In a letter to Swift of 12 October 1728, Pope asks, "Do you care I should say any thing farther how much that poem is yours? since certainly without you it had never been." See Jonathan Swift, *The Correspondence of Jonathan Swift, D. D.*, F. Elrington Ball, ed., 6 vols. (London: G. Bell and Sons, 1914), 3:303. Maynard Mack, *Alexander Pope: A Life* (New York: Norton, 1986), recalls Swift's explanation that he had suggested *The Dunciad* project to Pope, as well as Pope's observation that Swift rescued an early draft of the poem from the fire (442). I believe that in addition to these specific debts, *The Dunciad* is permeated with Swiftian imagery and with his characteristic use of literalized metaphor, and so even more thoroughly "Swift's" than Mack's discussion suggests.

8. Ehrenpreis observes that Martinus Scriblerus was originally modelled on Rabelais's Panurge (2:725). He notes that while the *Memoirs* never achieved the thematic unity of its classical and Renaissance predecessors, it eventually inspired *Gulliver's Travels*, Gay's *The Beggar's Opera*, and *The Dunciad* (2:726). Mack makes a similar observation (238). In his introduction to the *Memoirs*, Charles Kerby-Miller regrets that Swift's preference for the "richness, color, and broad humor" of Rabelais did not influence the *Memoirs* more directly; see Kerby-Miller, ed., *The Memoirs of the Extraordinary Life, Works, and Discoveries of Martinus Scriblerus* (New York: Oxford University Press, 1988), 71. The Scriblerian roots of *The Dunciad*, therefore, were also consciously Rabelaisian although Kerby-Miller notes that Pope, as chief editor, undoubtedly modified and refined the Rabelaisian elements of the *Memoirs* before publication (71).

9. For Swift's knowledge of the Renaissance humanists, see Jenny Mezciems, "Swift's Praise of Gulliver: Some Renaissance Background to the *Travels*" in Claude Rawson, ed., *The Character of Swift's Satire: A Revised Focus* (Newark: University of Delaware Press, 1983), 245–81.

10. Howard Weinbrot, in *Alexander Pope and the Traditions of Formal Verse Satire* (Princeton: Princeton University Press, 1982), argued convincingly that Pope's satiric persona is a mixture of the urbane, tolerant Horatian and the marginalized, angry Juvenalian or Persian personae. Pope borrowed elements of each, his satiric purpose determining which style predominated. I believe that *The Dunciad*'s narrator conveys a Juvenalian sense of outrage and alienation, similar to the prophetic perspective discerned by Thomas Jemielity elsewhere in this volume.

11. Peter Earle discusses this phenomenon and the difficulty of distinguishing between middle-class strata in *The Making of the English Middle Class: Business, Society and Family Life in London, 1660–1730* (Berkeley: University of California Press, 1989), 327–37.

12. See "Pope and His *Dunciad* Adversaries: Skirmishes on the Borders of Gentility" in James E. Gill, ed., *Cutting Edges: Postmodern Critical Essays on Eighteenth-Century Satire* (Knoxville: University of Tennessee Press, 1995), 275–300.

13. Pat Rogers, in *Hacks and Dunces: Pope, Swift, and Grub Street* (1972; abridged ed., London: Methuen, 1980), argues the appropriateness of *The Dunciad*'s setting in the Bedlam–Fleet Prison–Newgate locale, given the legal and economic problems of hack writers (152–60). Maynard Mack, in *Alexander Pope: A Life* (New York: W. W. Norton, 1986), finds the games of Book 2 an apt representation of "the rich absurdities to be unveiled when modern dunces are viewed against older traditions they no longer understand or follow" (467).

14. Ben Jonson, *Bartholomew Fair*, E. A. Horsman, ed. (London: Methuen, 1960), ironically invites a political reading of his play when a "Stage-Keeper" facetiously warns the audience not to "in themselves conceal . . . any state-decipherer, or politic pick-lock, so solemnly ridiculous as to search out who was meant by the Ginger-bread-woman, who by the Hobby-horse-man . . ." (12) in his satire of Puritan hypocrisy.

15. William Wordsworth, *The Prelude: A Parallel Text*, J. C. Maxwell, ed. (London: Penguin, 1986), 292, line 697. Pat Rogers, in *Literature and Popular Culture in Eighteenth Century England* (New Jersey: Barnes and Noble, 1985), distinguishes Wordsworth's treatment of the fair from Pope's in terms of both philosophical differences and the very different state of early nineteenth-century popular culture.

16. Alexander Pope, *The Dunciad*, James Sutherland, ed., vol. 5 of *The Poems of Alexander Pope*, John Butt et al., eds., 11 vols. (London: Methuen, 1963), 2.19–24.

17. "An Essay on the Dunciad an Heroick Poem" in *Popeiana VII: The Dunciad II, 1728* (New York: Garland, 1975), 15–16.

18. John Dennis, "Remarks upon Several Passages in the Preliminaries to the Dunciad," in *Popeiana VIII: The Dunciad III, 1729* (New York: Garland, 1975), 19.

19. Robert W. Malcolmson, *Popular Recreations in English Society, 1700–1850* (Cambridge: Cambridge University Press, 1973).

20. Sir Richard Steele, *The Spectator*, Donald F. Bond, ed., 5 vols. (Oxford: Clarendon, 1965), 3:476–77.

21. John Gay, "Saturday; or, The Flights," *The Shepherd's Week*, in Vinton A. Dearing and Charles E. Beckwith, eds., *John Gay: Poetry and Prose*, 2 vols. (Oxford: Clarendon, 1974), 1:119–23.

22. John Gay, "Book II: Of Walking the Streets by Day," *Trivia; or, The Art of Walking the Streets of London* in *John Gay*, 1:153, lines 343–50, 353–56.

23. In *Hogarth: The Modern Moral Subject, 1697–1732* (New Brunswick, NJ: Rutgers University Press, 1991), Ronald Paulson describes young Hogarth's Covent Garden address as "a ringside seat at the center of London fashion, theater, gambling, and wenching—and also law enforcement." Unlike the Scriblerians, Hogarth delighted in the spectacle of "Gentlemen and highwaymen, ladies and women of pleasure [strolling] the arcades, passing from coffeehouse to theater to bagnio to auction rooms and china shops" (204).

24. David Nokes, in *John Gay: A Profession of Friendship* (Oxford: Oxford University Press, 1995), discusses Gay's ambivalence toward the countryside as expressed in *Rural Sports* (106–107) and *The Shepherd's Week* (143–44); Gay's target was pretension and lack of decorum in all classes. In *Trivia*, Nokes observes, Gay reserved his chief derision for gentlemen who ride roughshod, in their coaches, over pedestrians (208–209). My emphasis is on the opposite end of the phenomenon: while the coach-riding aristocrats menace the less privileged by aggressive driving, apprentices and laborers threaten middling walkers by aggressive sports.

25. Emrys Jones, "Pope and Dulness," in Maynard Mack and James Winn, eds., *Pope: Recent Essays by Several Hands*, (Hamden, CT: Archon Books, 1980), 639.

26. Rogers argues contemporary association of mobs with anti-Papist sentiment as an important, if not the most potent, source of Pope's imagery (*Hacks and Dunces*, 112, 126–34). But W. A. Speck, *Stability and Strife: England, 1714–1760* (Cambridge: Harvard University Press, 1979), observes that after the Sacheverell riots of 1710, "there were no large-scale political upheavals; but there were demonstrations by Jacobite crowds in various centres, especially in the opening years of George I's reign," leading to passage of the Riot Act in 1715 (79–80). Given contemporary suspicion of Jacobite mobs, and persistent accusations by enemies such as Dennis that his writings aroused Jacobite unrest, Pope probably perceived the need to associate Whigs rather than Tories with mobs, or replace recent with previous associations.

27. In "The Deserted Village" (1770), Goldsmith describes participants in local pastimes, such as "the dancing pair that simply sought renown, / By holding out to tire each other down" (25–26). See Roger Lonsdale, ed., *The New Oxford Book of Eighteenth Century Verse* (Oxford: Oxford University Press, 1984), 524.

28. See, for example, David Blewett's introduction to Daniel Defoe, *Moll Flanders* (London: Penguin, 1989), 1–3.

29. Nancy Cotton, *Women Playwrights in England 1363–1750* (London: Bucknell University Press, 1980), 145.

30. James Ralph, *Sawney. An Heroic Poem*, in *Popeiana VI: The Dunciad, 1728* (New York: Garland, 1975).

31. Edward Ward, "Durgen or, a Plain Satyr upon a Pompous Satyrist," in *Popeiana VIII*.

32. Colley Cibber, *Another Occasional Letter to Mr. Pope*, in *Popeiana XV: Cibber and the Dunciad, 1740–1744* (London; reprint New York: Garland, 1975), 49.

33. Derek Jarrett, *England in the Age of Hogarth* (New Haven: Yale University Press, 1986), 157–59.

34. Leah S. Marcus, *The Politics of Mirth: Jonson, Herrick, Marvell, and the Defense of Old Holiday Pastimes* (Chicago: University of Chicago Press, 1986). Marcus describes the political expediency of James I's *Book of Sports*, and the ways poets both defended and challenged royal sanction of occasional, carefully controlled outbursts of "misrule" for the purpose of channeling subversive energy.

35. For a recent example of this phenomenon, see Felicity Rosslyn, *Alexander Pope: A Literary Life* (New York: St. Martin's, 1990), 87–96. Of the Fleet–Ditch diving contest, Rosslyn remarks that "the Dunces are at home in the ultimate realm of Dulness—where man finally abandons himself to decomposition, and his art is what enables him to do it" (96).

36. Colin Nicholson, *Writing and the Rise of Finance: Capital Satires of the Early Eighteenth Century* (Cambridge: Cambridge University Press, 1994), 152.

37. Regardless of whether the contemporary impression was correct that the rising middle class often wasted its discretionary funds on lawsuits and quack medicines, many other cultural observers, including Hogarth and Fielding, decried the apparent trend.

38. Ronald Paulson, *Breaking and Remaking: Aesthetic Practice in England, 1700–1820* (New Brunswick, NJ: Rutgers University Press, 1989), 50–51.

Notes on Contributors

ERIC V. CHAPMAN is the Chair of English at Menlo School in Atherton, California. He is completing a manuscript on *The Publishing Imagination: The Cultural Warfare of Alexander Pope and Edmund Curll*. He has published articles about Pope and William Blake and is pursuing studies of Eliza Haywood, William Hogarth, and satirical portraits of Pope.

CATHERINE INGRASSIA, an Associate Professor at Virginia Commonwealth University, is the author of *Authorship, Commerce and Gender in Early Eighteenth-Century England: A Culture of Paper Credit* (1998). She is currently working on a study of Eliza Haywood's fiction.

THOMAS J. JEMIELITY is Professor of English at the University of Notre Dame. Author of *Satire and the Hebrew Prophets* (1992), he has also written on Samuel Johnson, James Boswell, Edward Gibbon, Alexander Pope, and Evelyn Waugh. He is currently studying Alexander Pope's use in satire of religious and biblical material, with particular emphasis on *The Dunciad*.

LAURA J. ROSENTHAL is Associate Professor of English at Florida State University. She is the author of *Playwrights and Plagiarists in Early Modern England: Gender, Authorship, Literary Property* (1996). She is completing a study entitled *Infamous Commerce: Prostitution, Mobility, and the Ambivalence of Exchange in Eighteenth-Century Literature and Culture*.

GEORGE S. ROUSSEAU is Research Professor of the Humanities at De Montfort University. The author of studies dealing with medicine and the humanities, his most recent book, written jointly with Ray Porter, is *Gout: The Patrician Malady* (1998). He and Pat Rogers edited *The Enduring Legacy: Alexander Pope Tercentenary Essays* for Pope's tercentenary in 1988.

VALERIE RUMBOLD is Senior Lecturer in English at the University of Birmingham. She is the author of *Women's Place in Pope's*

244

World (1989) and of articles on Pope and eighteenth-century women writers. Her edition of *The Dunciad in Four Books* appeared in 1999.

CLAUDIA NEWEL THOMAS is Associate Professor of English and Associate Dean of the College at Wake Forest University. She is the author of *Alexander Pope and His Eighteenth-Century Women Readers* (1994) as well as of articles on Pope, Samuel Johnson, Elizabeth Carter, and women writers.

LINDA ZIONKOWSKI is an Associate Professor of English at Ohio University. Her articles on print culture have appeared in *The Eighteenth Century: Theory and Interpretation, Eighteenth-Century Life, ELH, Criticism,* and the *British Journal for Eighteenth-Century Studies,* and she has recently completed a book manuscript entitled *Professional Poets and Masculine Identity, 1660–1784.*

Index

Abjection, 226 n. 18; Cibber and, 98; prostitution and, 113. *See also* Subjectivity

Acting: early modern theories of, 89, 97

Addison, Joseph, 197, 204–5, 218 n.18

Aesthetic, 222 n. 20; Cibber's violation of, 86; individualism and, 84–85; Pope's construction of, 81, 86, 89

Allen, Ralph: Pope and, 39, 58

Anatomy, theories of, 39, 44

Ancillon, Charles d', 44, 46

Androgyny, 48. *See also* Castrati, Eunuch

Apocalypse, 166, 169, 238 n.42; characteristics of, 170–71, 173–74, 176, 179, 181–83, 236 n.24; fiction of, 176; as genre, 235 nn.7, 13, and 16; imagery of, in *Dunciad*, 177–78, 181, 217 n.17; imagery of, in *Mac-Flecknoe*, 14; Pope's use of, 170, 173, 183, 234 n.4; and prophecy, 168, 170, 172, 176, 235 n. 11; texts of, Biblical 170; texts of, structure of 182; texts of, judgement in, 171; writers of, 181, 183

Apology for the Life of Colley Cibber, effect on Pope, 94; Cibber's economic motivation discussed in, 117–19; Cibber's subject position in, 95, 97; masculinity in, 84, 105; theatricalization in 96–99; theatrical marketplace discussed in, 116–17. *See also* Cibber

Arbuthnot, John, 70, 219 n. 30

Arcadia, 34, 57–58; homosexuality and, 58–59; Pope and, 35, 60–61

Aristocracy: cultural authority of, 138, 139–40; in *Dunciad* 231 n. 25; education of, 141; effeminacy in males, 140–42, 145, 222 n. 23, 231 n. 27;

Grand Tour 142; imitation of laborers, 144; leisure of, 143, 197–98; masculinity and, 86, 139, 142, 144, 230 n.19; opera and, 140; poetry and, 132, 136; Pope and, 115

Ault, Norman, 109

Authorship, 162; Cibber and, 82; bourgeois model of, 146; class and, 86, 149, 203; constructions of, 27, 29, 136, 210 n. 23; gendering of, 129; independence in, 93; Pope and, 82, 93, 103, 135; professional, 15, 17, 24, 31, 93, 116, 130–31, 145, 148–50, 152, 157, 183, 194, 198, 200–201, 206–7; prostitution and, 106–7, 126. *See also* Poet

Bakhtin, M. M. : carnivalesque, 27, 148, 191, 240 n.3; grotesque realism, 154, 160, 207; on minenppa, 193, 240 n.4; Pope and, 192; Rabelais, attitude toward, 31, 189–91, 203–4

Barash, Carol, 85

Barrow, Isaac: in *Dunciad*, 18

Bartholomew Fair, 68; literary representation of, 17, 20, 194–96, 203

Bathurst, Allen Lord, 68

Baudrillard, Jean, 137, 230 n.22

Bel canto arias, 36

Benjamin, Jessica, 84–85

Bentley, Richard, 18, 26

Bertelsen, Lance, 28, 81, 84, 221 n.2

Bethel, Hugh, 22

Bible, scholarship of, 169–70

Biblical typology, in Dunciad 182, 234 n. 4, 238 n. 42; use of, 167–69, 176

Blackmore, Richard Sir, 78, 174, 200–201

Blake, William, 41, 58, 180, 235 n. 5

Blount sisters: Martha, 159; Theresa, 59; Pope and, 53, 156, 232 n. 12